PHILOSOPHY
OF THE
MASTERS

(abridged)

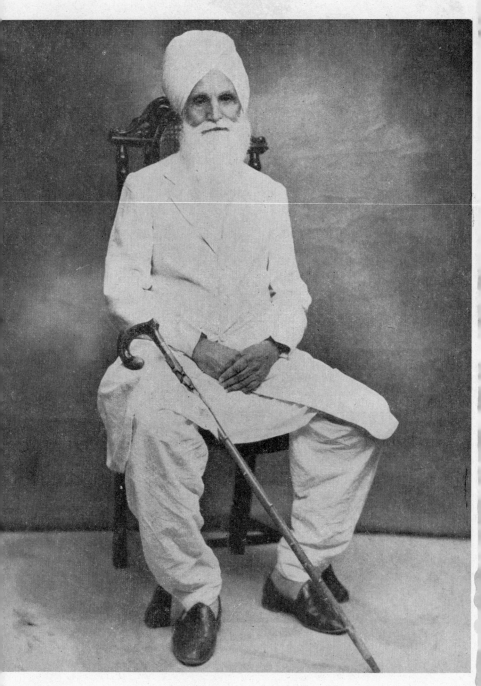

HUZUR MAHARAJ SAWAN SINGH

PHILOSOPHY
OF THE
MASTERS

(abridged)

Huzur Maharaj Sawan Singh Ji

RADHA SOAMI SATSANG BEAS
PUNJAB, INDIA

Published by
S.L. Sondhi, Secretary
Radha Soami Satsang Beas
P.O. Dera Baba Jaimal Singh
Distt. Amritsar 143204
Punjab, India

© 1973 by
Radha Soami Satsang Beas

First Edition   1973   5,000 copies
  Second printing   1977   5,000 copies
  Third printing   1984   5,000 copies

Printed at India Offset Press, A-1 Mayapuri Industrial Area, New Delhi 110064

TABLE OF CONTENTS

PREFACE

The Philosophy of the Masters was written by Huzur Maharaj Sawan Singh Ji, Sant Satguru of the Radha Soami Satsang Beas. The teachings of Sant Mat were practised and preached by him at the Dera from 1903 to 1948. During this period, he gained a large following in India and abroad by his divine influence.

His work is now being carried on by the present successor, Satguru Maharaj Charan Singh Ji, and the place is verily a haven of pilgrimage for tens of thousands of followers who come for spiritual guidance from all parts of the world.

The author was a Great Saint and a highly evolved soul. Consequently, his approach to the subject is fundamentally authentic and is based upon a background of direct personal knowledge and inner experience.

The preparation of the original work involved extensive research and labor by the author, and as a result of this, it comprises a complete encyclopedia of basic information on Sant Mat, the teachings of the Saints. Every aspect of the teachings is discussed in the minutest detail, and is lucidly and forcefully explained for the benefit of seekers after Truth.

The book in its present form was first published in the Punjabi language in 1943, in two large volumes with copious quotations from the Adi Granth, the Bible, the Vedas and various other Scriptures. It was later translated into English by R.D. Ahluwalia,

T.C. Aggarwal and others at the Dera, and published between 1963 and 1967 in five smaller volumes.

This abridged version of the Philosophy of the Masters is an attempt to extract from over 1300 pages of pure gold the essential nuggets of Truth. The reader is advised to go slowly and carefully so as not to miss the meaning of each sentence as written by this great Master or as quoted from a previous Master.

The topics covered in the five volumes of the Philosophy of the Masters in English, have been here organized into four sections.

The first section is an overview showing the structure of creation, the position of man, the challenge he faces to obtain release of his soul from the lower planes, and a brief description of how this salvation is accomplished through the science of Sant Mat.

The second section goes into detail on the relationships of the disciple to the world which will minimize the generation of new ties to this world in this life. With religion today generally unable to provide specific guides for moral behavior which would be accepted by society as "relevant", Sant Mat reaffirms the absolute morality of the ten commandments and the teachings of Jesus. In addition it clearly shows the spiritual reasons for these moral laws, thus combining reason with authority.

The third section deals with the disciple's efforts to still the mind and to know one's self. The same instructions as given by all true Masters wherever and whenever they have taught are given here.

The last section covers the disciple's relationships with the Lord and His representation as the Living Master. Assurance is given regarding the results obtained *in this life* by following the teachings of the Saints in the laboratory of the self. And in this respect we can do no better than to quote the author's own advice as follows:

> "The last request is that the reader should go through this book with reverence. He should prepare for returning to his Real Home according to the directions of the Teachings of the Saints and should reap the full benefit of the human body".

The present work—virtually a stupendous task—is the result of untiring zeal and hard labor for months together by Mr. John H. Leeming Jr., of Phoenix, Arizona, U.S.A. who has masterfully and painstakingly compiled abridgement of this wonderful source. We are greatly indebted to him for his labor of love in the service of the Master.

Secretary,   K.L. KHANNA
Radha Soami Satsang Beas,
27th January, 1973.

FOREWORD

Philosophy has been defined as a study to determine the nature of man and his relationship to the universe—both material and spiritual, in order to understand the origin and purpose of Life.

The goal of such a study is to establish from this understanding a set of rules of behavior for what we must do and must not do in order to achieve the purpose of Life.

How is such a study conducted?

Historically most philosophers have started with certain basic assumptions and then created an intricate network of definitions and arbitrary relationships to support the assumptions. They often resort to quoting ancient "authorities" when unable to otherwise prove their premise.

Gradually, in the area of understanding the material world, scientific approaches have taken over. Alchemy became chemistry, astronomy grew out of astrology, and mathematics grew as a tool to precisely express the newly understood relationships.

But Western philosophy has been unable to extend the scientific method into the areas of moral and spiritual relationships.

Since Man is composed of spirit, mind and physical body, he thereby gains knowledge in various ways. First, his physical senses make him aware of the material world around him. Next his mind handles thoughts and concepts which cannot be sensed or proven by the body. Similarly, the spirit can experience and understand that which is beyond the mind. The subtle comprehends the gross, but the gross cannot comprehend the subtle and infinite. Hence, that which is spirit can only be comprehended by spirit.

When the mind thru speech and writing attempts to describe and understand God, it can only describe and understand God as manifested at the mental world and below. Above that world and to the real home of the spirit, only spirit can comprehend. Therefore we must define God Himself as unknowable.

Religion then steps in to fill this void. However most religions are built on the experience or "revelations" of some bygone teacher and offer no scientific way for us to advance in our understanding.

In contrast, the Philosophy of the Masters provides the student with the key to the laboratory of mind and spirit, and the personal guidance of a teacher fully qualified to instruct in these subjects.

As with other philosophies there may be definitions new to the student, and there are many quotations from "authorities". This is, however, no less scientific than the introduction of new tools and references given the scholar as he progresses from general science to Physics. The initial arbitrary statements are soon demonstrated in the laboratory so the student himself may prove their truth.

Western philosophy and religion have failed in three major areas to provide the basis for a scientific approach. The first is the inability to explain, other than by the will of an arbitrary god or fate, the child born crippled or blind, the evil man living in luxury, the prodigy, the retarded, and all other "chance" elements that mold our life. Accept the premise of the soul returning for more than one life, with what ye sow in this life determining what ye reap in the next, and the science of cause and effect replaces the whim of fate or the need to propitiate a fickle and arbitrary god.

Second, man builds a religion from the teaching of a great soul or Son of God. After the passing of the founder, the followers become convinced that they have the only true teaching from the only true manifestation of God.

They become so convinced of this that they kill those who do not agree—all for the Glory of God!

If we accept the premise that God has even once manifested on Earth to teach those who would receive Him, then it becomes obvious that He must always be manifest in a living teacher. This is no more arbitrary than our need for a living lawyer or a living physician even though the writings of greater lawyers and doctors of past ages are still available. The actual presence of this Living Master is the heart and soul of the Philosophy of the Masters.

The third failure of Western thought has been the inability to connect the follower—in this life—to the power that is God. All teachings, which go beyond the mere satisfaction of bodily desires, promise salvation only after death. However, all Masters say to their disciples, as did Jesus to His closest followers:

"Unto you it is given to know the mysteries of the Kingdom."
                                                    Matthew 13:11

And so—the Philosophy of the Masters gives to the earnest seeker some knowledge of the Power that is God; the assurance that this Power can be realized in this lifetime; and the directions on how to start this course of study which is the chief purpose of human life.

The student is therefore invited to enter the laboratory of the Masters and make the experiment for himself. It would be well for him, however, if he would come, not proudly or arrogantly, but in the spirit of the great scientist, Alexander Agassiz, who said:

"Let the scientific student sit down before the facts, as a little child, and enquire of them."

It is useless to come to the Great Masters, unless one comes in that spirit.

This book is for those who are seeking—it will not be understood by all. One's needs, one's understanding is dependent upon the state of evolution of the individual soul. Neither the native of the jungle of Borneo, nor the denizen of midtown New York could survive in the other's environment. This is not to be derogatory, it is but a statement of fact.

Similarly, men will differ in their spiritual background, experience and needs.

For those who understand—give thanks for the Master's grace, and follow his instructions every day of your life. Truly, He has come for His marked sheep and will take them Home.

John H. Leeming, Jr.
Phoenix, Arizona

BOOK 1

AN OVERVIEW

CHAPTER 1

THE AIM OF A SEEKER

What is God? Is there any such Being in reality? What is the power that enlivens the universe and makes it carry on according to a plan? Is that power conscious or inert? If it is really inert, how then are the sun, the moon and the stars all revolving according to law? How are we related to that power? Whence did this universe originate, when did it come into being and how did such a thing happen? Such questions always face every individual. Book after book has been written on the subject. Many a man has had his day here and has departed. Many are still pondering over these questions but they remain ever fresh.

> "Centuries have passed in wranglings over the hows and whys of philosophy.
> But the discussion about God is still where it was in the beginning."

The mind of man is capable of great flights of imagination but the doubts it does not shed. The subject of God is not comprehended, and man continues to wander in the dense forest of his intellect.

There are theists and atheists. According to the latter, the existence of God is a mere fabrication of the timid. It is just a device to hide their cowardice, and a prop to lean on. Because God is not visible either with telescopes or microscopes, the atheists say that He can have no existence. Both the believers who believe in a God about Whom they have heard or read, and the non-believers, are unhappy.

If one is in a house that is on fire, he will first think of the quickest way of getting out of it before enquiring as to who set the house on fire and when it was set on fire. The answers to these questions can be determined after he has escaped from the burning house. In the same manner, we can find the answer to these questions after we have achieved our goal. The only thought that should occupy us at present is how to terminate this bondage and attachment.

Then why should we ask, "Why is this Path? Why is that Goal? How and when were this Goal and this Path made?" All this will be solved automatically when we reach our Destination. At present, the only possible answer to all these questions that arise in the mind is that God created all this out of His own Free Will.

Whatever actions are performed by the souls that have been sent to the regions of dissolution, their fruit will constitute their Fate, written in indelible letters by the pen of our Lord God. And by that Fate the souls have been sent into the upper or lower regions. It has become their destiny as a result of actions performed in their previous lives.

We understand that innumerable souls are living in Sat Lok—the region of Pure Spirit, free from dissolution, and also in the lower regions which are subject to dissolution. What was the previous karma or action, as a result of which these souls were placed in one region or the other? How did these regions come into existence? When were they created? The answers to all these questions are beyond the limits of time and space, and it is not possible for anybody to find them.

Hafiz says:

"You should think only of the bliss which you get from the Nam of your Master, and should pay no attention to the secrets of this universe nor of the regions beyond, for all this is beyond the ken of intellect."

The reply of perfect Saints to questions concerning whence this universe originated, and when and how, is that we should approach the Creator Himself for the answer. Those who have realized Him have annihilated their self. They have gone beyond the limits of time and space and the spheres of cause and effect.

"O mind, visit the place where you can see the Beloved; Give up this world so that you may see the other world."

On realizing Him these questions are automatically answered.

These interesting topics can be discussed at leisure when we reach the destination. At our present stage only those questions are necessary which relate to the *path leading to Him.* God cannot be known by reasoning, the reading of books and philosophical discussions. Doubtless, through them we can get an idea of His Reality and the existence of His power. But in order to realize Him as a fact we will need to experiment in the laboratories of the Saints and experience Him for ourselves.

For wordly progress our duty consists in so performing the actions that we remain within the bounds of laws of the society and sustain each other so that society may not split asunder. The rules of society include bodily, family, social, national and political rules. Similarly, the path of spiritual progress and emancipation has its laws. It comprises pure detachment.

Sant Mat gives true guidance, both in worldly and spiritual matters, and while strengthening the human virtues, turns the follower's thoughts to his Lord and takes him to Him.

The aim of a seeker after spirituality should be high. Unless there is some definite object or aim, it is useless to hope to achieve it. When his aim or object is certain then every effort brings him nearer to it. The condition of a common man is like that of a drifting man who floats in any direction the current takes him. We are floating in the river of traditions of this world. We follow the traditions. We do as our ancestors have done. We waste time in superstitions connected with the body. We never think of wants other than those of the body. We do not think of the soul or its plight. It is necessary to give up false beliefs. Adopt right beliefs. Follow the right principles. Understand the reality. If you do not understand it, enquire about it, so that you may clearly see the place you are to cross and there may be no obstruction in treading the right path. Those who follow a path followed by others without due consideration get involved in some superstition. Their progress stops and they do not get spirituality. It is therefore an essential condition of success to keep before you the ideal. Ask of yourself as to what you want to be. What ideal have you set in life? A large majority of persons are without an ideal and even if you find a man with an ideal he would consider the world as the ultimate goal. The seekers after spirituality would be only few. Have a peep inside yourself. What do you want to be? You ask for spiritual wealth with your tongue but wish for other things in your heart. Intellect says that it is good to attain spirituality, but mind is involved in the body and bodily pleasures and does not wish for anything else. How then can one seemingly engaged in spirituality obtain success? In the first place, you should have a clear-cut ideal and then a keen desire to attain it. It is only under such conditions that there can be a hope of success, but in order to obtain it you should lessen your love for wealth, woman and world.

The Sanskrit word for Spirituality means "Supreme Achievement." One should therefore discriminate between Supreme Achievement and an ordinary benefit. He should follow the path by which he may get the true, pure and highest benefit. He should eliminate everything that is not necessary and should assimilate the Truth.

Saints teach that true salvation (salvation of the soul) can be attained while living in this world, by means of a certain spiritual practice. This practice is called "Surat Shabd Yoga", which means the practice of uniting the soul with the Shabd (Word, Sound Current or Nam). By means of such practice one can achieve True Salvation even while living in this very body.

As the lotus flower remains above water while its roots are in the water, and a duck—although it is constantly in the water—flies away with its wings dry; in the same manner, one who performs Surat Shabd Yoga remains detached from the world and from its influence while living and working in it.

Kabir says:

"One who has been dyed in the Dye of Nam cannot be stained. He may live in the world, perform his worldly duties and activities, but his heart and mind will never waver."

Man has a physical body. He also has a mind and an intellect, as well as a soul. With the body he accumulates wealth and all other physical amenities. Body is served by body, and mind is served by mind. But soul is by far the most precious of the three. And it is a Master who gives us the gift of knowledge of the soul. That is why a person should offer his body, his wealth and his mind to the Master in order to achieve the gift of Nam.

Remembrance of the Lord and praise of His Name lead to various benefits, according to the Gurus. All desires, ignorance and cares are destroyed, and death and rebirth ends. All good intentions are fulfilled. The heart is filled with happiness, bliss and joys. The lotus opens and egotism disappears. The fear of death is overcome and one does not go to hell. He crosses the world of phenomena in safety. The Lord is seen everywhere and in everything. One not only crosses the world himself, but takes others also along with him. He is saved from the depredations of the five robbers (lust, anger, greed, attachment, and vanity), and attains the stage of easy and natural trance in meditation. He is beholden to the Lord. The remembrance of the Master is remembrance of the Lord. The true Gurus, therefore, take care to explain the benefits of remembrance of the Master.

CHAPTER 2

THE STRUCTURE OF CREATION

At this stage, only a brief description of the structure of creation is necessary. Actually the higher realms are such that no sort of understanding can be conveyed to human intelligence. Only as one travels upward with his Master from plane to plane can their nature and extent be comprehended.

The lowest division is called Pinda. It is the region of gross physical matter, with a limited admixture of spirit which is necessary to life. All of the untold millions of universes known to our astronomers are but a very small portion of the grand total of the Pinda Region. And Pinda is but a speck floating in the Brahmand Region.

Brahmand is the next higher division. It is divided into four Regions with gradually increasing intensity of spirit. The first of these spiritual regions is called Sahansdal Kanwal, meaning "Thousand-Petaled Lotus". It is the region known as the Astral Plane and is the "Heaven" of most worldly religions. It is here that one first meets the Radiant Form of one's Master. The name of the Lord of this region is Niranjan, literally meaning "pure".

There is then another man hidden inside of this physical man, a much finer body, called by the Masters the astral body, or light body. It is so called because when seen, it appears to sparkle with millions of radiant particles resembling star dust. It is much lighter and finer than the physical body.

This astral body every person possesses and uses here and now, although he may be entirely unconscious of it; and it is through and by means of this finer body that the mind and soul are able to make contacts with the physical body and the outside world. This finer body takes shape and colors in harmony with the character of the individual. On the astral plane, where we function in the astral body, no deception is possible. Everyone is seen just as he is, for the astral body reveals his true nature. The astral body has its five senses, just as has the physical body. When the physical body dies, this finer body remains as the instrument of expression in that higher realm of life called the Astral Plane.

The second spiritual region is called Trikuti, meaning "Three Prominences" or three mountains. It is known as the Mental or Causal region and is the region of Universal mind. The name of the Lord of this region is Brahm or Onkar.

Inside of the astral body, and quite distinct from it, there is still another body, much finer and more subtle than the astral. It is called by the Masters the causal body, and is so named because stored in it are the real causes, or seeds, of all that is ever to take place in one's life. The causal body is as much finer than the astral, as the astral is finer than the physical.

In this body, a perfect record is left of every experience of the individual, running through all the countless ages of his existence. Out of all these experiences character is formed, and from that character all actions flow. If one is able to read these records, as the Master and many others can do, he can see exactly what that man has done, or had done to him, during his entire past. Also what he is going to do in the future. It is all there, the past in a visible record, and the future in seed form.

After the physical, astral and causal bodies, the mind is the fourth unit in the total constitution of man. The mind is still finer than the causal body, more subtle, and in closer proximity to the soul. If we are on the physical plane, we must have the physical body, the astral body, the causal body, and the mind. If we are to manifest in the Astral Region, we must temporarily leave the physical body. If we go higher to the Second Region, Trikuti, we leave the astral body behind, and function with the causal body and the mind. When we leave Trikuti on the upward journey, we discard both the causal body and the mind, leaving them behind in Trikuti. We do this because we no longer need them in the regions above Trikuti.

The creator and supreme ruler of these three lower regions (Pinda, Sahansdal Kanwal, and Trikuti) is Kal. They are the regions of Mind and Maya, of time and mortality, of karma, birth and rebirth. They are in truth but a reflection of the higher regions and are therefore termed an illusion or unreal in comparison with the regions above.

The next higher, or third spiritual region is called Daswan Dwar, meaning the land beyond the "Tenth Gate". It is here that the returning soul bathes in Mansarovar or the pool of Immortality, removing forever the ties to the lower regions. The Lord of this region is known as Par Brahm. Between Daswan Dwar and the next region is Maha Sunn, an area of intense darkness which the soul can cross only with the help and the light of the Master.

The fourth spiritual region is called Bhanwar Gupha which literally means "revolving cave". The Lord of this region is Sohang, meaning "I am that". When the soul meets the lord of this region it recognizes its true grandeur.

This is the top region of the Division of Brahmand. Both Pinda and Brahmand are subject to dissolutions. There are two kinds of dissolutions. One, called simple dissolution involves all regions up through Trikuti. This occurs only after many millions of years. The second, the grand dissolution, occurs after immeasurably long periods of time and includes the physical universe and all four regions of Brahmand. After a period of darkness, a new creation takes place.

The highest of the three grand divisions is Sat Desh. It is the only perfectly pure region. It is the realm of absolutely pure spirit and is the region of Truth, of Ultimate Reality. It knows neither death, nor dissolution, nor change, nor any imperfection. It is the great center about which all other worlds revolve. It is the grand capital of all creation, the abode of the Supreme Creator—Lord of all. No sort of understanding of it can be conveyed to human intelligence.

From the center of light, life and power, the Great Creative Current, the Shabd or Word, flows to create, govern and sustain all other regions. Surat (soul) and Shabd (Sound) are both of the essence of the Lord. God himself is Shabd as well as Surat. They are an inseparable three-in-one. The Sound is in reality God-in-Action. He projects Himself into everything and revels in this play. He is the worshiper as well as the worshiped.

The Grand Division of Sat Desh is divided into four distinct regions, but the difference between these subdivisions is very slight. The returning spirit comes first to Sach Khand, the fifth spiritual region. The True Home of the Soul. The Father's House, from which long ago we descended to seek experiences in the lower worlds. It is the Home to which the Great Masters take their disciples and it is where the Master's responsibility ends. By attaining this state, the soul enters into communion with the Lord. The devotee and the Lord become one and never separate again. The ruler of this region is Sat Purush. He takes over the responsibility of guiding the soul to the end of the journey.

The sixth spiritual region is Alakh Lok, meaning the Inconceivable Region. The next highest is Agam Lok, meaning the Inaccessible Region.

The Highest Region is called Anami Lok, or Nameless Region. Home of Radha Soami, Lord of the Soul—Supreme Creator. Although the name Radha Soami (Lord of the Soul) may be ascribed to the Supreme Creator, it is fully recognized that no name can describe Him. No thought can embrace Him. No language can tell of Him. He is the formless, all-embracing ONE. He is the impersonal, infinite Ocean of Love. From Him flows all life and spirituality, all truth, all reality. He is all Wisdom and Love and Power.

"He creates Himself and knows Himself.
He separates the earth and the skies.
He spreads the canopy of the heavens.
He upholds the skies without pillars.
He makes the Shabd His insignia.
He creates the sun and moon and illumines them   A
By His own light."

CHAPTER 3

KARMA AND TRANSMIGRATION

At the time of creation a portion of the infinite number of souls decended into the material regions and put on the wrappings or bodies necessary to work in the causal, astral and material planes. These bodies dim the light of the Soul so that it has forgotten its original splendor and its true home.

The souls in Pinda have been here for eons and have experienced life in all forms as governed by their desires and actions. Through an endless series of births and deaths we have left one body only to be born into another. This has been called the Wheel of Eighty-Four, or the cycle of 8,400,000 species of life into which the soul may have to incarnate. The eighty-four lakh species of life have been described in the Hindu scriptures as:

30 lakh species of trees and plants (1 lakh equals 100,000).

27 lakh species of insects.

14 lakh species of birds.

9 lakh species of life in water (fish, etc.).

4 lakh species of other life, including quadrupeds, human beings, etc.

Saints of all communities have accepted and preached the principle of transmigration.

"Transmigration is simply the coming of the soul into different species to enable it to carry out its allotted task according to its own karma. The soul emerges from the great ocean of life and returns to it.   12

In India almost all religions, namely, Hindus, Jains, Buddhists, Sikhs, and others, believe that a person undergoes pain or pleasure as a result of his own previous action and he bears the consequences of the actions performed in his present life, in the future.

Jews, Christians, and Mohammedans do not believe in the transmigration of the soul, nor in the law of karma. They believe that God is the Creator and the Lord of the entire universe. Just as a potter makes a pot or unmakes it at his will and the pot has no say in the matter, so is it up to God either to grant Salvation to His creatures or to keep them all in ignorance. It is also their belief that God being independent, nobody has the right or power to interfere with His actions nor does anybody know about His doings. These matters are beyond human ken and would best be left alone.

The Saints have very clearly indicated the pros and cons of the law of karma. It is a theory of cause and effect, which operates throughout the universe. Emerson and other philosophers, and also professors of physics, have called it the law of compensation. 'As ye sow, so shall ye reap.'

Whatever a person speaks has a two-fold effect. One is the action, and the other is the reaction. The reaction resounds in and near the speaker and creates the same type of thought-currents in his environment. Thus whatever thoughts—virtuous or wicked—emanate from him, they engender their exact resonance. This is an inviolable and unrelenting law, which

operates in connection with both animate and inanimate objects alike.   It cannot be erased.

Karma is also a process of working out one's
credits and debts.   If we take from somebody, we
have to give to him in return, and under this principle
fate karmas are formed; and by this our ups and downs
in life can be explained.   Pleasure and pain, poverty
and riches, sickness and health, taking and giving,
are all the result of such actions and have to be paid
for.   If one is not able to pay off in this life, he will
have to do so in some future life.

A person dies but the scroll of his actions does
not perish.   The account of all such deeds is imprinted upon the soul which, after death, is still enveloped
in an astral and causal body.   The soul leaves the
body at death, but the accounts remain with it until
they are cleared.

Shamas-i-Tabriz says;

"We live in this universe, and in various births we wear different garbs.   Sometimes we come into one specie and sometimes into another, but we are all a part of the Creator.   In
other words, we came into this world and we left this world
hundreds and thousands of times, because this universe is a
workshop with exits and entrances."

Karma or action is of three kinds: Sinchit,
Pralabdh and Kriyaman.   Sinchit is the store karma;
Pralabdh is the fate karma; and Kriyaman is the fruit
karma.   Store karmas are the results of actions of
past lives, which have not yet been paid for nor assigned.   Fate karmas constitute that portion of the
results of actions in past lives which have been allotted to our present life, and on account of which this
human body has been given to us, that is, for under-

going the results of good and bad karmas according to our fate. Kriyaman constitutes the new karmas resulting from actions which we perform in this life. In other words, while undergoing our destiny (fate karmas), we are daily incurring new karmas as well, the results of which will be undergone in the next life as fate, or part as fate and part as Sinchit, in some future life.

What is really meant by 'past karmas'? The Scriptures tell us that God gives us a physical body— either in the human form or in that of a lower specie— and we come into this world in order to reap the fruits of an allotted portion of our past karmas. In whatever manner He wishes us to do this task, we do exactly that way, because that is the way it is written in our Fate. Nobody can escape his Destiny or Fate. God alone is free, and He manages the whole world by His command.

Our own past actions are responsible for the good and the evil, the pleasure and the pain that we undergo, as well as for our being born into this world in a high or a low specie. "As ye sow, so shall ye reap." We are happy as a result of good actions, and we are miserable as a result of our own bad actions, because we must bear the fruit of our own actions in thought, word and deed.

One cannot escape the result of his actions by performing them in secret. The consequences of such actions have to be borne some time or other. It is therefore clear that whatever weal or woe, joy or sorrow, we experience, it is all due to our own actions, and we should not blame anyone else for it. How can a person hope to achieve good results out of bad actions. Anyone who does is laboring under a mistaken idea.

To cry to the Lord for forgiveness and to think that we can then commit more sins is a mistake. Diseases are punishments for sins. When there has been a sin, it can only be atoned for by undergoing suitable punishment. The root cause of all sins is identifying oneself with the body. Unless we rise above bodily considerations, thoughts of sensual pleasures and desires to enjoy them do not disappear.

> "Many a seeker gets into trouble, because his search for pleasures leads to disease. The desire for pleasures does not go without submitting to His will. Till then one wanders."   A

Dhrita-rashtra (a king who was blind from birth) was once asked to what action in a past life he ascribed his blindness. He replied that he could see as far back as all the actions of his past one hundred lives, and in all these lives there was no act which could have resulted in his blindness. Lord Krishna then granted him his own inner vision for the purpose of seeing beyond his last one hundred lives. Only then did Dhrita-rashtra find that in well over a hundred lives back he had performd a bad deed for which he was born blind in this life. What can one do about the store of karmas lying latent through hundreds of past lives? The cycle of karmas is constantly on the move, and the results of our actions are brought forth and have to be paid for even after hundreds and thousands of lives.

We are all bound down by our fate karmas. Many people are good, and they perform good actions because of their fate karmas. Others are bad and they perform bad actions on account of their fate karmas. They are all powerless to do otherwise. Even if an opportunity to do a good deed comes their way, they ignore it. They do not feel the necessity of the Master and the Lord.

Karma is administered by Kal, the Lord of Death, who administers the three worlds, that is the material, astral and causal regions. Kal was created by the Supreme Lord; he administers the three lower regions under His orders. He dispenses justice (karma) impartially. In compliance with the orders of the Lord, Kal asks all living beings after their death to render an account of their good and bad deeds and he then deals with them accordingly. Hells are meant for the sinners and heavens for those who have performed meritorious deeds. When one's stay in these regions is over, he has once again to tread the eternal wheel of birth and death.

Kal has two powers, namely, Time and Space. These provide the warp and the woof of the creation. Space helps in spreading the creation, and time is ever bringing about changes.

"God Himself forces His creatures into destined paths of karmas over which they have no control and which cannot be effaced. Whatever is destined to take place, must take place."
                                                                    A

"We have to meet certain people; we have to part from others. This meeting and parting is also in conformity with the Law of Karma. It is on this basis that the functions in and of this world are performed."
                                                                    A

Kal administers as he is directed to by the far higher True Being (Sat Purush) and he is not the creator of the soul. He can neither create nor destroy a soul. It is only the body that belongs to him. He assigns

a body according to individual karmas and takes it
back after the allotted span is over. He has no control over the soul, because souls are the children of
Sat Purush and are immortal.

No specie below the human form is free to act.
But human beings have freedom of action, consistent
with their fate karmas. They can therefore take
advantage of the power of freedom of action to a
certain extent.

Human birth is obtained only through great
good fortune. On getting it we should follow the
spiritual path and the teachings that are preached by
the Saints. Human birth is rare. It cannot be had
again and again. If we miss this opportunity we
would regret it very much later on.

> "The rung of the ladder from which the hand has slipped can-
> not be caught again; even so is the human life wasted."   A

Human birth is the top of creation. It is obtained
only by great good fortune. Human birth provides
us with an opportunity to meet the Lord. Guru
Arjan Sahib says:

> "For many births was I a moth or insect,
> For many births was I an elephant, a fish, or a deer,
> For many births was I a serpent or a bird,
> For many births was I grass and trees.
> Now there is an opportunity to meet the Lord,
> This body of glory has been obtained after long ages."   A

Man is engrossed, body and soul, in this world.
He does not think of that other abode where he will
some day go and live.

> "To the abode, he is to leave, he is attached;
> For the abode, where he has to go and live for ever, he cares
> not."
>   A

It is, therefore, necessary that before leaving this world man should make some provision for the hereafter.

"A journey to a strange land lies ahead of all;
O ignorant one, beware, for death is near!"

But the question arises as to how can one do it? By attending Satsang and by fully imbibing its teachings, we are able to gain freedom from some of our karmas. However, the shackles of our karmas, or the results of our own actions, are very strong.

There are people who are not destined to meet a Master in this life on account of their Fate Karmas. Such people would not care to meet a Master, even if He were in their very midst. As a result of such an attitude and on account of their Fate Karmas, they continue their wandering in the cycle of births and deaths in various species.

We are powerless to change our destiny. Whatever is destined in our Fate must happen. We shall meet the Master and remember the Lord only if we are destined to do so. People who follow the dictates of the mind have worldly thoughts and objects dominating them. And those who follow the dictates of a Master have the predisposition for God-Realization imprinted on their minds.

"Only if it is in our Fate do we go to a Master, do we accept Him as a Master, do we surrender ourselves completely to His Will, and also does He unite our souls with the Audible Life Stream."   A

The ocean of karmas is fathomless. It is almost impossible to obliterate all the store karmas. But when we meet a true Master, He clears the accounts of all our karmas by inculcating in us the spirit of doing actions without any thought of reward. When we do our spiritual practice according to the instructions of the Master and surrender ourselves completely to Him, we cheerfully undergo our fate karmas and create no new karmas to be undergone in a future life. The store karmas are gradually destroyed by the practice of listening to the Shabd. Sometimes the Master helps us in bearing the load of our fate karmas so that what might have been a fatal stab becomes a pinprick, with the result that we undergo our karmas without much pain or mental anguish.

In this manner all our karmas are eventually liquidated by the Grace of the Master. At last we are relieved of the load of karmas and achieve Salvation by crossing the ocean of Life. Only while living in this world and doing desireless actions do we become 'actionless'.

Action is inherent in the mind and in the body. So long as the mind is not conquered, it is difficult, if not impossible to be karmaless. Mind is restless. It is impossible to make it motionless even for a second. Therefore, it is impossible for anyone to be free from mental or physical action. However if a person offers all his actions at the altar of his Master, then whatever action he performs is without any punishment, and he will without doubt obtain release from the cycle of transmigration.

At the last moment of life, the Lord of Death, or Kal, does not come to take away the disciple of the True Master. The Master Himself comes and takes the soul with Him. Kal does not come near a devotee.

"This ego is a chronic disease,
Which yet can cure itself with ease,
When grace divine from Lord descends.
Through Guru's Word the soul ascends,
From self thus gets release."

A

CHAPTER 4

THE NEED FOR SPIRITUALITY

The whole world is full of worry, anxiety and tension. Except for the realized Mahatmas (great souls) no one is free from them. This is a proof of the world's bankruptcy of spirituality. The reason for this chaos is the disturbed state of the people. The world has progressed in every other way, but in the realm of spirituality people have remained ignorant. They have explored the rivers, mountains and oceans but not themselves. What is the purpose of all the sciences except that man should know himself?

> "The purpose of all knowledge is this, and only this. You should know what you are on the day of judgment. You may know the value of everything but if you do not know your own value, you are ignorant."

We know about other sciences but we know nothing about our soul, yet the soul is the power by means of which we know about the sciences and because of which the mind and the intellect work. Man is ignorant since he does not know his own value. Man may obtain control over all worldly things, but if he does not know his own soul his whole life is useless.

> "For what is a man profited, if he shall gain the whole world, and lose his own soul."
> B

To the common man the religious rites are more important than the Lord, and a person who believes in some bygone Mahatma or has faith in his religious books is considered a religious man. This narrow-mindedness is like a parasite which feeds on religion and sucks its blood to the extent that the real spirit leaves it and only the skeleton remains. Within the fort of sectarianism the frenzy of religion is a madness as great as that of a rogue elephant. Thus sectarianism becomes the keeper and the usurper of religion, and external rites replace the true religion. Sectarianism preaches the superiority of caste due to birth and turns its face away from the Reality of religion. The worshipers of sectarianism, attracted by the external appearance, begin to consider the rites and rituals as the be-all and end-all. They think all else is ignorance.

Therefore, religion, which was founded to help the progress of the human soul, becomes its prison. According to sectarianism it is a sin to think of anything else other than a particular creed. People show respect to their own bygone Mahatmas (Great Souls) and religious books and have hatred for others.

The purpose of human life is to achieve communion with the Lord by engaging in and remaining happy in His remembrance and by loving Him and His creation. But man, by turning his face away from the Lord, has become devoid of love and has become the enemy of man. Instead of becoming lovers or devotees of the Lord, men become the protectors of false faiths and, in fact, quite wordly. What is worldliness except turning away from the Lord and loving and listening to someone else?

"Know ye what is worldiness! 'tis severing one's relationship with God, harboring any thought except of love towards Him, and listening to things other than His praise."   5

All the world is running about in search of happiness and peace. The bodily pleasures are

momentary and are ever-changing. Whatever pleasure is felt through the senses is due to the attention
of our mind being concentrated on the objects that
give rise to the pleasure. The sense pleasures are
like a dog that crunches a bone. Its mouth bleeds
and it enjoys the taste of its own blood but thinks
that the enjoyment is from the bone.

We do not enjoy any peace because we are not
connected to our spiritual Source. This inner restlessness is influencing the world and, as a result of
it and despite our being the sons of the same Father,
we have forgotten the Fatherhood of God and the
Brotherhood of Man and how to have brotherly
feelings for each other. This is leading to conflict
between brother and brother, one society and another,
one race and another, and one country and another.
One thirsts for the blood of the other. Outer religious
teachings and warnings do not lead to mutual love.

Some believe in the motto, "Eat, drink and be
merry," according to the so-called western light.
They say that there is no need for God. All look
to the shell of the walnut and are trying to digest it,
but this cannot be done. No one looks to the kernel,
for protection of which the shell was made. Because
of this conflict, we have forgotten God and are going
away from Reality.

All religions preach the same ethical and spiritual
truths for men. Their principal teachings are that a
man should be of good conduct, have faith in the Lord
and attain communion with Him (merge into Him).

However, the present-day religions ask us to worship some by-gone Mahatmas such as Christ, Buddha,
Krishna, Rama, Kabir or Guru Nanak and so forth;

but they do not tell us how these Mahatmas attained spiritual eminence and how we can have access to them. They stress the necessity of having faith in one religious scripture or another, but they do not tell us how we also can have the experiences mentioned in them. They tell us how to cross the ocean of existence and what the ship is like in which we have to travel to do so, but they do not take us to the ship. They have nothing in which to cross the ocean of this world. They do not even know about the journey across the ocean, nor do they know how to control the angry waves and the furious storms of the ocean.

With the world in such a condition, the Saints point to the Reality and speak of an easy path to Reality which is inside every man. This path, they say, has been created by God and has been in existence since the time of creation. It is not man-made. Saints say that God exists and that all religions try to establish communion with Him. The path of communion with God is called Religion. 'Religion' comes from the Latin word 'religare' which means 'to bind' or 'to unite'. The real purpose is hidden in the root of the word. Religion means 're-uniting with God.' This Spiritual Path is the same for all. He who remembers God and enters into inner communion with Him is the devotee, whether Hindu, Sikh, Muslim or Christian.

The Lord created human beings, and only later did they become Sikhs, Muslims, Christians, Buddhists and so forth. There were no Sikhs five hundred years ago, no Muslims thirteen hundred years ago, and no Christians two thousand years ago. Three thousand years ago no Buddhists were to be found.

Many races existed before the Aryans founded Hinduism. Men are men, whether of East or West, and all are one as there is Soul in each of them, and that is a particle of the Lord.

The Saints tell us that God is to be found inside the temple of the body. Both the soul and God are present in the body, but there is the curtain of egoism between them and for this reason the soul cannot see God.

> "Both live in the same house, at the same time, but do not see each other."   A

One may belong to any religion, and in order to attain communion with the Lord it is not necessary to give up one's creed or caste. Man can meet the Lord inside regardless of caste or creed.

It is very necessary that Spirituality should be preached again so that mankind may rise above this degradation. We should emphasize the life of the spirit so that the sufferings of mankind may be relieved and man may be saved from the evils of egoism.

Unless a man consciously goes inside, has communion with the Lord and becomes like Him, all his efforts will be of no avail.

The Lord is an ocean of limitless, boundless and all-pervading void. Unless we have complete silence within ourselves, our soul cannot experience that Silence out of which arises the Voice of Silence or the Shabd, by contacting which our soul becomes merged in Silence. This is the reality of Silence. However, the intellect cannot grasp that which is eternal and immortal. That can be grasped only by the soul, and can be seen only by going inside. We cannot imagine God, since He is beyond the reach of the human mind and intellect.

"By thinking one cannot obtain any conception of Him, even though one thinks hundreds of thousands of times."   A

That knowledge is blessed and really praiseworthy which is utilized in trying to understand the Lord and in singing His glory. All other knowledge becomes the cause of our shame, for by swelling our ego it leads us millions of miles away from the reality and only the pride of knowledge remains.

We can realize Him by devotion and love, but not by thinking. In order to realize Him, we should reach the regions of pure consciousness inside ourselves. Spiritual life is the name given to a life of communion with God; not to a life spent in merely thinking about Him.

CHAPTER 5

THE NECESSITY FOR A LIVING MASTER

The formless Lord pervades everywhere, but in spite of this, unless we become directly connected with Him, we do not receive any virtue from Him. Electricity is present everywhere, but we cannot derive any light or other benefits from it unless we know the location of the switch. Even if we know this, it is of no use unless there is a light bulb properly connected with the switch. When the connection is made, electricity does its proper work. It lights our dark house. It alleviates the heat of summer. It cooks for us. It runs our factories. Similarly, if we are connected with the Lord, our actions will bear fruit.

Master Is The Lord

The perfect Master is the Lord in human flesh. He is the Shabd personified, "the Word made flesh." Unless we are familiar with the human Master, how can we realize His subtle form, which is the Shabd? The Shabd and the perfect Master are the two means of taking the soul to its original Home. No one but the Master can reveal the secrets of Reality, and without Him no one can gain release from the bondage of mind and Maya. No one can meet the Lord except through the Shabd, and it is only the Master who can connect the soul with the Shabd. This is the only purpose of their manifestation in this world.

Human beings are endowed with the gifts of intelligence and discrimination to a far greater extent than all the other creatures in this world. All other creatures are, therefore, not worthy of our devotion. Actually, devotion to them would pull us down.

The relationship between beings of the same species has a great deal of power in this world for creating love and attraction. We are on the physical plane, and we can only love one who is also on this physical plane. We are human beings and we should love only a human being. We have not seen the Lord. How can we offer our love to Him? In other words, it is clear that in order to love the Lord we must love Him through one of His manifestations. Such a man is the Master.

The question arises, why should a man worship another man? The answer is that there is a great difference between one man and the other. A Master has assumed the form of a man, but he is not an ordinary man. Internally He is always in conscious contact with God.

To our limited understanding, the Master may appear to be finite. Actually, he is Infinite. He is the medium for attaining God-Realization. He is the medium for taking us from the physical to astral, from astral to causal planes, and even further up— stage by stage—to the Unlimited Power above, by means of his instructions and discourses.

If one were to assert that he worships and contemplates on the form of God, which is omnipresent, it can be said that at the most he contemplates on the form of a vacuum or of the ether. Besides, it is not visible to our sense of sight and it will not be helpful in awakening in us the currents of spirituality.

A Master has two forms. Externally he is a human being; but internally he is, in fact, God. He is in the form of a human being outside; but he is God in man, or God plus man. He has contact with human beings on one side, and with the Lord on the other. From this point of view he has two aspects. One is that of a human being, and the other is that of God. His real form is Shabd. Shabd creates the physical body and dwells in it. "And the word was made flesh, and dwelt among us."

A Master is the medium through which individuals are connected with God. In other words, God, Shabd, and Master are three different forms of the same Lord. If we offer devotion to Shabd in the physical form, which is the Master, we are then immediately connected with the Lord inside. Devotion to the Master is, in fact, true devotion to the Lord.

A study of the ancient history of India will reveal that in prior ages education was imparted by the Masters in places far removed from human habitations, and the student was wholly occupied physically, mentally and spiritually in the service of his Master. Later this type of education began to disappear slowly and in its place idol worship started. In the present age, such rendering of service to the Master has altogether disappeared except in the case of a rare few. Now God Almighty, in His abundant Grace, has sent His own Incarnations into this world to preach the doctrine of Master-Disciple Service. This tradition of Master-Disciple relationship continues today.

The perfect Master or Sat Guru has a very clear inner vision and can at once see who is fit for this Path. Those that are ready are accepted. He, in His grace, chooses them and makes them followers of the Truth.

"When the disciple is ready, the Guru appears"

When our soul grows weary in its search for the Lord, and is anxious to return to its home, when our eyes long to see the Lord and we hunger for Him, then, in order to fulfill our intense desire, He incarnates as a perfect Master or Sat Guru. In order to release the seekers from their bonds He himself comes as a redeemer. He gives the seekers instructions according to their development, and connects them with the Lord.

The secrets of spirituality, or of the practical means by which the soul can become united with the Lord, are given out by a living Master only. This teaching is imparted through an unspoken language. There is no spoken language by means of which it can be imparted. Religious books merely give a few hints about the ascent to the spiritual regions. The scenes witnessed by the soul with the help of the Master in the subtle regions cannot be fully described. The books, being inanimate, cannot help the soul in its ascent. In the writings of the Saints there is a reference to internal experiences. The bliss of these experiences can be had by internal progress and not otherwise. It can be achieved through the Sat Guru only. It cannot be had by reasoning. Holy books and scriptures describe it to a certain extent only; but it cannot be experienced except through a living Master.

The Need For A Guide

Spirituality is a difficult path and cannot be trodden without the company of a Master.

The soul is covered with three sheaths, namely, the gross, subtle, and causal bodies. One can, without the Master's help, reach the subtle and causal regions. His original home, however, is beyond the three regions, in the fourth region. There are many entanglements and obstructions in the gross region. If we reach the subtle region, there are numerous misleading and distracting devices there, and it is difficult to escape them. And beyond that region it is impossible to enter the region of pure consciousness all alone. To walk on this path is to tread on a razor's edge. There is danger at every step. He who wishes to know the reality or to get true knowledge and to meet the Lord should seek a perfect Master who knows the way. It is said in the Katha Upanishad:

"Arise, awake, learn the true knowledge quickly. Seek a Master who has knowledge of what is beyond, since the Mahatmas say that the path is sharper than the edge of a sword and it is very difficult to tread it."

It is impossible to realize the Lord without a Master. A disciple needs the help of the Master at every step. Maulvi Rum says:

"Search for a Master, because to tread this path without him is full of risks and dangers. If you tread this path without a Master, Satan leads you astray and throws you in a well. If the protecting hand of the Master is not on your head, then the voice of Satan will worry and lead you astray. Many wise men trod this path, but were led astray by the Negative Power (Kal). There are Shabds (Sounds) of Kal

inside us, which are imitations of the Lord's Divine Sounds.
They lead you to destruction."

"Follow the Master, since without Him the journey
Is full of sufferings, risks and dangers;
Whoever went this way without a Master,
Was misled by the evil ones and thrown in a pit.
O fool! If you have no Master, the voice of evil will keep
    you confused;
The evil ones will lead you astray and cause you suffering.
Many wiser than you have tried this path before.
The voice of evil comes as the voice of a friend;
It's a friend who leads but to destruction."

Without a Guru all actions and observances are
fruitless. Without a Master all worship is a waste.
Unless the internal eyes are opened and unless one
knows the reality, one cannot gain emancipation.
It is, therefore, necessary to take shelter with some
Guru who can turn us away from external practices,
connect us to the inner practice of Nam and take our
soul to its original Home, beyond the lower universe.

"There is utter darkness without a Master.
One cannot understand without a Master.
Without a Master the soul is not realized.
Without a Master release is not attained.
Seek a Master, meditate on truth.
When you meet a Master,
The Shabd will remove all your sufferings.
Let the Master dwell in the eyes.
Let the Master dwell on the tongue.
O! praise the Master always.
They who have not seen the Master,
They have done nothing.
They have wasted their lives."   A

To try to walk on that path by oneself results in
being led astray, and one has to repent for this mistake.

If one has the Master by his side, he can easily reach the home of the Lord. If it had been in our own power to go back, we would not have remained separated from the Lord.

"Nothing except the grace of the Master can kill the ego;
Hold fast to the garment of the Redeemer.
Go and sleep under His protection;
It may be that He will then grant you release;
Go on cooing like the cuckoo day and night;
Seek the secret of the hidden treasure from the Master.
Go from door to door and street to street;
Search for Him time and again;
Do not turn your face away from the Saints;
Then leave the rest to God."   5

Sight is a great blessing to us. A sightless person longing for sight, cannot see and wanders about in the dark. If he recovers his sight by an operation, he feels greatly indebted to the surgeon. The inner eye is millions of times more useful. Without it one cannot see beyond this world. One cannot see the Lord. Without Him we have been wandering from birth to birth. The Master opens the inner eye or the knowledge-center. This inner vision is most essential, but it is highly regrettable that we, engulfed in Maya, do not experience it.

"They are not blind
Who have no sight.
O Nanak, blind are those
Who are separated from the Lord."   A

When making preparations for a journey, we consult various directories. But if someone tells us about a person who has already visited the place and the country to which we want to go, we would not only consult the directories but would also consult that person, because he has seen and known everything for himself. If, on contacting him, we learn that he is again visiting that country and is willing to take us along with him, we would gladly accompany him. We can, to some extent, check his facts with those given in the directories. If the facts and directions are corroborated by several directories, we are all the more satisfied. The souls of the Saints visit the spiritual universes and regions. They can, therefore, give us the information needed for our own journey to those regions.

Religious books are like directories. They simply point out the way. The Saints-incarnate take us to the higher regions in the ship of Nam. We can obtain tickets or passports from them and cross in their ship of Nam or Shabd. They are themselves the captains. We can thus reach the region of the Lord.

It is obvious that if, for instance, we had to visit London, we would first consult a directory to find where it is situated and the route we should follow, where we would have to change and at which port we would have to embark, and to which company the ship belongs. We would have to obtain a passport, for if we did not have a passport we could not start our journey. Similarly, we have to obtain 'permit' from a Saint (the Deputy of the Lord) to enter the realm of the Lord. This passport or permit is initiation. One has to have the permit stamped with the seal of the Sat Guru (Master). This fact has been mentioned by various Mahatmas in their hymns. Their writ runs throughout all the universes and regions since they are the duly appointed Deputies of the Lord. When we get their passport, no one can obstruct us in any of the universes or regions.

We can further illustrate the necessity of a Guru by another example. One wishes, let us say, to fly in an aeroplane. But the pilot has locked the door and engine of the plane so that no ignorant person can get in and possibly be injured. A person who does not know how to operate a plane does not even know how to board the plane. But even if he were to do so, the aeroplane would not start, since the engine is locked. Even if it were to start, the ignorant person does not know how to take it up or bring it down. Even if he were to take it up, he would not know the conditions in the upper regions. There would be nothing but certain destruction for him.

This human machine is similar. In the first place, the soul cannot concentrate itself at the proper place unless proper instructions have been given. Even if it should do so, however, it could not climb into the ship of the Shabd. Even if it should somehow be connected with the Shabd, it has no knowledge of the higher regions and does not know the direction to be followed in order to go up or to come down. If the pilot (Guru) takes a new man with him in the plane, unlocks it, and takes him up on a few flights, the new man might then be able to fly the plane by himself.

For traveling through the spiritual regions it is very necessary to have a pilot who knows those regions and who has often traveled through them. If he is with us, the journey becomes possible. If such a Mahatma were to invite us to accompany him and we should say, "No, thank you, we will fly our plane by ourselves," we would be very unfortunate.

"Seek a Master for this journey;
Without a Master it is full of risks and dangers."   5

"Even if there be hundreds of moons;
Even if there be thousands of suns;
With all their light,
There is darkness without a Master."   A

"Where there is no Shabd,
Darkness abounds.
Nothing is gained there,
And coming and going do not cease.
The Master has the key;
No one else can open the door.
When one is fortunate,
One meets a Master."   A

Scriptures And Learned Men Cannot Take The Place of Guru

Guru is the name of a very pure spiritual being, who has access to Sach Khand (True Region). He has experience of the gross, subtle and causal regions. He has experience of spiritual matters and is free from the bondage of the senses. Unless we become connected with such a person, our spiritual aspirations do not awaken. The guru, in fact, is a glowing lamp whose light rekindles the lights that have blown out. A burnt-out lamp cannot do this. Many persons say that we can light the lamp of knowledge by merely reading religious books. They say that we need no Guru and that the books will serve the purpose of the Guru. Let us consider what these books are. They are invaluable records of the spiritual experiences of Saints and holy men. It is, therefore, good to be fond of reading such religious books. We must have respect and love for them. But persons who depend upon books alone have yet to understand the difference between insentient and sentient beings.

Books stimulate the desire to hear about spirituality and to understand its principles, and to read accounts of the lives of Saints. All this can be of great benefit to us, but it cannot activate the spiritual life within us. We can obtain this spiritual life only from some spiritually realized soul. Only a burning lamp can light another lamp. It is impossible to get life from inert matter. Similarly, spiritual knowledge cannot be attained by the mere reading of religious books, were it even for millions of years.

Spiritual knowledge cannot be taught. It is a 'touch' which can be had only from a man of realized experience. "Spirituality cannot be taught but caught." The experience of Saints cannot be had except by revelation. It is not simply a matter of knowing it; one has to realize it as an experience.

> "The thing you want is at one place,
> But you search for it at another;
> How can you ever find it?
> O Kabir, if you want to find it,
> Take one with you who knows where it is.
> He will then show you the thing you want.
> It is a long, long way to go,
> But he will take you there in a moment."

In order to learn how to cook well, one has to work under an expert cook. When studying medicine or engineering, one has also to do practical work. One cannot become a doctor or an engineer by mere reading. One needs the help of a teacher in all the external sciences. How much more is a teacher needed in the case of the abstruse and difficult spiritual science? For without a teacher, when we shut the eyes, we see only darkness within us. A teacher is needed to show us how to see the inner light. One needs a teacher in every line. Some say that no spiritual teacher is necessary, and that they can acquire spiritual knowledge by themselves. They are like a person who refuses to drink water out of the well of some one who is willing to serve him, but insists upon digging a well of his own. This shows that he is not thirsty as yet. Those who do not need spirituality do not need the Master either.

That knowledge is within you. But unless you know the method of going within and opening the knot of consciousness and gross matter, you remain without realization of it. If spiritual knowledge were to be had from books, the learned ones would have become self-realized. But they are no more than walking encyclopedias, and are as lifeless as a mansion of bricks and stones. The brain full of book-knowledge is like a donkey that is carrying a load of sandalwood but is unaware of its scent, or like a spoon that remains in the pudding day and night but does not know its taste. If one could become spiritually-minded by reading books, there would be as great a flood of spirituality as there is a flood of books. But how many really enlightened souls do we come across in this age of books? Hardly any.

Whenever Saints come into the world there is a flood of spirituality. Numberless seekers are dyed in the color of the Saints and turn to the spiritual life. A soul can get spiritual uplift only from another soul. An intellectual teacher cannot do this. One may be very intellectual or learned, but unless he is himself spiritually evolved, he cannot help another. It is very easy to give discourses or talks on spiritual matters, but it is quite another matter to lead a spiritual life. No one can become spiritual by simply studying books on the science of spirituality. Any claim to spirituality based on such a study would be pretentious.

In the Bhagvad Gita it is said:

"You should prostrate yourself before a perfect Master and carry out spiritual practices and serve him. Only a Guru who knows the reality can impart this knowledge to you."

We cannot gain knowledge of the spiritual path without a Master. It is very necessary to know a Master. Jesus Christ said:

"No man cometh to the Father but through me."

"He who does not know the Son,
does not know the Father."

"He that receiveth you receiveth me, and he
that receiveth me receiveth Him that sent me."

A search through the scriptures of all the religions shows that all lay emphasis on the point that no one can gain release without a Guru.

"The Shastras, Vedas and Smritis all say the same;
Hold fast to the belief that there is no release without a
Master."   A

In the religious scriptures of the Hindus the necessity of having a Guru is also strongly emphasized.

"God cannot be realized without initiation, however much one may meditate on Him. Unless you are initiated by a true Guru, you cannot realize Him because He is so subtle that He is beyond the reach of imagination."   F

There is no instance in history that tells of any man making the spiritual ascent without a Guru. Saints who possess knowledge from the time of theii birth are rare. They do not, however, go against the tradition, and for this reason they also adopt a Guru. Kabir Sahib, for example, adopted Gosain Rama Nand as his Guru. Christ was baptized (initiated) by John the Baptist. It is a historical fact that such Saints, although they had knowledge from the time of birth, remained in the company of Saints and derived benefit from them. Guru Amar Das said that it is ordained by the Lord from the beginning that He cannot be realized except with the help of a Guru.

This being so in the case of those who are born Saints, it follows that a Guru is all the more necessary for common people.

Past Saints

A patient cannot take medicine from a past physician, however proficient he may have been. No one can get his case decided by a departed judge. No woman can marry a dead person and beget children of him. Similarly, perfect Mahatmas came in their own time and redeemed those who came in contact with them then. After the expiration of their period they left the world and merged in the Lord. Before departing, they passed on their work to others. Only man can make another man understand. This is the law of nature.   The Lord works in this world of matter through living persons.

Many believe that past Mahatmas are even now present in the spiritual regions and can help us.   This matter should be considered calmly.   Those perfect Masters fulfilled their mission and merged in the Lord and left the remaining work to some other Mahatmas.   One Mahatma finished his work and handed over the office of Guru to another according to the direction of the Lord, so that the work of connecting the souls with the Lord and redeeming them could continue.   Even if a past Mahatma wished to redeem a person, he would work in accordance with the law of nature and carry out his mission through a living Mahatma.

We can take the help of past Masters only after ascending to the regions where they are.   We are, however, in this gross world, while they are in the world of the spirit.   If we think that past Mahatmas can help us from the spiritual regions, we are acting on inner feelings, imagination and inferences.   And unless our inner eyes are opened, we are unable to be certain whether our inner thoughts are from the Lord, from a past Mahatma, from some imperfect soul, or if they are only waves of our own subconscious mind.   It is wrong to act on the waves of the subconscious mind, and one is likely to be misled by them.   Moreover, when we have not seen a past Mahatma, the anti-power or any other soul can claim to be that Mahatma and deceive us.   As we cannot positively recognize him, we are likely to be deceived.

Let us consider whether it is logical to think that past Mahatmas can act as Gurus and that it is not necessary to have a living Guru. If a past Mahatma can do so, surely the Lord Himself could give the necessary spiritual instructions. Then why did any Mahatma have to come here at all, as the Lord could always do so?

If, however, there was a necessity for a Mahatma at any time in the past, it follows that there is a necessity for one even now, just as there was before.

If the Lord wishes to make people understand, He must take human form. This is the law of nature. He has to take the form of a Saint or a Holy man.

This does not mean that the past Mahatmas are dead. No, they are immortal and have crossed the gross, subtle and causal regions. They are united with the Lord and are indistinguishable from Him. If they are supposed to be wandering in the lower regions, what was the use of their perfecting the practice of listening to the Shabd?

It is no use getting entangled in long intellectual arguments. It does not help or carry us forward. Seek the guidance of a living Mahatma who can tell you the natural and easy method of uniting with the Lord. You need not wait for another life after you die here. If you try, you can succeed here and in this very life.

A disciple should have one Master only. The disciple should continue to contemplate on the form of the Master who initiated him even after the latter leaves this world, and he will succeed. The Master, when He initiates a disciple, takes His stand by him. He dwells in his heart. He is the ideal. The disciple will succeed because of this fact. He will gain inner experience. He will lack nothing. A Master never dies. He is imperishable. He is a principle or an ideal, which never dies. He merely gives up the body. A disciple may serve and live in the company of another holy man. He should, however, maintain internal connection with the Guru from whom he received initiation, and always fix his attention on His form. He is present in his heart and will look after every one of His disciples. If one were to shift from one Master to another, he would never gain anything.

The Guru of the time is the Guru with whom the disciple has a *living* connection. Gurus of the past are no longer Gurus, because they are not living.

Both are necessary in their own spheres. By reading the history of the past Gurus and their beautiful hymns, we can realize the necessity of a living Guru and to some extent we understand his mission. The real benefit of spirituality, however, can only be had from the Guru of the time or the living Guru. The Guru who initiates a person is his present Guru or Guru of the time. Even if there be more than one Guru at one and the same time, a disciple should have one Guru only, just as a woman should have one husband only. Contemporaneous Gurus fill their respective disciples with their own higher consciousness. One cannot gain emancipation without this. Gurus stress the need for this again and again. Maulvi Rum says,

"Do not rely on your intellect or ability or cleverness. Do not break your relationship with the prophet of the time."

Master Is Love

The Master is deeply concerned about his disciple. He wishes the disciple to make progress in all respects. Sometimes he is angry with his disciple for the disciple's benefit, but the heart from which this seeming anger emanates contains a never-failing fountain of love for the disciple. The words may appear to be harsh but they are saturated with love. And it is for this reason that a devotee finds even these harsh words to be sweet. A sign of Guru Bhakti is that whenever a Guru uses harsh language or is angry, the disciple takes it to be sweet and is not offended.

A lover loves his beloved very much. A glow of happiness lights up his face as soon as he sees his beloved. But the Master has a unique spiritual beauty and magnetic power of attraction. His form radiates thousands of blissful currents of attraction which invigorate the body and the mind.

Even if one were to see the Master's face at all times, or for hundreds of times and with hundreds of eyes, the mind would never be satiated, because every time that face is seen it is beheld with a new light and a greater radiance.

Love for the Master is sweet and magnetic, and is able to bring happiness to the disciple. On beholding the Guru, there is an indescribable ecstasy which is spontaneous and permeates every pore of the body. Even by having a small taste of this ecstatic state the soul is steeped in the Master's love.

A king once went to a foreign country. Before he left, he asked his queens what they would like him to bring for them. One asked for clothes, another for delicious foods, yet another for useful articles, another for articles of beauty, and still others for diamonds and jewels. The youngest queen, who was generally considered a fool but who in reality was the shrewdest of all, said, "O Emperor! Come back yourself and keep me at your feet, and I will have everything I could wish for." The king came back and sent the other queens the presents they had requested and then went to the youngest queen with all he had. How fortunate was that queen! The king had the feeling that he should give all he possessed to her because she truly loved him. The queen sat at his feet, and touched the feet of her all-bountiful lord, and enjoyed his loving gaze. The other queens received a few gifts, but she had the love of her lord. Of what use were the gifts without the lord?

Kal does not wish that anyone should go out of his domain, because the life and gaiety of this creation is due to the souls that are in it. He accordingly misleads the souls in a variety of ways by means of the mind and the Maya. For this reason the True Being sends his incarnations, the Saints and the Masters, from time to time to emancipate those who are in the clutches of delusion. Without taking refuge in such Saints one is not freed from the bondage of death.

Briefly, this book advises you to rouse yourself, be awake and search for the Saints who are spiritual kings—in the streets, cities and countries—wherever they may be, and follow this Path which is like the edge of a razor and in following which attachment to the body has to be given up. Such a Master will not only teach you the way from darkness to Light but will also guide and accompany you in the various regions and spiritual realms.

"He will be with you in the material and spiritual regions so that you may not wander from the Way."

"And wherever the account (of our actions) is asked from us, there He stands (to help)."   A

Connect your soul with Him and be happy. Saints are our true guides and leaders. Learn from them how you can become passive and can attain absolute stillness and silence inside to enable you to obtain the bliss of the Light of lights.

"He is the wise and true Master,
Who shows us our home within our body.
There rings the melody of the five Shabds;
There is the beat of the drum of Shabd.
The worlds, underworlds, islands and seas
All make one wonder-struck.
A deep and subtle melody plays there,
And a king sits on the throne of Truth.
Hear the music of the Sukhman,
In the region of the void,
Hear the unutterable music,
And the desires in the mind will die out.
The lotus will be upturned and will be filled with nectar;
Then the mind ceases to wander,
And the eternal music never leaves us.
It is with us from the beginning through the ages.
All who realize the five Shabds
And go back to their original Home,
Have found the Shabd which leads them Home.
Nanak is the slave of such perfect Masters."   A

CHAPTER 6

SANT MAT—THE SPIRITUAL SCIENCE

Sant Mat is another name for Surat Shabd Yog—
Yoga of uniting the soul with the Sound Current or
the Holy Spirit. It is the inner experience of connecting the soul with the Lord. This experience is far
superior to creeds and faiths. We call this Sant
Mat or the Teachings of the Saints. These teachings
deal with the real principles of Spirituality. They are
much higher than the religions, since they simply
state theories, beliefs and miracles.

The teachings of the Saints are natural and have
existed from the beginning of the world. They came
to this world along with man. The teachings or the
method for the soul to return Home was created at
the same time when man was created. This is a certain
and never-failing Path wich can never change, which
has been in existence from the beginning and which
cannot be altered by anyone. Gurus, Saints and
Mahatmas, who are indistinguishable from the Lord,
have shown this path. It is natural and every individual can follow it. It is not man-made but God-made.
No one need believe in this path blindly, for it can be
experienced within one's own self.

A true science never requires anything to be taken
for granted. The teachings of the Saints are as exact
as mathematics. Whenever anyone has followed
these teachings, he has come to the same conclusion
as all others who have done so.

The real purpose of leading a spiritual life is that man should tear away the veil of Maya (Illusion) and Matter, and recognize Himself as the Soul, which is superconscious and is a particle of the ocean of Superconsciousness, so that he may blend into that Ocean and take on its color and qualities. In other words, the spiritual drop blends into the ocean of the Lord.

Spiritual life, with the help of the Master, leads one to the Almighty in a short time. This cannot be done in any Religion by one's own unaided efforts. A true Master is needed.

Surat Shabd Yog is easy. The Path is the same for everyone, whether poor or rich, whether of low caste or high caste, whether literate or illiterate, whether of the East or the West, the North or the South. The practice of Surat Shabd Yog leads to the enjoyment of bliss in this very life. It is easy and natural, like other laws of Nature, for those who understand it correctly and practise it correctly and diligently engage themselves in practice.

Yogas are of many kinds: Pran Yog is the practice of breath control; Hatha Yog consists of physical postures. Both of these concern the gross or physical body and are of low merit. Those that pertain to mind and intellect concern the astral body. Anand Yoga pertains to the causal body. This is superior to all other Yogas. The path of the Saints is Shabd Yoga, which is the life-breath of all Yogas. No outer practice is involved in it. The Sound Current is heard with the ears of the soul. We gain this exalted state without expenditure of any kind. The Sound is really the manifestation of the Lord. It comes from the highest region and the soul is connected with it.

Surat Shabd Yoga is easy to practise. One does not have to undergo suffering while practising it, as in other yogas. One does not have to make any effort except that of listening to the melody of the Shabd with close attention. A child, youth, or an old person belonging to any sex, caste, creed and country can practise this Yoga. One does not have to undergo hardships as in Hatha Yoga. One can practise it while living at home and carrying on one's worldly duties. It is not necessary to change one's religion in order to practise it. Anyone belonging to any race, community, religion or faith can practise it.

There are three phases of Surat Shabd Yoga, namely simran (repetition or remembrance), dhyan (contemplation) and bhajan (listening). Simran consists in repeatedly remembering a certain specified thing. The full details of this practice can be obtained from a perfect Master. In the beginning simran is practised by means of spoken words. Later on, however, it is performed by means of the 'tongue' of the soul. When it becomes firmly established and the power of remaining in concentration is developed, inner light appears and also the beautiful astral form of the Master. This form pulls the soul towards it and in this way, contemplation is completed. The object contemplated upon, the contemplation and the contemplator become one. The ideal, the contemplation and the doer become one.

When a disciple remembers an ideal again and again and fixes the eyes of contemplation on it again and again, the Nirat or soul's power of sight, will visualize its shape and absorb its effect. In this way, the soul and the soul's power of seeing rest in 'calm fixity' and the Divine Melody is heard during contemplation. The seeker should fix the attention of the soul on the Melody described by the Master. The power of speech should merge in simran or repetition, the power of sight in contemplation, and the power of hearing in the Shabd. The disciple should seal his tongue, eyes and ears with simran, contemplation and the Divine Melody.

> "Close the three apertures (ears, eyes and mouth); make no loud recitations.
> Close the outer apertures and open the inner ones.
> Close the three apertures and repeat the Name of the Immaculate One;
> The inner apertures will open only when the outer ones are closed."
>   4

These three practices are done at the eye center, also called the Third Eye and the eight-petaled lotus center. The eye center is between the two eyebrows. For the practice of Surat Shabd Yoga, it is necessary to obtain initiation from a perfect Master or Saint. Progress in this Yoga is made in the company of Saints. When the Lord sends His grace from His original Home, then only one gets the blessing of meeting a true Master and of being in His company.

Initiation

Initiation is mentioned at several places in the hymns of the Gurus. The Master gives to the disciple His spiritual light. He makes him fit to lead a spiritual life.   The Gurus describe it as the 'gift of life'.

"He gives the gift of life;
He teaches devotion to the Lord.
He unites his disciple with the Lord."   A

"Those only meet a Master,
Who are so destined.
The Name of the Lord is the nectar;
It is given at initiation."   A

Initiation can be had from a living Master only, and not from the so-called preceptors who merely whisper a mantra in the ears of the disciples. This gift of life or ray of life can be obtained from a living Guru.   The life-giving impulse can be obtained only from a living being; it is impossible to get it from books or scriptures.

"One meets a Master,
And gets initiation.
He surrenders all,
And enjoys the inner life."   A

At the time of initiation, the Master imparts the secret knowledge of the heart. It then becomes possible to make spiritual progress by following the Master's directions. After explaining everything, directions are given which help in repetition, contemplation and manifestation of the Inner Shabd or Divine Sound. They help the disciple in his inner ascent. At the time of initiation the Master gives the ray of life and connects him with the melody of the Shabd. He then establishes a subtle link with the disciple, guides him and takes him to the original Home. However learned, religious-minded, self-disciplined or respected a man may be, he remains deluded by the mind and Maya. In these circumstances only a Master can connect him with the inner Shabd. However virtuous a man may be, he cannot, by his own efforts alone, contact the Sound. Unless the Master gives him the gift of the ray of life and initiates him, he cannot contact the Divine Sound.

At the time of initiation by the Master the soul becomes fit for being connected with the Shabd. This moment is considered as the moment of birth in the Master's family. After a disciple is connected with the Name by the Master, he begins to progress on the spiritual path and to get control over his weaknesses. When the seeker progresses on the spiritual path by following the directions of the Master, he does not remain subservient to the body. On the other hand, his soul tends to soar to the spiritual regions, to break off all the ties with the earth and to dwell more and more in the higher regions within.

This gift of the Name is given to a conscious being, and is meant to awaken him to a new life by its animating impulse. How soon one obtains the benefits of initiation depends on the person initiated. It depends on his inner spiritual condition. The inner condition is different in different persons. Certain persons are fully ready, while others are less so. The Master 'injects', as it were, his consciousness and light into the soul of the disciple at the time of initiation. This injection of His own consciousness and light permeates the disciple like leaven, and produces a new spiritual consciousness and light as the practice of Nam is continued. The spiritual light of the Master gives a new life to the soul of the disciple and begins to free it. Consequently, the disciple begins to have a feeling of fulfillment. This gift of the Master cannot be taken away. Time and Maya cannot destroy this seed, this ray of life. The disciple, once initiated, will certainly progress, sooner or later. He will one day certainly reach his true Home.

For the practice of this Yoga it is necessary to have a secluded spot away from noise. To achieve inner seclusion, the Masters teach a perfect method by which the disciple closes the outer doors and sits in one-pointed concentration. He is asked to practise at a fixed time, morning and evening. At that time, one has to gather one's attention at the seat of the soul, which is behind the eyes, mid-way between the two eyebrows. The Hindus call it the Third Eye or the eye center. It is not necessary to put pressure on any vein or other part of the body. It is sufficient if you fix your attention at that point in the body.

This is the point which is referred to by Lord Krishna as being in the middle of the root of the nose. During this exercise one performs the simran, or repetition, as directed by the Master, and also contemplates on Him. He should not let any other thought enter his mind. In this way, he should gather together at the eye center the consciousness, which normally pervades every pore of the body, and fix his attention at the eye center. The full details of this practice and also of the difficulties and obstructions that may be experienced, are described by the Master at the time of initiation, so that the disciple may avoid them. The Master also helps the disciple internally and protects him.

It is dangerous to practise this Yoga without

initiation, after merely reading books or after hearing about it from others.   All Saints give the same advice. They say that one should seek a Master for this journey because, without a Master, this path is full of risks and dangers.

Practice

What is the sign of success in the practice of this Yoga?   It is that one loses all consciousness of the body.   In the beginning the hands and feet become numb, and then other parts gradually become numb. The currents of consciousness which flow downwards and give life to the body gather together at the center of the soul—the eye center—and the rest of the entire body loses consciousness.   Unless one rises completely above the nine doors (the eyes, ears, nostrils, mouth and two lower apertures), one remains ignorant of the divine vision.

"Unless a man rises above consciousness (of body),
He remains without the divine vision."

Kabir Sahib also says that the soul which is wandering around in the nine doors cannot find the invaluable treasure.   He says:

"O fair damsel, you have searched in all the nine doors,
But have not found the precious treasure.
O Kabir, the nine doors hold it not;
It is inside the Tenth Door."   4

When the powers that normally operate at or through the nine doors gather together, the divine melody is heard and the inner light is seen.   The connection with the gross senses ceases, and the

subtler regions come into view. The soul, mind and
intellect all become finer and purer.

> "There the soul, mind and intellect find their real and proper
> form."   A

All the faculties of the devotee improve. The
faculties of his soul and mind become finer. The
intellect is sharpened. On listening to the melodies
of the Divine Sound, the mysteries of all the higher
and finer spiritual regions are revealed.

Everything is inside. Those who know the
method of going inside can find and possess
everything.

> "There is everything in the body,
> Vast lands, regions and under-worlds.
> The life-giver resides in the body,
> And sustains all.
> The treasures of spirituality are inside the body;
> The springs of devotion are also there.
> In the body are the nine regions of the earth,
> And all of its crowded commerce.
> In the body is the treasure of the Name,
> But can be found only through the Shabd of the Guru." A

In the regions of the soul, there are beautiful
heavenly regions and also their rulers. There are
many mountains and rivers and seas and deserts in
the way of the soul, and these cannot be even imagined.
This world is like a piece of seaweed in that ocean of
creation.

> "Inside man, are seas, deserts and mountains;
> All faculties of thought and imagination are overwhelmed to
> stillness, seeing them.
> In the vast empty space of the Fifth Region,
> This earth would look like a thin hair in the full-flooded ocean."5

Any left-over rambling tendencies are ended by listening to the Shabd, which resounds in all human beings. Then only comes complete concentration. This Sound Current is the heritage of all. We do not hear it, because our attention is extroverted This Divine Melody resounds at the headquarters of the soul in the body and can be heard at the eye focus by going within.

The Sound Current has the force of a magnet, which attracts the soul and makes it still. Then the soul passes through the Sound Current, to the place from which it emanates. This place is the origin of the whole world. When a person listens attentively to the Heavenly Sound, he begins to be enraptured by its bliss and automatically turns his back upon the world.

When the soul by means of simran or repetition is gathered at the eye center and crosses the starry regions, the sun and the moon, it beholds the astral form of the Master within. This form accompanies the disciple to the ultimate Home. The attention of the disciple then becomes strongly concentrated. He reaches this stage by means of simran or repetition. Simran is not much needed thereafter. The disciple worships and meditates on the Guru, and by degrees the two become one. He merges in the Master. The hint given by the Gurus when they say: "Leave yourself and merge in the Guru" refers to this state. In this way, the disciple automatically finds his way to the higher regions.

When one gets the company of the inner Guru, he looks one-pointedly at his form and into his eyes, and as a result of the wonderful light and magnetic attraction of the Master he reaches a high degree of concentration. His soul leaves the body easily and rises to inner regions and sees various scenes there. Besides this there is no other method for easily concentrating and seeing the beautiful sights of the inner regions. Simran and contemplation are now complete and the music of the Shabd, which was dimly heard at first, is now clearly heard. It intoxicates the mind and gladdens the soul.

The purpose of simran is to collect the soul behind the eyes so that this earthly vessel, the body, may be vacated at will. The purpose of contemplation is to hold the soul still in the upper regions. This results from fixing the attention on the radiant form of the Master. The function of the Divine Melody is to take the soul up to the higher regions. When a disciple has access to the radiant form of the Master, he may consider half the battle as won. After this, the act of rising to higher regions is both easy and joyous. The Master takes the disciple along with Him by the radiance of His light and the wonderfully sweet melodies of the Divine Sound. They enter the region of the thousand-petaled lotus, which is in the center of the astral region and is very brilliant. In this region the Negative Power places certain obstacles in the disciple's way. But the Master removes them and takes the soul across.

After passing through many other spiritual regions, the Master takes the disciple to Sach Khand, the True Region.

The Kingdom of Sach Khand is within us, but it cannot be entered without knowing the proper way. We should go within. The way to do this is the practice of listening to the Shabd. It is only by this practice that we can obtain release from the mind and Maya, pain and pleasure, duality and birth and death.

In conclusion it may be said that the teachings of the perfect Masters of the highest order have always insisted upon two basic points or principles.

The first is the absolute necessity for a *Living* Perfect Master who can take the souls of his disciples back to their Original Home in the highest heavenly region. These Masters point out that a doctor who died two thousand years ago cannot heal people who are today suffering from disease. No more can a Master who lived some hundreds or thousands of years ago give people of today the true initiation or baptism, or connect the souls of the seekers with their Creator and thus set their feet on the path of true and final liberation or salvation.

The second is the importance of Shabd or Nam, commonly called in English the Sound Current or the Audible Life Stream. It is the Nad of the Vedas; Bang-i-Asmani or Kalam-i-Ilahi of the Mohammedan Saints; the Tao and the Way or Celestial Sound of Lao Tze, the great Chinese spiritual Master; and the Holy Ghost, Holy Spirit and Word or Logos of the Bible. The Shabd is the Supreme Creator Himself vibrating and resounding throughout the whole creation and inside every human body. It is upon its wave that we have to return to our Original Home. Only a living perfect Master is able to put souls in direct contact with this Shabd or Nam which ultimately leads to their release from the cycle of birth and death.

BOOK 2

RELATIONSHIPS TO THE WORLD

CHAPTER 1

THE WORLD IS NOT OUR HOME

This universe is unstable and perishable. It is continually changing. It will not be tomorrow as it is today. There is no stability in this world. It is the land of death, and like a house of sand it can be destroyed at any time.

Whatever is seen here is some day going to perish. Every object in the universe is short-lived. Kings, subjects, houses, palaces, those who dwell in them, all the objects of the universe, gold and silver and their wearers, this body, clothes, men and women, all are perishable. The people have forgotten the Lord because of these entanglements. No one really deserves to be loved here. Many have gone, some are going and the rest are ready to go.

> "Neither wealth, wife, riches, house nor anything else will accompany us. Know this for certain." A

> "We see people die every day, but live in the hope that we will live for ever. What can be more strange?" D

> "You are a guest for the night, but hope to live for ages; The houses and riches which you see, are like the shade, cast by a tree, which is constantly moving." A

But still we remain engrossed in this universe. Our wealth, our wife, our riches and our houses are not ours, and nothing will go with us when we leave. Why, then, are we so fond of them?

We are wasting our invaluable time on objects

that will be left behind, and do not think of that which will accompany us. The body that comes with us does not accompany us. Its form and its youth will not remain the same. How can reliance be placed on relations and objects connected with this body? It is a question of the value of life. We should keep in our minds that which we really wish to know and the ideal we wish to reach. He who remembers death remains free from the bondage of the world and cannot do any evil action.

Human birth is an opportunity for meeting the Lord. He who does not engage in devotion to the Lord and does not practise the Name wastes his life. Human birth is rare. Do not waste it. Spend it in devotion to the Lord.

In this perishable body only the soul is real and immortal, and one should care for it with true devotion.

Devotion

The quality of devotion is working instinctively in all human beings. It is a natural inclination in everybody to live in communion or in happiness and joy with somebody else, because man by nature is a social being and is not content unless he is able to become one with the object of his affection. Till such a time he remains restless and his mind wavers.

In this world people have devotion of various kinds. Some are devoted to amassing wealth. Others are happy in devotion to their family. Still others take pleasure in becoming great in the eyes of society and try to acquire knowledge and artistic abilities.

The devotees of wealth, work day and night cease-lessly and are able to amass some wealth, but this leads to a desire for amassing more and more. If we are able to save a thousand dollars, we are then naturally inclined to save more hundreds of thousands, and this money-amassing obsession completely over-powers us.

One who is greedy cannot, because of that greed, freely use his wealth, nor can he leave it. He is, therefore, burning in the secret fires of his greed. When one devotes himself to wealth, he is always afraid of thieves and is constantly thinking of how to keep his wealth safe in vaults or strong boxes. This worry becomes a part of his life. He is also afraid of this wealth being taken away by the powers that be. All comfort and peace of mind are destroyed by the constant worry.

A greedy person is extremely selfish because he is not capable of using his wealth for his own needs, and will not dole it out amongst the poor or others. So it is true that wealth is not worthy of our devotion. We were not born for amassing wealth, because wealth is like a shadow that lengthens and shrinks at different times, and when wealth goes, it causes a mental dis-turbance. Actually, wealth is for the use of man, and man was not born to be its slave.

Our relatives, our family and our community— all are subject to extinction by death. Nobody is free from death, and everybody is going his own way. If all these people are subject to death and separation, why should one attach oneself to them? They all have different temperaments and naturally there are differences of opinion. Consequently, devotion to them cannot be unchanging or always the same.

Devotion to one's community and to one's family is better than devotion to one's own self. And devotion to one's own nation is still better. But this has natural pitfalls because it gives rise to favoritism and group rivalry. Sometimes one has to do desirable and undesirable things in order to keep up his own reputation, for he is always concerned about the criticism of others.

Yet it is desirable that a person engaged in devotion to his nation or country should be fearless of all criticism, should stick to his principles, and should not be afraid of any adverse opinion. Truth will not diminish and should never be abandoned.

People who are absorbed in devotion to their own family often create enmities with others. People who are devotees of their country also quarrel with each other and with other countries. The fire of war and enmity in the world is entirely due to the pugnacious tendencies of such people.

Similarly, those who are proud of their intellectual attainments are often fond of arguments and wrangling, which lead them farther away from the Truth. Such people always try to fight on the plane of intellect. The egotism of knowledge swells their heads, and they are so intoxicated by it that at times they even forget their principles. Brother becomes an enemy of brother, and by the help of science, technology and learning, weapons of destruction are produced. This type of knowledge is constantly on the increase and is a cause of conflict and misery.

All these things—wealth, family, intellect, and so on—may be good for our own use and happiness, but they must be used properly; and because it is not possible to do so, they are not worthy of our devotion. They are incomplete in themselves, and are not permanent.

Amongst all the types of devotion, the highest is that which is offered to God (Sat Purush), who is One, Unchangeable and Indestructible. He is the Creator of all, and we are all His children. By loving God we are also able to love all His creatures, because we are all brothers and God is the Father of all of us. Through this love there flows the current of the Fatherhood of God and the Brotherhood of Man.

You cannot see your face in ordinary plate glass, but if it is chemically made into a mirror, you can see your face in it. In a similar manner, if a pure heart is filled with devotion and love, that heart is able to see in itself the image of God.

We should be devoted to that which is sublime, beautiful and perfect, which has a power of attraction like that of a powerful magnet and can draw the minds of others into its own, and which fills our minds with a peculiar happiness and tranquility.

Detachment

Absence of attachment is detachment. Attachment is another name for longing or desire for material objects or persons. One becomes detached when he is able to take his attention away from these objects. A person with discrimination knows that this world is impermanent; it is all illusion and subject to dissolution. When detachment is achieved all these worldly objects and relations lose their importance, and all the ties of attachment are automatically loosened.

When the mind is diverted from worldly objects and relations and is attracted towards a higher aim, that is also detachment; in other words, the mind is removed from the worldly longings and is restless in the feeling of separation from the Lord. The awakening of such love is the key to detachment. Saint Augustine says:

> "It is the great evil of man to desire to enjoy the things which he ought only to lose, and to lose those which he ought to enjoy."

In fact, everything pertaining to this world should be discarded, and everything pertaining to Spirituality should be imbibed. That is real detachment. In order to meet God, one should detach oneself carefully and with discrimination. Then alone will he receive the real benefit; that is, he will be able to rise above the cycle of birth and death.

> "If one acquires detachment of the mind through careful discrimination, he is free from the cycle of birth and death." A

In order to be truly detached, it is necessary to be detached from everything in this world. And to do this it is not necessary to leave one's home, society or other connections. What would happen if one were to leave his hearth and home? The mind would create new ties even in a jungle, not only with the surroundings but also with abstract desires. Saints do not advocate that type of detachment. The real detachment is to detach one's soul and mind from the love of the world and its objects.

A person appears in this world and then vanishes from sight like a bubble. What happens prior to

his birth and after his departure?   The desire to know
the secrets of this mystery of life arises in the mind of
a seeker.   In that state his mind is naturally detached
from worldly illusions and he tries to engage himself
in a search for a much higher Being.

When one meets a perfect Master, then alone
will he be able to understand fully the implications and
the meaning of true detachment.   Then he need not
try to run away from the world and leave his household
in order to lead a life of detachment.

> "O my mind! If you meet a true Master you need not run
> out to achieve detachment, because He is the bestower of
> all gifts and is the treasure of all comforts, and is the fountain
> of Elixir, running at all times to take the devotees into life
> Everlasting."   A

In the company of a Master, the soul of a disciple imbibes the qualities of God and all other tastes
in the world become insipid.   The devotee is engaged
in worldly pursuits, but within himself he is above
their ties because of detachment.   He lives in the
world but he is not a man of the world.   He realizes
that God is the highest goal, and he forgets his world
in remembrance of Him.   So even while living in the
world, he cannot forget Him

The truly detached person knows that one day
his own body, his house, his palace and all his worldly
property—all attachments—have to be left behind,
and nobody knows when this will happen.   Therefore,
he lives in this world in name only and gives more
attention to the purification of his soul, for he does
not wish to barter his soul for the sake of this world.

> "For what is a man profited, if he shall gain the whole world,
> and lose his own soul?"   B

One who has reached the stage where he can see his Master within at will, is always a detached person. He will completely disregard the criticism of others. A truly detached person is one who has a strong desire to meet the Lord and for whom it is not possible to live without Him. He thinks of Him with every breath and considers life useless without Him.

"The world is all illusion without service to the Master. Without Shabd nobody can cross the ocean of this world. He alone is fully detached who is fully engrossed in Shabd, because this Shabd is true. Shabd is my Master and Shabd is my Spiritual Guide who is as deep as the sea. This world is a desolate land without Shabd. Only a truly detached person can attain the state of Sahaj.
So says Nanak, O ye! take it as true!"   A

Such a person, having realized his self, lives desirelessly in the world of desires. His mind is in contemplation day and night. Such a person is really detached and merges in the Lord. One who has renounced all desires and is also free from the attachment of illusion, is detached from all directions and really has detachment ingrained in his mind. Such a person is very fortunate.

CHAPTER 2

ACTION WITHOUT DESIRE

Before we are able to understand the doctrine or the principle of desireless action, we must understand what really is meant by the word "action". Action means something done. Before you do anything, there is a desire, an intention or an urge in your mind. The desire is first formed within the mind, and then it is executed outside. A simple example will make this clear:

A person got it into his head that he wished to kill another person. This constituted his intention or internal action. In order to execute or fulfill the desire, he took up a weapon and killed the man. This was the external execution of that internal action. The internal action emits certain currents (the effects are in one's aura even if one does not execute the action externally), so that it makes a deep impression not only on his mind but also causes a disturbance in the environment around him.

We should therefore keep careful watch over our mind and consider how we can attain the state of desireless action. The teachings of the Saints and those contained in our religious Scriptures enable us to make the proper choice.

Action plays a great part in spiritual matters. A man has a physical body, but he acts through his mind. Whatever mental attitude one has, becomes manifested in action. "Thought is the keynote of our

success" was said by the great philosopher, Emerson.
Therefore, the actions of a person are governed by his
thoughts.   And good or bad actions are the results
of the same degree of good or bad thoughts which
he entertains.

Consequently, a person becomes a good or a
bad person as a result of his good or bad actions.
And all this is done in accordance with one's own
desires.   Actions, therefore, mould our lives in virtuous or evil directions so long as we perform such
actions with desire.

We have to act for the benefit of our own body
and for the benefit of others.   Otherwise, we would
be a burden on society.   Therefore, it is essential
for human beings to act.   History reveals that Saints
have always practised and approved of such actions.
To remain "actionless" while acting is the main
puzzle which must be clearly understood.

A person who has conquered his mind will be
able to control his physical actions.   One who is
free from attachment and hatred is a genuinely
actionless person.

How can we attain this reactionless state?   How
can a person be released from the bondage of attachment?   How can the cycle of births and deaths, which
is the necessary consequence of our actions, be made
to cease?   And who can understand the enigma of
'reactionless action' even while acting?   All these
questions are answered in the Scriptures by a simple
reply to the effect that these things can be understood
only if one becomes a Gurumukh.

What is a Gurumukh?   One who surrenders
himself to a Guru (Master); that is, one who lovingly

and implicitly follows the instructions of a Guru. The Guru bestows the Gift of Nam, by the practice of which one burns away his ego, and attains the true state of "Actionlessness". Thus, by the Grace of the Master, the load of karmas is lightened.

"Man does not become karmaless (without action) by simply renouncing actions or by not doing them, because a man cannot live even for a second without doing some action. The mental currents create actions in man at all times. One who forcibly suppresses his physical self from performing actions is deceiving himself, for his mind cannot be restrained permanently in this manner. Therefore, that person is really great who conquers his mind by withdrawing it from worldly desires and thus acts with a disinterested or unattached mind. That is to say, disinterested as far as the fruit of action is concerned, but interested in serving the Lord only. He performs his prescribed duties as indicated in his moral or religious code, because to act is far better than not to act. The body is given to us for the purpose of action, both internal and external." C

Actually, all actions that are performed under the influence of the ego—whether good or bad—are equally responsible for the ties of attachment which bind an individual to this world. Good and bad actions are equally responsible for binding a person. The fetters may be of iron or may be of gold, but both have the same effect of binding. Good actions may temporarily give us a reward in heaven, and bad actions may bring us the punishment of hell, but the bondage of transmigration remains.

All religions have laid great emphasis on desireless actions. The Bhagavadgita, or the Song of the Lord, is replete with teachings of desirelessness or desireless action. It says: "In this world one should take refuge in God after renouncing all desires and all actions arising therefrom."

Hindu Philosophy also teaches that in order to attain Salvation it is necessary to get rid of all desires and the fruits of all worldly actions caused by such desires. The same teaching of karmaless action is contained in all holy books.

> "The aim of human life is that a man should put his mind to yogic action. He should have fraternal thoughts for all fellow beings and should consider himself to be present in all, while everything pervades in him."

> "O Arjun, under the influence of your ego you believe that you should not fight. This idea of yours is fallacious, because the action which you do not wish to perform, you will have to do under the compulsion of your nature."   C

So long as a person considers himself to be the doer, he is weighed down by the shackles of karma. A person who renounces all desires and the fruits of all his actions, becomes independent of all actions and their results.

> "O Arjun, one whose mind has no thought that 'I am doing it' and whose mind is not engrossed in worldly attachments and worldly desires, such a person—even if he should kill somebody—does not kill anybody and is not bound by the result of this action."   C

> "O Arjun, renounce all self-interest and consider reward and punishment alike. Engage yourself in spiritual practice and then perform the action. Such action is free from effect, and you should perform all your actions in this manner."

> "Those persons who do karmas in this manner are freed from the ties of transmigration and attain the highest form of Salvation."   C

Progress of all kinds—intellectual, physical, religious, spiritual and moral—is possible only with good health. A sick man cannot engage himself in any religious activity. He will be unable to do anything for his country, to earn his own livelihood, to work for society, community or religion. He cannot even engage himself in his own spiritual upkeep. How then can he realize himself!

Food is very necessary for preserving the body. Without it, the body cannot be maintained. It should be light, easily digestible and taken in such a quantity as does not exceed our needs.

One should not eat only for taste. We should see that the food which we take is neither excessive nor insufficient for our body's needs. It should also contain ingredients producing energy essential for the upkeep of the body and the brain. A tasty food taken in excess is harmful. For brain and mental work, one should eat nuts, fruits, apples, grapes, milk, almonds, etc. For persons engaging in physical labor, butter, carbohydrates, rice, sugar, etc, are necessary. Similarly, strength-giving and bone-forming foods like wheat, milk, butter, etc., should be taken.

We must have plenty of air, water and carbohydrates. Air is foremost, without which one cannot live. Water comes next. Both are free gifts of nature. Carbohydrates found in cereals are third in importance.

Whatever is necessary for man to eat is found in fruits, vegetabls and cereals, butter and milk. Wheat is considered to be the best energy producing food among cereals. Wheat flour from which the bran has not been separated is most beneficial.

Wholesome food should be prepared from vegetables and cereals purchased out of the hard-earned income acquired by honest means. The person preparing should have wholesome ideas and he should repeat and remember God's Name with a peaceful and tranquil mind while preparing the food. The effect of these measures is reflected in the food and in those who eat it. By taking such food there would be peace in their minds and they would readily engage in remembering the Lord.

The Saints* teach us that we absolutely cannot make spiritual progress if we kill animals for our food. In Kal's world we must take life in some form to support our bodies, but daily meditation will take care of any karma due to taking necessary food from the vegetable kingdom.

Also, it is absolutely necessary for spiritual progress that one earns one's own living honestly or by one's own labor. Only such persons can worship, whose earnings are honest.

"For meditation, take food which is honestly earned so that your grief and suffering may not increase."

Honestly-earned food produces a peculiar light in us. Food is like a seed. As the seeds are impure or pure, their fruits will produce bad or good thoughts in our minds. By intake of food earned both by hard labor and by honest means, we shall be inclined to contemplate and remember the Lord. By eating hard-earned bread we begin to imbibe good virtues. God has given us hands and feet. We should earn our food by their proper use. We must not covet

*There is ample evidence that Christ taught and practised the vegetarian diet, but that it was dropped from the teaching of the church in the 4th century in order to gain acceptance by the Emperor Constantine.

or desire the wealth of others. To beg is to be under obligation and is to depend on others. Be content with whatever you get. Do not depend on anyone. Do not be tempted by the luxurious living of others.

When a person looks to others for his living, he does not remain independent but becomes a slave of others and indulges in undue flattery. By not using his hands, feet, brain and ears, he becomes incapacitated.

It is necessary to earn money for one's living by fair means. Money earned by foul means is really not wealth but blood of others. Guru Sahib said that money is necessary for living whether one is a begger or a rich man. To conceal one's riches and to show oneself as a detached person is to deceive the world. If one depends upon others through his lazy habits, he too deserves condemnation. Saints have always taught that one should earn one's own livelihood.

If one is engaged in business or a profession and does his work with love, he will never cheat anyone nor deprive other persons of their rightful due. The world is always prepared to listen to the message of love because it is inherent in all of us; and if we practise it daily it becomes manifest in us.

Surrendering everything to the Lord is the first step towards the path of Devotion because if everything is surrendered to Him in all humility, we are released from the load of karmas and become worthy of realizing Him within. But so long as the record of karmas is not obliterated internally by destroying our ego, we cannot become actionless. Actions are pure only if performed without any desire for reward. And one who performs his actions in this manner is action-less even while acting. Such a person achieves God-Realization.

An action can only be performed through inten-tion or desire, and without these no action can be executed (because whenever a person acts, it is difficult for him to get rid of the thought of reward or punish-ment.)

If, therefore, a person wishes to perform a desi-reless action, he can only do so by complete detach-ment from the world. So long as a man has not achieved such a state of desirelessness, he should do his best and leave the results of all his actions in the hands of his Almighty Father. In that way he will not be subject to the consequences of his actions. In addition to this, he should engage himself in spir-itual practice according to the instructions of a per-fect Master, because when he has made some progress in the Spiritual Path, his karmas will begin to dis-appear.

If it were necessary to renounce everything in this world in order to obtain the state of desirelessness, it would be exceedingly difficult, if not impossible, for everyone to be able to do so. Very few indeed would be able to achieve it, and all praise would be due them.

At the moment, however, we have to consider how the large majority of people who regard such renunciation as beyond their reach, should achieve desireless karma. For such persons it is necessary to perform all action in the Name of God. To obtain release from the fetters of Karma, it is necessary for such persons to engage in spiritual practice according to the instructions of a perfect Master and to inculcate in themselves the spirit of devotion to the Lord and the Master.

> "Whatever you do, whatever you eat, whatever you give, whatever you worship, whatever penances you perform, O Arjun, surrender them all to me, because by doing so you will be free from the consequences of actions (you will be actionless) and, traversing the path of Renunciation, you will attain liberation and will merge in me." C

CHAPTER 3

DO NOT INJURE THE FEELINGS OF OTHERS

In order to tread the Path of Spirituality it is necessary to abstain from injuring the feelings of others and to imbibe the virtue of sympathy with others and to hearten them. Injury to the feelings of others produces darkness in the heart, while sympathizing with others and keeping them satisfied fills the heart with light. Injury to feelings of others results in impurity and disfiguration, while sympathy leads to beauty and decoration. One leads to hardening and difficulties, while the other leads to softening and simplicity. Injury to the feelings of others means causing pain to their hearts. This takes three forms:

(1) *Mental:* Control your mind so that the thought of injuring others does not enter it.

(2) *Vocal:* Keep watch on your tongue so that it may not utter any improper words. It should not be soiled with impolite or abusive words. Abuse is one, but its reverberations are many. Evil words lead to disputes, disharmony and sufferings. An angry man, in uttering improper words, uses the basest of abuses and wants to win the field, but a saint admits defeat and keeps silent. Abuses are like live coals and emit smoke of anger, rage and backbiting. One can be called a sadhu only if he gives them up.

"The abuse is one when it comes, but many when it reverberates.
O Kabir, if it is not returned, it remains one only.

Abuse leads to disputes, sufferings and disharmony.
He who admits defeat is a saint; he who quarrels is mean.
Abuse is a live coal and anger, deceit and backbiting are smoke.
He who remains aloof from them is called a holy man."   4

"Drink wine and burn the carpet. Set fire to the Ka'aba. Become the dweller of the idol house. But give up injuring the feelings of others."

(3) *Bodily or Physical:* Control the body so that none of the organs, hands or feet may cause harm to anyone. To cause pain to another man's heart is violence which is forbidden. He who wounds the heart of others by his words or actions is a great sinner.

Forgiveness

Forgiveness means to forgive the faults of others, and to have no thought of it in the mind thereafter. Persons without forgiveness fight each other and exterminate themselves. Millions of persons perish because of lack of this virtue.

A person of forgiving nature is calm, humble, patient and forbearing. Even among great difficulties, he does not give up forgiveness and is always cheerful. There are two powers in the world. One is justice and the other is forgiveness born out of mercy. Justice is good, but that which can be achieved by forgiveness cannot be had by justice. To err is human. It is not at all uncommon for man to err. If errors are to be invariably punished, it would result in extirpation of the erring individuals. How can blood be washed with blood? If we demand justice, it punishes the guilty. The guilty man undergoes the punishment. This, however, does not remove the hatred against the complainant and the spirit of revenge is there. The resolve to take revenge for getting him punished is very much strengthened. Whenever he passes by the complainant, the mental desire to take revenge always springs. He gets no rest until he avenges him. This leads to retribution by the other side. The dispute thus increases, as justice cannot remove the thought of ill-will and revenge. But if we forgive any person out of kindness and mercy, it has great effect. The dispute is settled. The thought of revenge does not arise. On the other hand, the person forgiven feels grateful to the person forgiving him, and has a feeling of friendship for him.

The feelings of inflicting punishment and taking revenge spread unrest, uneasiness and disorder in the world. The reactions correspond to the thoughts sent out, and they affect us accordingly. If you send out currents of love you will get those of love as reaction. If you have thoughts of hatred against anyone, you will get the same in return. Actions beget reaction. If you propagate thoughts of love, you will get the fruits of love. If you sow thorns only, thorns will grow. Practise forgiveness, and people will forgive you. You reap what you sow.

"O Farid! how can you expect grapes after sowing thorns; How can silk be the product of spinning wool?" 13

If we will not think ill of anyone, our love would be universal. When we will forgive the guilty and not wish ill for him, we will have no enemy. A forgiving person is always happy. It is impossible to describe the happiness, calmness of mind and peace which result from forgiveness.

It is only a brave man who can forgive. This is beyond the power of a weak man. The Lord is kind and compassionate. Where there is compassion, there the power to forgive can arise. For this reason, the great Saint Kabir has assigned a very high position to forgiveness. He goes to the extent of saying that the Lord Himself dwells in a forgiving person. Where there is forgiveness, the Lord is there in the form of mercy.

Ibrahim Adham, the King of Bokhara, had to remain with Saint Kabir for a number of years. After serving him for some time, he appeared to be very calm, quiet and serene in nature. One day Kabir's wife, Loi, requested the Saint to initiate him. Kabir, who was aware of Ibrahim Adham's inner progress, said, "The receptacle is not yet ready." On Loi's insistence the Saint said: "When Ibrahim Adham goes out of the house, throw a basket of sweepings over him from the roof." When this was done, Ibrahim exclaimed: "O! How I wish I were in Bokhara. Then I could have taught the guilty person a lesson." When Kabir was told of this he remarked: "Did I not say that the vessel was unclean?"

After a few more years had passed, the Saint one day told his wife, "The vessel is now clean." Loi said, "Outwardly he is still the same and renders service as quietly as he did before." On hearing this Kabir said, "The previous time you merely threw house sweepings on him. This time throw a basket full of filth and, concealing yourself, listen to what he says." When Ibrahim came out of the house the Saint's wife threw the filth on his head, spoiling all his clothes. Looking up quietly he said, "I am grateful to the person who has thrown this rubbish on my head. May God's grace be upon him."

Forgiveness extinguishes the fire of anger. There is no other way to calm it. Man remains ignorant of the reality, owing to the veil of egoism. This can be understood on meeting a perfect Master only. The fire of desires and egoism is extinguished. Anger can be given up by giving place to forgiveness in one's mind by the grace of the Master. Egoism and anger leave the mind wherein contentment dwells.

The highest embellishment of forgiveness is the divine glory of the Saints and they preach its practice.

Sweetness

By sweetness is meant sociability, civility, broad-mindedness, polite speaking, cheerfulness and for-bearance. It is necessary for a beautiful face to have good habits, otherwise the beauty is useless. If there is a beautiful house in a beautiful city, but only owls reside there, what is its beauty? There may be a green tree, but if there are no flowers or fruits on it, then of what use can it be? A gold watch which does not tell time, or a beautiful lamp which does not give light, is of no value. Similarly, a man may be very beautiful, and may wear costly clothes, but if he is not social, is not good-mannered, courteous and polite, then he is without human virtues. What makes a man really a man are his sociability and cheerfulness.

The bounties of the Lord are reserved for the person who greets others with a cheerful heart and an open mind.

If a man is handsome or rich, this concerns himself. If he is social and cheerful, he influences others. If he is always cross and has wrinkles on his brows, nobody wants to see him, to say nothing of meeting him. Sweet speech full of humility goes to the bottom of another man's heart, and this is the real glory and embellishment of man.

Shah Farindu was asked as to how he supervised his servants. He replied, "By politeness and forbearance." He was then asked as to how he solved his difficulties. He replied, "By leniency and kindness."

However serious the difficulty, use politeness, sweetness and melody. It can succeed better than use of the sword or violence. The wound inflicted by a sword heals in course of time, but that caused by a sharp word becomes fresh every time you remember the words. It is, therefore, necessary to watch the speech so that no harsh words are used. Think before you speak. Even if there is an occasion, ask to be excused, as a matter of courtesy. It tastes sweet to take bitter pills from a cheerful person. It, however, becomes difficult to take even a sweet thing from the hands of a rude man.

The mind is like a crow, which has no other wish than to annoy people. But as soon as it is steeped in love, it becomes a swan and troubles no one.

The heart is the true mosque of God. It is the temple of the Lord. Everyone's heart is the Lord's tabernacle. He who causes pain to hearts strikes and breaks that temple. He who causes pain to others not only desecrates and ruins the temples of others, but demolishes the temple of his own heart also.

The world is like a machine and we are its parts. Even if one part is injured, the machine cannot run properly. Even if one organ of the body ails, the whole body becomes restless. The world is like a body of which we are parts. How can we be happy if we injure any organ? If one understands this, he does not injure any living being or any other animate object, to say nothing of injuring a man. His whole way of thinking, speaking and acting changes. Mind, speech and body are the means of doing both evil and good. A man becomes the doer of evil and good through them. To think ill of others is a sin of the mind. Jealousy, hatred and enmity are evils of the mind. Harsh words, criticism of others, speaking ill of them and abusing them are sins of speech. Wrong actions are sins of the body. These include adultery, killing and violence.

When you meet another person cheerfully, you shower flowers, and the other man becomes full of its scent. Be cheerful like a flower. Whoever would meet you would share your happiness.

We should not be of hasty temperament. We should be courteous in our daily behavior. Whoever comes in contact with you would be pleased with you. To be courteous on a particular occasion is called politeness, but when one is always courteous and mild he is called civil. This virtue is very helpful in spiritual matters.

Continence—Chastity

Continence does not mean that one should merely control his lust and sensual passions. It means actually to withdraw oneself from all the sense desires. If we listen to sensual talks with our ears and see things with our eyes that stimulate passions and yet avoid sexual urge, it would be like putting one's hand in fire and hoping that it will not be burnt. One should therefore withdraw one's attention and thought from all things which stimulate passion in order to achieve success in one's celibacy. The aim of continence is to try to seek God because it is a powerful medium for the goal of His realization.

In the eyes of the Master, if a man and woman are to live together, it is absolutely essential that they be legally married.

Chastity is the most beautiful flower of all human virtues. It makes an angel of a man or woman. Its beauty lies in its own purity. It has the quality of keeping the soul and the body free from any blemish and defeat. Chastity consists in having no thought of connection with any person other than one's own wife or husband. It needs very great restraint because chastity may be destroyed by even thinking an evil thought. Fruits remain fresh on the trees, but once they are plucked their freshness is destroyed. One may preserve them for sometime by placing them in a jar of honey. Similarly, chastity of a man or woman, once broken, can be protected only by devotion of a very high order. Such a devotion has a protecting influence for the soul, just as honey has for plucked fruit. We are otherwise destroyed like a moth in the fire.

If after marriage a woman gives her entire love to her husband and the husband gives all his love to his wife, then what is left to give others? A faithful wife or husband is ready to do everything possible for the other. How can they then love the Lord or His creation? They cannot consider the entire humanity as their family as they themselves are moving in a narrow sphere. As their progeny increases, their love for the all-pervading Lord decreases. How then can they attain truth?

What then is the remedy for married persons? How can they realize the Lord? There is only one way—it is that their connection with or devotion to each other should not be based on satisfaction of their lust, but they should lead a life of restraint with the only object of producing offspring. Their sexual desires should be on the basis of scriptural injunctions. They should have marital relations only once a month until such time as a child is conceived, whom they should be able to bring up and make self-supporting.

The aim of human life is not the production of children alone. Our main aim is to unite the soul with God. A person on the spiritual path should always have this goal in view. The relationship of man and wife after a certain age, say 40 or 50 years, should be discontinued. One should then, while earning his living with his own labor, dedicate his time to the service of the Lord and His creatures. All saints and great souls have followed such a path. They led a married life of restraint up to a certain age and thereafter they gave up this aspect of their activity. Swami Ram Tirth said that as long as men and women do not learn to live as brothers and sisters and lead lives of purity they cannot hope to make any progress. Lives of persons, who have tasted purity of existence, have been happy, healthy and without worries. To consider our elders as mothers and others as sisters or daughters will raise a man to a high moral ideal and will relieve him from many troubles of the world. It also increases his mental and physical strength. Others remain weak, unhealthy and are victims of many troubles.

This continence cannot be practised by control of body alone, for control of mind is essential for the control of the body. Continence should therefore be observed with mind, speech and action. If one controls the body but thinks of sensual pleasures, it is harmful, for the mind pushes the body in that direction.

Dr. Nicholson writes, "It is a medical and physiological fact that the best blood in the body goes to form elements of reproduction in both sexes. In a pure and orderly life, this matter is re-absorbed and it goes back into circulation ready to form the finest brain, nerve and muscular tissues. This matter carried back and diffused through his system makes a man manly, brave and heroic."

If one remains celibate, even simple food is sufficient to keep fit and healthy and one will not need medicines and so forth. His life will become pure, his heart and body will be strong and he will attain long life. He will also be able to control his anger and his sense organs. He will have a pure, clean and good heart. He will be virtuous, non-violent and of a good moral character. Thus his children will be a valuable asset to the coming generation.

Keep the company of pure men. If you cannot meet them, contemplate lovingly on the Master. In this way, your inner dirt would be washed. Do not, therefore, permit anybody to spoil your chastity. In order to be chaste, you should avoid the company of such persons as are given to sensual enjoyments. The poison of their lustful ideas will surely affect those who come across them. You should always keep the company of pure and chaste persons. If you fail to get such company, meditate on the form of the Master with love and devotion. In this manner, your inner impurities will gradually be washed out.

Charity

The Lord is bountiful. He is the giver of all blessings. We always pray, "O bountiful Lord, give us" and He always grants us boons.

Whatever He is giving, is for all. Whatever we have, others also have a right to it. We should share and enjoy. We all belong to the Lord. If we really become His, then all become our partners and nobody will seem to us to be outside the sphere of the Lord.

To share one's hard-earned income with the helpless and the sick and to spend it on the poor, the downtrodden and orphans is called charity. Charity is very necessary for the good of the world. Charity is a meritorious action. By charity, fragrance and freshness increase while stinginess leads to stinking. It is like well water which remains cool, fresh and sweet as long as the well is worked. Charity is sharing wealth with the needy and spending it on good works. He who does not spend in charity, wastes his wealth on unfruitful actions. Kabir Sahib has said:

> "When water increases in the boat or wealth in the house,
> To take it out with both hands is what the wise do."

Guru Nanak says, "Perform charity with due caution. Sow the seed of charity in the field after examining it." Charity should be given only to such of the needy, the helpless and the orphans, who are not engaged in evil deeds. Serve the hungry and the thirsty. What is the use of giving wealth to those who already have it? To perform charity without due consideration, is like sowing seed in barren land.

By subscribing to institutions other than the needy, the seeker after spirituality is, in a way, sowing seed in barren land.

To earn by one's own labor and to share it with the needy leads to acceptance at the door of the Lord. An old man went on pilgrimage to Mecca (Haj). In his dream he saw two angels. One asked, "How many persons have come for pilgrimage?" The other replied, "Six lakhs." The first one asked, "How many are accepted?" The other said, "None." He, however, said that there was a cobbler in Damascus who did not come, but his Haj was accepted. On enquiry it was found that he collected the money for Haj but as his neighbors were hungry he spent the money on them.

True charity consists in earning not only for our own subsistence, but in spending part on others for spiritual good and without expectation of reward.

As to who is entitled to receive charity can be known from a holy man only, so give in charity after enquiring from him. They do not covet your wealth as they have the wealth of Nam. They are care-free. They will distribute the money given by you to the hungry and the thirsty and thus do good to you. You would thus become the cause of making them happy and earn their grace.

The highest form of charity is soul charity or giving of Nam. This can be done by Masters only.

They do not accept any consideration for the same, and are happy in giving it. They confer a great boon on the world but do not even mention it. They give life and persuade persons to engage in devotion. These Masters help millions by making a gift of the ray of Nam.

Humanity

Humanity simply means love for the Lord and His creation. Its other name is sympathy or compassion, fellow-feeling or heartfelt attraction. Its proof is that one's heart melts like wax on seeing the suffering of another. The other man's suffering appears to him as his own. He heartens him, feels sympathy for and is attracted to him, and takes steps to remove his sufferings. A man should feel for others and consider their sufferings as his own. Sheikh Sa'adi says that if there are no feelings of kindness, mercy or love, then there is no difference in such a man and the figure of a man on the wall. Both are useless.

"The heart without love is like a graveyard; just like the bellows of an ironsmith which breathes though lifeless."

The fire of love being kindled, other virtues and gifts come of themselves.

"Love, and all things shall be added unto you."

God is Love and the world lives by Love. It is therefore the duty of a human being to love. One who loves never injures the feelings of others.

Not to hurt the feelings of others by thought, words and action is good principle. This can only happen when we have love for the Lord who pervades all. A seeker after spirituality never hurts the feelings of others as he believes that all are His creation.

LOVE

It is not easy to understand love because its true nature and greatness cannot be described in words. It is a pure and delicate feeling or emotion, which can be experienced only by one who is in love. It is beyond the capacity of the tongue or the pen to describe it in any human language. Actually, love is another name for God. And just as it is not possible to reduce God's greatness to mortal dimensions, so also is it not possible to describe adequately in any words known to man, the grandeur and sublimity of love.

It is the natural desire of all human beings to be happy, and happiness is the fruit of concentration of the mind. This treasure of concentration and happiness of mind can easily be obtained through love, because these qualities are the natural attributes of love. Without love, everything in this world becomes subject to miseries and misunderstandings, which cause domestic quarrels, religious disputes, bloodshed and even wars among the nations.

God looks on all beings as the same. No one is better or worse than another. In His eyes there are no nationalities, races or creeds. For Him, all are His creatures. A person who understands this Truth is not capable of hating anybody. He is a lover of God, whose Light shines in all human beings. He loves everybody. People of all faiths—Hindus,

Mohammedans, Sikhs and Christians—are the recipients of His love. All religious scriptures, Saints and Masters have always preached this Truth: We should love every created being. According to the Bible, Christ said:

> "Ye have heard that it hath been said, thou shalt love thy neighbor and hate thine enemy. But I say unto you, love your enemies, bless them that curse you, do good to them that hate you, and pray for them which despitefully use you, and persecute you."

Wherever there is love there is life. Where there is no love, life is worthless. Actually, a man is not a true man unless he has within him the divine spark of love. God, in the form of love, is within everybody. Those whose eyes are open see all human beings as manifestations of God, like rays of the sun or the waves of the ocean. They know that the same spark of love has created them all. Therefore, who can be low or who can be high? Men in different positions of life and in different countries are all one in His eyes; and differences of caste, creed or country can never be of any importance to those who possess the quality of love. There is one God in heaven and one family on earth. Maulana Rum says:

> "The current of love from the one God is flowing through the entire universe. What do you think when you look at the face of a man? Look at him carefully. He is not a man, but a current of the Essence of God (Love), which permeates him."

Love is the richest of all treasures. Without it there is nothing; and with it there is everything. He who does not have love in his heart is not entitled to call himself a human being.

Love is not dependent upon anything else. It is an ocean of faith and fortitude. It is an ocean of strength and faith. It imparts peace and serenity to the mind and to life. It is of real and lasting value. All the things of this world appear beautiful when there is love. By the currents of love the entire atmosphere is charged with joy, and the spark of God's light is visible in love.

Love For The Spiritual And Love For The Physical

Love is of two kinds. One is physical and man-made and the other is spiritual or divine. Physical love is the love of worldly people who are continually tied to the world and its objects. Divine love is that of the devotee of the Lord, and it establishes a permanent connection with God.

The physical kind of love is of two types. One is that love which is caused by some special action, quality or circumstance associated with an object or a person.

A person may be a good artist or painter. Someone else may love him because he may be able to make use of his art by getting from him a beautifully painted picture or an artistically illustrated book. His love is based on this one purpose alone, and as soon as that purpose is fulfilled, his object being attained, his love for the artist is gone. This shows that his love was of a selfish nature and was not for the painter or the artist.

A man may love his wife only for the fulfillment of his sensual desires. As soon as his desires are fulfilled or the woman becomes unfit for that purpose, his love for the woman ends and he would like to enter into a new relationship with someone else. This would mean that his love was aroused by lower desires and was not for the wife at all.

Similarly, if a servant works well and obeys our orders, we love him. But when he becomes superannuated or indolent, he is turned out. When a horse is beautiful and has a good and fast trot, we love it. When it becomes weak and old, we try to get rid of it. Our love is not for the servant or the horse, but for the work they can do for us.

One person may be a beautiful singer and may have a sweet voice. Someone else loves music, so he also loves the singer; but as soon as the voice or the sweetness of the voice is gone due to illness or some other reason, his love also goes. Still another person may be handsome or beautiful and may be loved because of that quality. But if this quality should disappear (because of illness, accident or old age), the love for that person would also disappear, since he was loved for that quality alone. Normally, this is the state of love in the world. People love because of superficial beauty or external show. This is not true love.

Superior to this is the second type of physical love which is neither dependent on, nor created by any material circumstance, action or quality, and consequently does not vanish with them. Such a love is distinguished by one sign. It comes into being spontaneously, without any external cause. This love comes from the heart with strong currents, and in it there is no motive of gain or selfishness. This is known as natural love, and once experienced it becomes a permanent feature. True love remains constant.

Such a love is superior because it is neither dependent upon the quality or actions of its object, nor upon its transitory nature. Not only that, it does not cease even after death, because it merges into the soul. This degree of love is not found in the other type.

If one loves another without any selfish motive, he does not bother about the qualities of the beloved, and is always prepared to disregard the qualities for the sake of love, because the qualities without the beloved have no meaning or value for him. The heart of such a person is brightened by the light of love, and the beloved appears to be the center of all qualities and attractions to him. He loves for the sake of love alone, and is not dependent on the qualities, which are of no importance to him.

The second kind of love is divine Love. It also is of two types.

Divine love is free from the mixture of illusions and is always pure in the regions above; but in the regions below, love is mixed with physical matter and the low desires of animalism.

Generally, people love God because they are attached to His creation. He is the Sustainer of the universe and looks after sinners as well as Saints. He bestows health, children and various other gifts and comforts. He is the Forgiver of all evils.

But if one were to love God—not for His gifts but for love alone—then such a type of love would be very high.

The true and real type of love for Him is that by which the heart is attracted towards Him without any selfish motives. Such a love is produced in the mind of a person who is without any desires. Without any apparent reason the attraction is there. It is beyond description, and even if we were to try to describe it, the description would be incomplete. In fact, it is not possible to describe this lofty type of love within the limitations of worldly words or ideas.

If you were to ask what is true love for God, and what is the way by which one can be attracted towards Him, it would be difficult to give the answer in mortal language. The flow of tears from the eyes does not reveal the depth of love. The lover's feeling of restlessness is no indication of the intensity of his love. But if one were to follow the path of love for the Lord, the soul would then perceive a spark of the flame of this love. But the influence that this love exerts in man cannot be described by intellect.

All Saints love God for His sake only. Their love is very different from the love of ordinary people. When conditions are favorable and one is placed in comforts of life, then it is easy to love God. But the Saints do not waver in their love for Him even when they are deprived of comfortable circumstances. They sacrifice their body, mind, wealth and even their lives for the sake of love for the Lord.

Actually, love is not true love if it varies with changes in conditions, or vanishes in the face of adversities. True love is everlasting. It cannot be destroyed even by tempests of hardships. Such love is a guiding star for the world and its ignorant people. It cannot be valued in terms of money, but one may nevertheless be able to perceive its greatness and superiority over the ordinary type.

"Love is not love,
That alters when it alteration finds,

Or bends with the remover to remove.
It is an ever fixed mark,
That looks on tempests and is never shaken.
It is the star to every wandering bark,
Whose worth's unknown, although his height be taken."

To obtain a further understanding of love it may be studied in a series of examples—love and lust, love and attachment, love and beauty, love and knowledge, love and detachment, and finally the true divine love.

Love And Lust

Love is not the name for sensual desires, in which there is a preponderance of lust. The expression of love that is produced as a result of physical attractions is not the true form of love. Rather, it is the cause of one's fall in the eyes of God.

Love and sensual desires are two different things. There is a world of difference between them. One is a unique life-giving current, while the other is a filthy evil that drains life out of the body.

Lust is always for selfish gains. A lustful person tries to make the other person the object of the satisfaction of his desires. But true love aims at giving happiness and comfort to the beloved. Such a lover has the quality of enduring pain in order to give pleasure and happiness to the beloved, and is happy in the will of the beloved.

The innate quality of a man is love. But this very power or current of love, if directed towards sensual desires, removes a person from the path leading to God-Realization. This misdirected energy is term-

ed lust.   But when this very current of love forsakes
the pleasures of the senses and is directed towards
God, it becomes the True or Divine Love.

Love And Attachment

Love is not attachment.   There is a vast difference between the two.   In attachment one is entangled
with his body, wife, children, relatives, religion, caste
and country.   In other words, one has a feeling of
indifference or estrangement regarding everything
that is not related to his attachments.   Attachment is
finite, and a person in that state cannot be guided by
real knowledge.

There is a strong feeling of selfishness connected
with attachment.   But in love one sees everything
with the same eye—whether it is a human being or a
beast.   He loves all alike; in fact, he loves the entire
creation.

The ideas of selfishness and of a limited sphere
of interest enter into attachment, and to fulfill these
ideas man may stoop to evil designs and actions.   The
result is misery and nothing else.   Love is free from
this dross.   A lover loves all.

In attachment, one falls low.   He cannot look
at everything with a disinterested eye.   The world of
attachment is like a bargain counter, where one gives
only in exchange for gain; otherwise he has nothing to
give.   Love knows only how to give.

A lover also knows that the true love, which is
God, is within every creature.   He loves everybody—
the good and the bad—without any idea of gain.
Love is the support of life.   It is the giver of energy.

Love in which there is even a small amount of selfishness or selfish desires, or even a tiny thought of some bargain, is not real love. True love is only for the sake of love itself. The only wish of a true lover is to be united with the Beloved. Love is awakened when the currents of love, which emanate from the Beloved, enter into our hearts. This is true love, and it is not dependent on any outside influence.

There is no question of gaining anything in love. It is not something that can be bought in a grocer's shop. Love is a matter of "giving", and not of "taking". Surrender your body, mind, life, beliefs— then only will you know the bliss of walking in the precincts of Love. Sarmad says:

> "I gave my body, I gave my life, and I also gave my beliefs. The whole world is entangled in these things, but all these entanglements have been removed from me. What greater blessing could anyone wish for?"

Love And Beauty

Physical beauty is subject to destruction, but true love or real attraction never perishes. Beauty may perish, and even good works may cease. Graceful actions and attractive deportment may be no more, and even the beautiful face may vanish; but true love lives so long as the lover is alive. Even after his death love does not disappear, but merges into his soul. True love never perishes, because it is part and parcel of the soul. Physical beauty is temporary. It may be glamorous today and gone tomorrow. After youth and good health pass away beauty fades; but love remains forever.

Physical beauty rests on a weak foundation and is ephemeral. But love is the natural quality of the soul and is eternal. A life full of love enhances beauty, and beauty of this kind radiates soul force. Beauty of this type has a unique attraction, because it produces love. If beauty is not dyed with the attraction of soul force, love does not exist. A humming bird loves only live flowers. It is not attracted by artificial flowers or by those painted on a wall or on a piece of paper.

Love never perishes, even if the bones of a lover are ground fine like powder. Just as the perfume of sandalwood does not leave it, even if it is completely ground up, similarly the basis of love is the soul, and it is indestructible and therefore eternal. Beauty can be destroyed, but not love.

Wherever there is love there must be beauty. Love brings joy and luster to the eyes. The currents of love emanate from Saints and men of God. Their beauty is doubly enhanced. Their love is of the soul and not of the physical body. Such persons are handsome or beautiful despite their color or physical deficiencies. They have developed the inherent love of the soul, and their physical body is dyed deep in the Spiritual Color which reflects real inner beauty.

Love And Knowledge

There is a vast difference between intellect and heart. It is as great as the distance between the earth and the heavens. Knowledge is connected with a person's intellect and is of a restless nature. It tries to take a person towards cleverness, and establishes a stronghold of selfishness in him. But the heart is connected with the inner currents emanating from a place where love and devotion are generated.

In the path of spirituality, the heart is more effective than the brain. Intellect merely brings light, but the power of spirituality is produced in the heart. Intellect is the cause of one's attention being scattered out into the world; but love removes us from this completely, by the concentration of attention.

"Hundreds of thousands of clever acts and intellectual acrobatics are responsible for our ties to this world. And not one of them is the least bit of help to us in meeting the Lord."A

The way of finite knowledge and the way of love are different. The former scatters one through the desires of the mind, while the latter teaches one to concentrate on one object only. The former asks you to see the world and fill your mind with the different kinds of knowledge that exist in the world; but the latter says that the Beloved is the fountain of all knowledge, and that you should dance attendance in the lane of love and concentrate on Him within yourself. The former persuades you to associate with your friends and companions; but the latter warns you to remain away from friends who would lead you astray from your Beloved.

Intellect goads you to achieve a high status in this world and to become a leader of your country or creed; but love says, "Sit in a lonely corner and be happy in the remembrance of the Lord of all regions." Limited knowledge asks you to acquire intellectual superiority and proficiency in the arts; but love wishes only to take you on the path where the soul is truly enraptured in divine ecstasy. The human intellect considers it impossible to meet and see the Lord, because intellect is limited. But love beholds to its heart's content, His manifestation in both the worlds.

Due to their limited knowledge, the majority of the people do not believe that there could be a living Master in the world today. But love says,"You should remove the bandage of ignorance and selfishness from your eyes. Then only will you see not one but many perfect Masters. It is due to our own faulty mind and intellect that we fail to meet a perfect Master."

Intellect believes that comfort and happiness in this world are entirely due to wealth. But love says that real happiness is in concentration and stability of heart, and one should not run after the worthless treasures of the world.

The human intellect goads us to remain in comfort and to pamper ourselves; but love says, "Sacrifice your head and your dear life to your Beloved." At most, the intellect will take you to the pleasures of heaven. But love says that to ask for anything except the Beloved or to desire anything else is the cause of misery, pain, and sorrow. Therefore, one should never desire anything else.

Does this mean that knowledge and intellect have no merit? All Saints and holy men teach the people of the world through their discourses. They differentiate between Truth and untruth by intellectual reasoning. If that is the case, then how is it that knowledge described above is depicted in such disparaging terms?

Limited knowledge cannot see beyond the physical self and keeps one devoid of love for the Beloved.

A man may be very learned and also highly intellectual, but he cannot reach the gate of the Beloved by mere learning. So long as he does not merge himself in the Lord, who is all Love, he cannot be successful, and his intellect will beguile him towards the wrong path. If, however, knowledge is used without the negative influence of the intellect, then it can be free from its limitations and dross. Otherwise, one will always remain submerged in sensual pleasures. But one can have communion with God, who is omniscient, if the mind and senses are under the control of knowledge. Such a state can be achieved only by one who is guided by a living Master. Then he really meets his Beloved.

A man's intellect is limited. It cannot see beyond the world and its objects. Only true love can reach beyond these bounds, because love transcends all limitations and sees things which an intellectual cannot conceive of, even in his dreams. Shamas Tabriz has described the difference between knowledge and love in the following words:

"Knowledge says that the world is scattered in all the six directions—north, south, east, west, above and below—and that there is no path leading beyond this. Love says 'There is a path and I have been on it many times'. "

"The human intellect says that there is nothing beyond this body or physical life. It is followed by death and nothing else. The path of love is full of the thorns of troubles, and one should not tread that path under any circumstances."

"But love says, 'Thorns there may be, but there are also life-giving flowers on that path. In love one goes beyond this body, because then only can one find the life eternal. There fore, do not be afraid of the thorns of this apparent death'."

"Without the help and guidance of a Master, the soul is unable to reach the goal of love. Limited knowledge and intellect alone cannot reach the place where only ecstasy and madness of love can go. The heart of a lover cannot be trapped by the net of the body and physical attractions, because it has already reached a place which is nameless, limitless and beyond the reach of matter."

We should contemplate and think of the Master with discrimination, because by this means alone can we achieve grace in His Court. We should carefully try to understand the meaning underlying the writings of wise and noble men and thoroughly consider them in all of their aspects. When convinced that the path of Spirituality is the right path, only then should we follow it and in good faith. This is the only way to tread the path of God and Spirituality. Except for this, all other paths lead one towards the Negative Power.

Love And Detachment

Real detachment is not merely running away and leaving everything. Rather, it is that pure state of the mind in which all desires are burnt up by going beyond all attractions of the world. But without understanding, detachment is an impossibility. When such a state is combined with the longing to meet the Lord, it is called love. Therefore, love and detachment are not two different qualities. They are two separate names for the same state of mind.

One may be termed a devotee or a lover in proportion to the degree of his detachment. Those who do not possess love for God in their hearts do not have even a particle of detachment. As the mind becomes free from desires, to that extent is it filled

with love.   One who is steeped in attachment for the
world cannot be a lover.   You should bow before
God by saying good-bye to worldly desires; otherwise
the prayer is not genuine.

Detachment and true love are one and the same
thing.   So long as the mind does not have an aversion
to worldly desires it cannot attract love.   No doubt
it has been noted that sometimes devotees, in the
beginning, in spite of being detached, do ask God for
material necessities.   There is no harm in this, provided, one is treading the spiritual path with the proper
attitude and not for the fulfillment of any desire connected with the senses.

> "I need only the bare necessities of life; that is, wheat flour,
> a pinch of salt, a little pulse—as much as will keep me alive.
> Then I also need a bed, a pillow, a mattress and a blanket to
> protect me against the wind and cold.   I do not want any-
> thing else except the privilege of being devoted to Thee with
> all humility.   I have no other desires except Thy Name." 4

In the Bible, Christ says the same thing in even
stronger terms:

> "Think not that I am come to send peace on earth: I came
> not to send peace, but a sword.   For I am come to set a
> man at variance against his father, and the daughter against
> her mother, and the daughter-in-law against her mother-
> in-law.   For he that loveth father or mother more than me
> is not worthy of me: and he that loveth son or daughter
> more than me is not worthy of me."

Actually, a detached devotee never seeks anything
from the Lord.   He asks for only Him, because
everything else is transitory and is the cause of pain.

> "To demand anything from Thee beyond Thyself will cause
> nothing but worry and pain.   Oh Bless me Thou with Thy
> Blissful Name that I am rid of the craving of my mind." A

Such a devotee does not ask for anything from the Lord, because he does not feel the need. His pains, worries and prejudices are all destroyed. Whoever has tasted the Elixer of Love will not run after anything else, and whatever he says will be acceptable in the Court of the Lord. This means that a devotee of this kind will not pay any attention to any material thing.

Divine Love Is God

Prior to the creation of this world, God was a vast ocean-like All-Consciousness. He was all love, all bliss and self-sufficient. God was everything in Himself and was in a state of blissful quiescence, and His basic form was Love. It was not love for any other being, because none existed. It was for Himself. It was part and parcel of Himself, and He did not have to depend on anything else for this. Such is the indescribable condition of Love. But we may illustrate it to some extent by an example:

Suppose that you are in love with the Lord and have completely merged yourself in Him. Then your own self has been forgotten, your body and mind will be numb, and everything will be forgotten except your love for Him. You then lose yourself in the bliss of contemplating on His Love, so much so that there is no difference between "I" and "You", and you become Bliss incarnate.

You cannot describe that state of mind, because God is Love and Love is God. Both are one and the same, and both are indescribable. God, in Himself, is a deep ocean of Love. We cannot compare the bliss of contemplating on His Love with any other type of happiness or bliss.

This Divine Love is a quality of such a kind that it cannot be described in speech or in writing. If anything, it can be compared to a magnet which has extremely powerful attraction. Love was in the beginning of the world, and its influence is even now permeating all material and spiritual regions, whether visible or invisible. That is how all things are attracted towards each other and the world is in existence.

The foundation of True Love contains no trace of selfish aims or desires. Like God's Love for us, our love should also be expressed and offered to Him without any selfish motive or desire for reward.

Whatever people may say about love, their words are not the path of love. The roots of love are in the Infinite, and its green leaves are spreading beyond limits. The tree of love is not supported either by the earth or the sky. Though it is described to a certain extent in the Scriptures, the people of learning are unable to give a faithful description of it, because it is indescribable. Only a rare person (a true Master) can impart the knowledge of love correctly to a true and real seeker. The worldly people are all ignorant of it. Hafiz says:

"If you wish to join my class, throw away all of your books. The knowledge of Love is not found in them."

There is no difference between Love and God. God is Love, and Love is God. Both are beyond thought and description. The Elixir of Love can be tasted only by inner experience. All descriptions of Love are far from the Love itself.

God is Love and the soul is a part of Him. The

qualities of God are therefore naturally found in man. The entire universe is being sustained by love. In other words, it is a form of love. God created the current of love in this world, and by this current the world is kept in existence.

God is Love. God is also Nam and Shabd. In other words, Love is the treasure of Nam and it contains that most powerful elixir by obtaining which all our evil tendencies are destroyed.

Love is the inherent quality of the soul. Love is the sustainer of life, just as a lotus lives on water, its growth is in the water and it blossoms through the currents of water in it. Similarly, love is the life of the soul, and the existence of the soul is dependent on love of God. The soul becomes happy when love takes hold of it. Guru Nanak says:

"God is the Elixir of our life and you should love Him. As your love for Him increases, your soul will blossom on the water of love like a lotus."

Love is that which transforms the small drop of the soul into the ocean of God.

BOOK 3

SELF UNDERSTANDING

CHAPTER 1

VIRTUES

There are many virtues in the Lord. The soul that imbibes them finds the Lord and is dear to Him. She is the happy bride who is dear to the Lord.

The Lord is the store house of all virtues. Those virtues by imbibing which the soul is honored at the door of the Lord are classed under fourteen heads in the Adi Granth. They should be carefully considered and imbibed.

(1) Repeat the Name and feel the presence of Parbrahm (transcendental Lord).

"The virtuous one found the truth by giving up desire for evil. She dyed her mind in the shabd of the Guru and uttered the words of love and endearment with her tongue."

(2) One should give up egoism and sing the praises of the Lord, and love Him.

"He gets the Name by service of the Master and it is enshrined inside him.
Mind and body become peaceful and the fire of desires is extinguished.
He who gives up egoism attains utter peace."

(3) Do not injure the feelings of others.

"Do not speak harshly to any one, as the Lord is in all. Do not break anyone's heart as all are ture pearls."

(4) Do not be rude but use sweet words.

"Ask the blessed bride what has made her dear to her Lord. It was contentment, simple dressing and sweet speech."

(5)   Live in awe of the Lord.

She dwells and works in awe of the Lord.
She gets great bliss here and in His court hereafter by entering the gate of salvation.

(6)   Live within His will and give up otherness.

"She is truly embellished,
She is incomparably beautiful,
She alone is the ever-happy bride,
Who is approved by the Lord."

"The ever blessed bride who loves the Master is always full of compassion.
The words of the Master are jewels and he who accepts them enjoys the nectar of the Lord's love."

(7)   Give up desires and evil.

"The virtuous one found the truth by giving up desires for evil. She dyed her mind in the shabd of the Guru and uttered the words of love and endearment with her tongue."

(8)   Give up egoism and do not talk ill of others.

"If you wish to enter the paradise of Eden, treat the creatures of God with kindness."

(9)   Do good even to the evil-minded.   Do not indulge in wrath. Live in humility and think of the self.

"Do not be cross with anyone but search your own heart. Live humbly in this world, O Nanak, and thus obtain His grace."

(10)   Give up lust, wrath, greed, attachment and evil thinking and serve in humility. Abstain from coveting the wife, wealth and possessions of others. Do not indulge in evil thoughts or back-biting and live in peace.

If one removes lust, wrath, greed and attachment, gives up evil and self-seeking, becomes humble and serves the Lord, then he is dear to Him.

(11) Adopt truth, contentment, compassion and forgiveness.

"Ask the blessed bride what has made her dear to her Lord. It was contentment, simple dressing and sweet speech."

(12) Give up doubts, seek the Lord, know yourself, consider the Lord as Omnipresent and all-pervading and serve the Saints.

"Be you the slave of the Saints, their contact leads to Peace. The best of all virtues, however, is that the Lord is near you."

(13) Become the dust of all, consider all as friends, see the Lord in all and do not injure any being.

"There is one Light. That One dwells in all hearts. See the same Brahm (Lord) in all.
The soul and the Lord are one and pervade all. Bow to all."

(14) Admit death as a fact and give up longings for the future.

"Accept death as the first basic fact and give up longing for the future.
Become the dust of all men and then come to Me."

Austerities

The meaning of austerities is to undergo physical or mental hardships or to perform any practice that removes egotism. To live in jungles and subsist on roots and fruits, sitting in fire, exposing oneself to fire, to lie on nails fixed in the ground, to remain standing with one hand raised, to sit in water and to undergo other physical and mental sufferings are called austerities. The purpose of performing these austerities is that the mind may become pure, and that lust, anger, attachment, greed and egotism may be removed so that realization of the Lord may be attained.

In the religion of the Saints, no importance is attached to austerities that cause pain to the body, since by exposing the body to water and fire the inner fire is not extinguished, nor by keeping the hand raised is egotism removed.

If one's goal can be achieved without causing suffering to the body, then why undergo such suffering?

> "He who follows the path taught by the Master wears the coat of knowledge stitched with the needle of meditation and the thread of shabd. He uses compassion as a rake and the body as firewood and ignites the fire of the eye center. He bears love for Him in his heart and contemplates in trance on all the four ages. All yoga is included in the Name of the Lord to whom belong this body and life.
> O Kabir! when He has compassion, He leads him to the true ideal."   4

Gurus describe the real austerities through which the cycle of birth and death is ended and the soul reaches the door of the Master. The greatest of the austerities is the Master's service, through which the Lord dwells in the heart. In this way one reaches the door of the Master.

> "The Master's service is the best of all austerities. The Lord dwells in the heart of the man who performs such service and removes all his sufferings. He sees the Lord as the door of the Truth."   A

The teachings of the Saints say that only those repetitions, austerities and services are beneficial which are dear to the Lord. They remove the feeling of selfishness and separateness.

> "Repetition, self-discipline and obedience to the Master are the austerities to be performed by the devotee.
> O Nanak, service is done to develop the soul. This is acceptable to the Lord, and one then finds reality."

Sincere love is the essence of all repetitions and austerities. He whose mind is pure and who contemplates with love and devotion on the feet of the Lord must be considered to have performed all repetitions and austerities.

Cleanliness

Cleanliness is also an essential part of religious duty. It is of two kinds, internal and external. The physical body, house, clothes, etc., are of the second category, and purity of mind and the senses is of the first category. External cleanliness is essential for internal purity, and has a very considerable influence over it. Cleanliness is next to Godliness. Both internal and external purity are essential. The cleanliness of body, clothes and house are very necessary for bodily health. It can be done by a daily bath, by brushing the teeth, cleaning the clothes with soap and water, and by living in an open and sunny place. The body is full of many pores, through which perspiration comes out and the outer atmosphere affects the body through them. One must keep them clean and healthy. Pure food is also essential.

For perfect purity, clean conduct, pure food and good character are absolutely necessary.

Inner purification can be had by purity of the mind and senses, i.e., by attaining the truth or practice of Nam and Shabd.

It is necessary to be clean both inside and outside. Have a clean body, speak good words. But unless pure thoughts arise inside, nothing pure can come out. It is, therefore, imperative that the thoughts should

be pure.   Out of the fullness of his heart a man speaks.
Therefore, be pure of heart and tongue.   If the heart
is not clean, how can the soul be clean?   Do not utter
any unkind or harmful words.   Use words that sound
sweet to all.   Cleanliness of the heart consists in not
entertaining any evil thoughts.   Unite yourself with
the Name and thus get rid of all impure thoughts and
attain cleanliness or purity of the soul.

In reality, persons of low spirituality are un-
touchables, rather than sweepers, cobblers, minstrels
and bards.   The real seeker should therefore undertake inner purification according to the directions of a
Master and thus realize the Lord.   He should drive
out all thoughts except those of the Lord, so that the
Lord may reveal Himself.

> "Clean the cell of the heart for the Beloved,
> Banish all thoughts of others to make room for Him."

Gurus describe the clean body as one in which
the true Name of the Lord is dwelling.   True cleanliness is achieved by the inner practice of the Shabd.
That heart is pure in which there is devotion for the
deathless Lord and Master.

Humility

In order to be deserving of the Lord's grace we
have to empty the heart of vain glory for, unless a
vessel is empty, it can contain nothing.   If we have
humility, Kal and Maya cannot affect us.   All the
Saints have adopted it and adorned themselves with it.
What is false pride or vainglory?   To be proud of a
virtue we do not possess, or we possess merely as a gift
from some one else, is false pride.   We do not deserve

to be respected or honored because we belong to a
noble family of great deeds or because our ancestors
selflessly gave in charity.

"By whose grace you have a beauteous face,
Always remember that wonderful Lord.
By whose grace you have got this good species,
Always remember that Lord day and night.
By whose grace you have a diseaseless body,
Contemplate that Lord with love."   A

Another person is proud of his knowledge and
talent. He is not entitled to this pride. This is due
to the teacher who taught him and the intellect given
to him by the Lord. Of what should a man be proud
in this world? People are proud of wealth and
property. These are evanescent like the declining
shade. People are proud of youth, which is lost in
disease and old age. In the first place, these do not
remain the same but if they do, it is only for a short
time. They fall like leaves of a tree.

From the above discussion it is clear that it is
not proper to be proud of worldly pleasures. The
thought of countless bounties of the Lord and our
innumerable sins and defects makes us beggars at
His door. We should therefore think as to which of
His bounties we are acknowledging and what we are
doing for them. As long as we believe that whatever
good or evil we possess is not because of us but from
Him, we cannot be proud of anything. What are the
bounties which we have not received from the Lord?
Having received them what have we done to show our
gratitude and in respect of which of them? If this
line of thought leads to pride then the thoughts of our
defects and ingratitude is a sure remedy.

Egoism or pride is not liked by the Lord. He showers His grace on those whose mind is full of humility and meekness.

> Water does not accumulate at high places but does so at low places;
> He, who bends, drinks; the stiff-necked remains thirsty.   4

Pride goes before a fall and a proud man does not imbibe the virtues of others. The humble and the meek can get spiritual wealth from the spiritually-minded persons. After finding the path he should in all humility assiduously tread it. This is due to the grace of the Lord and the Master. If we do not take a humble and meek attitude before doing a good deed, do not retain it while doing it, and do not consider it a gift by the grace of the Lord and the Master after it is done, it is snatched from our hands by pride amidst our rejoicings. The way to God is firstly humility, secondly humility and thirdly humility. Again unless humility precedes, accompanies and follows every good action which we perform, pride wrests wholly from our hands any good work on which we are congratulating ourselves.

Only an ant can pick up sugar from the sand, no elephant can do so. Similarly persons proud of wealth, race or family cannot gain any virtue or learn any lesson from the creation of the Lord. Only a humble person can derive this benefit.

Even if you have many good qualities, you should lead a life of humility and consider those qualities as a gift from God, because God loves the humble. Remember this well in your heart and do not enter into unnecessary disputes or critical discussions, because such discussions lead nowhere. They may be compared to churning water. Those who seek the Lord do not run after outer show and glory. They remain happy in the will of the Lord and the greatness of their soul can be glimpsed in whatever work the Lord puts them on.

We try to make a show of avoiding the gaze of the world and hiding ourselves but in reality desire that it should run after us and find us out. We sit in meetings on a back bench or on a low seat so that we may be seated in the front or on a high seat. True humility never makes a show nor indulges in humble words. A really humble man not only wants to hide himself and his virtues but also tries to keep himself out of the sight of the world.

We always say that we are nothing, we are of no consequence and others are better. But if others say the same thing about us, we would be very sorry, as we think that our state is quite the reverse. Those who really inwardly believe that they are the lowest are really spiritual.

It therefore behooves us not to utter words of sham humility. If we do utter such words they should represent our real inner feelings. We should not lower our eyes unless our mind accepts humility and poverty. Unless we feel a genuine desire for humility and poverty we should not express it. A truly humble heart desires that instead of his saying so, others should say of him that he is the most inconsequential and unimportant person. If any one says this of him he does not feel offended but is happy to feel that there is at least one man who thinks of him as he himself does.

In true humility we need not pass ourselves as fools or parade ourselves as wise men. Just as pride is opposite of humility, so deceit, pretence, cleverness, show, hypocrisy, cunningness and worldly crookedness are opposite of calmness and right conduct. If the worldly wise, in order to gain their ends, dub right conduct as mean and foolish, the truly humble person should bear the backbiting and criticism cheerfully. The cause of this backbiting is not in him but in others.

Some persons under the cover of humility give up inner prayers because of being imperfect. They do not think themselves fit for them. Some say that they do not advise others as they themselves are not perfectly faultless. Some do not wish to use their talents in the service of the Lord because, they know their weakness best and are afraid lest while doing service they should feel proud and while showing light to others may ruin themselves in the fire of pride and conceit. These thoughts do not arise when one is truly humble. These are reasons for one being idle and a coward. Such, on one hand make a great show of feelings for the Lord and his incarnation, the Master, and on the other hand, under the cover of humility, want to keep themselves deprived of the great humility which He in His mercy wishes to shower on them. The Lord and Master desire that we should be perfect like Him and thus obtain His grace.

The man who has no confidence in himself puts forth arguments and reasons for not doing his duty but a man of prayer, although he feels utterly incompetent knowing full well that he is not fit for it and cannot perform it, surrenders with full faith and fortitude everything to the Lord and His incarnation the Master, and engages himself in carrying out the directions for fulfilling the task given to him by the Master.

Humility is not weakness. It is such a powerful thing that all the powers of the world have to bow to it. Man conquers himself with pridelessness. No one can defeat a prideless man; as behind his humility is acting the secret power of the Lord. Humility is an ornament of great men.

We should make our hearts the source of love for the entire universe and should have so much humility that even if a person does evil to us, we should return love for the same. In truth, one who is embellished with humility loses the capacity of stinging others. Even if any one harms him, he does not think evil of him.

True humility produces sweetness in our heart and the words uttered by us would be sweet. All life currents would also be delicious. The sweetness would be the same for all. Our neighbors and others would feel its sweetness. All our sayings and actions, whether great or small, would be full of humility. They would dye our relations and others in the same hue.

The humility of Tulsi Sahib appears from the following verses:

I am unwise, helpless and of humble heart.
By taking refuge in the saints I have recognized the Master.
The Master is unfathomable ocean of peace.
He put me in the right path.
I bow at his feet again and again.
I humbly sing the praises of the saints.
Considering me humble he opened my inner vision.
I again sang the praises of the refuge with the saints.
I am thy slave with the whole of my mind.
Considering me low you have found me.
I am your slave for ever and for ever.

No one can cross without a saint.
Saints are merciful and compassionate.
By taking refuge with them even the low caste swim across.
There can be no beginning or end without a saint.
Tulsi the helpless has taken shelter with You.
Whatever is done, is done by saints.
Without the saints, path cannot be found.

The following quotations are all from the Adi Granth:

"O my Lord, please listen to my one supplication. You are happy in your Home, whereas I am wandering homeless."

"What should a poor girl do if she is not able to win the favors of her Lord? She tries hard, but does not find a place in His court."

"I was not able to commune with my Lord tonight, and my entire body aches. What is the state of those women who pass their nights alone!"

"O my Lord, what qualities should I acquire to be worthy of meeting Thee? I am ignorant. I am not beautiful and have no wisdom."

"My devotion and love for the Lord have helped me in giving up all passionate desires and feelings of anger. The Lord has become happy in seeing me in my beauty and devotion."

"The Lord's commands are sweet, and my negative desires and feelings have vanished. I am now the beloved of my Lord, and my mind is rid of all worries."

"One should make a fan of his hair and should serve the Saints with it."

"I feel happy and contented with Seva, such as to fetch water, to pull the rope of a fan, or to grind corn for the Saints. All high positions such as kingship, the possession of wealth or property and positions of power, are worth nothing except being thrown into fire."

"Make me the humblest of the humble, for the humble are all dear to God."

"O my Friend! I would wish to be the dust of thy Feet at all times."

"That friend who is with me in the beginning, in the middle, and at the end of my life is a welcome friend of mine."

"He alone is my friend who is near me at all times."

"The devotees of the Lord are always happy. They are just like small children—free from the net of Maya (Illusion) and above worldly desires. Just as a father keeps his children happy and in comfort, similarly God keeps His devotees always happy."

"Just as a child respects his father, similarly a devotee lives in accordance with the commands of his Guru. No secrets remain between the two. Nanak is happy because all his desires are fulfilled."

Truthfulness

All our efforts are incomplete without truth. Truth is the crown of all. This is the secret of all practices. All other worship is mere hypocrisy.

To have a truthful life is the goal of human life. Truth is everywhere. It should be separated from untruth and experienced inside. The heart wherein it dwells also takes its form. God is truth. One should be truthful in His eyes as He loves truth. It does not matter what religion you follow.

We have to consider here as to what is truthful speech, i.e. speech which is made by a truthful person. To describe a thing exactly as seen or heard is truthful speech. Besides speaking the truth, our dealings should also be truthful. We should have truth as our ideal while thinking and base our conduct on it. In this way, our hearts, thoughts and conduct become truthful.

"He who has true attention has right conduct.
He is in communion with the Lord at all times." 4

In speaking the truth, compassionate considerations should be kept in mind. In fact, truth is that which does not injure the feelings of others. Whatever is uttered should come from the heart and should not injure anybody's feelings.

The opposite of truth is untruth. Not to relate what one has seen or heard or done is called falsehood. A false person is a hypocrite. He looks with his eyes down and has no light on his face. He is always planning and scheming. He is always afraid that his falsehood may be detected. In order to hide one lie he has recourse to hundreds of them. He loses his peace of mind in scheming all the while. Doubts and suspicion become his second nature. He accordingly trusts no one. His relationship with others is based on selfishness. He is not confided in by anyone owing to his conduct, nor does he confide in anyone. Deceit, fraud, hypocrisy and cunning become staple food of his life. His life becomes a burden to the world. If a liar meets a liar they like each other, but if a liar meets a truthful person, their relationship snaps.

Truth can stand on its own legs but not so the untruth. A truthful man is steady, patient and firm in his determination. An untruthful man falters at every step and is not steadfast. While the truthful man is fearless and has no qualms or hesitation, an untruthful man is always afraid and never looks anybody in the face. The truthful man is brave and courageous. But the untruthful man is a coward and an idler. A truthful man is free from cares because of his fearlessness, which produces detachment in attachment. The truthful man gives up flattering, cajoling, theft and secrecy.

From the above it is clear that a truthful man can succeed in the spiritual field. As truth dwells in him, he speaks the truth. He himself treads the path leading to the Lord and guides others to it also.

"He is whom the truth dwells, practises Nam truly and speaks the truth.

He himself treads the path of the Lord and guides others on this path."

A

Such a person in a way becomes related to truth. Whatever he says comes out to be true. He is happy in the enjoyment of bliss of truth, both outside and inside. Owing to leading a truthful life he becomes fearless and peaceful as he is connected with truth which is eternal and never changing. All the world is happy in having him. By speaking and seeing the truth his mind and body become true. He preaches truth and is embellished by it.

One who is truthful and contented and speaks the truth is dear to the Lord. He never suffers separation from Him. Truth has nothing to fear. It is not affected by curses nor can Kal harm it. When a true devotee meets the Truth (Lord), he merges in it.

Contentment

Contentment means satisfaction, agreement, being contented with what one has and being satisfied with it. If one does not gain his object in spite of effort, or succeeds to a very small extent only, and yet remains calm and collected and does not feel troubled in his mind, he is said to have contentment. When one is surrounded by troubles on all sides, is not honored by anyone, is talked ill of by everyone and is faced with defeat on all sides, but does not feel aggrieved by the thought that others are happy, then it is a sign of contentment.

It would, however, be a mistake to infer from all this that contentment means idleness or slackness. To seem contented and to grieve in secret and to feel jealous is to show oneself in different colors and to deceive the public. A contented person on getting nothing even after making efforts does not blame the Master or the Lord. He tries seriously to accomplish the task. Failure or success leaves him unaffected.

> "When one fails in spite of effort,
> Know it to be the will of the Lord."

Only a contented person can put in ceaseless efforts for serving others. He observes truth, never attempts evil and does good actions and earns merits.

> "They earn contentment who sincerely contemplate the truth.
> They do not do any evil acts and earn merit by good acts."   A

He is very patient. Even though possessed of respect, prestige and strength, he forgives the faults of others. He feels happy when others progress and get honor, and has clean intentions. Even on getting honors and glory he loves others and treats them kindly. Although learned and wise, he respects other learned men and tries to imbibe their virtues as a duty. He is beautiful, but does not indulge in sensual pleasures. He is always patient, modest and scrupulous. Such a person is not only contented, but has other virtues also. He is satisfied with his wife and considers those older than he as mother, and younger ones as sisters and daughters. He lives on the income earned by him by his own labor. He enjoys his simple fare as a sumptuous dinner, and drinks water as if it

were nectar. He is not envious of the good life led
by others. Omar Khayam says:

"In this world, he who has half a bread and has a place to sit,
He is not anybody's slave or master.
Tell him to be happy as he has sufficient in this world."

If one is poor while doing meritorious deeds and
the Lord has given him contentment, he is really rich.
A rich man without contentment is a beggar and very
poor, for the hunger of such a man would not be
satisfied even if he got all the good things of the world,
as none can be satisfied without contentment.

"Put on the ring of contentment and garment of humility." A

This is necessary so that while trying, one may
not become ungrateful or blame the Lord, or he may
not slowly wither on getting less than expected or by
being a failure, or he may not give up the effort and
admit defeat. One should be content with what he
gets from his meritorious deeds. One should
patiently attend to his duty. He should ward off the
attacks of greed and covetousness by the shield of
patience, so that, in the end, the drop of soul may
mingle with the ocean of the Lord and become blessed,
and may not become dry like a rivulet. Sheikh
Farid says that contentment naturally makes a man a
true creature of the Lord, and he unites with the Lord
and grows into an ocean.

All desires vanish on getting the wealth of contentment. When one is desireless, worry disappears and
mind becomes restful. Those who desire nothing
are real kings.

In Summary

In the Mahabharat, Bhisham describes to Yudishtra the characteristics of those in whose company one loses the fear of life and death, and gains salvation.

"They are vegetarians. They love or hate no one. The virtuous life is dear to them. Their senses are under control. They regard joy and sorrow alike. They are truthful and benevolent. They accept no charity from others, while they are themselves charitably disposed. They serve their guests. They afford comfort to everybody. They help everybody. They are courageous. They follow the path of Truth. They are the friend of all, and in time of need are prepared to sacrifice everything. They remain steadfast on the path of Truth. Their conduct and bearing are in accordance with the tenets of their religion. They talk ill of no Saint nor Seer. They are a menace to none, nor are they frightening. They live a noble life with determination, and bear a feeling of non-violence (absence of hatred) towards all. They are free from lust, anger, attachment and ego. They do their duty and follow religion for its own sake, and not for securing fame and wealth. They are naturally inclined towards religion. Just as they have their daily bath, eat their daily food and satisfy other physical needs, so also is religion part and parcel of their daily life. They have no fear, sorrow or ire. They are truthful and honest. They do not rejoice over gains, nor do they grieve over losses. They are of even temperament and maintain their equanimity under all conditions. The pairs of opposites such as gain and loss, joy and sorrow, love and hatred, life and death, fail to perturb their mind. They are firm and strong in their resolve. They attain a high state and tread the path of Truth with great resolution."

CHAPTER 2

MEDITATION

There are 24 hours in the day and the Saints teach us that if we are to make spiritual progress, we should devote two and one-half hours each day to meditation. This is our tithe of 10 per cent of our time—withdrawn from the world and devoted to realizing the Lord.

The technique of meditation taught by the Masters provides a practical way to withdraw our attention inside and to use this daily period for our true work.

When you visit your elder or your superior, you look at him with respect and attention, and try to prevent any other thought from entering your mind at that time. But when you sit in devotion in remembrance of God, how many thoughts and ideas—even of an impure nature—enter your mind? How great is the injustice you do unto Him? How can this be avoided?

From time immemorial, man has been extroverted, observing outside objects through the sense organs. Three sense organs are chiefly responsible for drawing our attention, namely, the tongue, the eyes, and the ears.

With our tongue we talk to the people of the world. With it we repeat our thoughts and ideas about the world, and communicate with the world. In this manner the impressions of the world enter our mind and intellect.

With our eyes we see the objects of the world, and their forms get imprinted on our mind. With our ears we listen to the voices of the world, and by listening to them constantly we become one with them.

Our eyes are responsible for 83 per cent of the impressions imprinted on our mind, our ears for 14 per cent, and the remaining 3 per cent are formed by the other sense organs of the body put together. If our attention ceases to go out and we thus stop the entry of impressions from outside, we can, with an inward gaze, realize the Truth. It is for this reason that Saints always impress upon us to shut our eyes and our ears while doing Meditation.

Whenever we wish to withdraw our consciousness inwards, the thoughts of the world invade us. These are the impressions that have continually entered through the sense organs. Thus, the affairs of household, office, shops and other places, also the forms of relatives, friends and foes that we have been seeing project themselves on the mind's screen and obstruct concentration. The first step for spiritual uplift, therefore, is to eliminate them.

The removal of the impressions that are formed in our subconscious mind and which come before us involuntarily is the second step. It is only after the devotee has ascended the two steps, that he can become introverted or turned inward.

The power of speech of the tongue should be utilized in Simran; the power of the sight of the eyes should be used in contemplating the form of the Master; and the power of hearing of the ears should be spent in listening to the Sound Current. These three practices are absolutely essential, and are the keys to successful Meditation. These will be discussed in detail.

The Scriptures detail many a benefit from Meditation. When an overwhelming adversity besets your path, when there is no other help, when foes hotly pursue you; when close relations desert you, when all hopes are dashed and when all avenues are closed, if you still remember God, no harm shall ever touch you. The Lord is the strength of the weak. He is eternal. He is known through the Guru's Shabd.

A person may have many kingdoms; he may rule vast dominions; he may have access to all luxuries; he may own many gardens and orchards; he may enjoy many privileges; he may revel in the pleasures of the world; yet if he has not the remembrance of the Lord, he is doomed to sub human form in his next birth.

When a person is depressed for want of food and resources; when even the last penny has left him; when he is without a job; even then if he gives place to the Lord in his heart, he shall forever be freed from want.

When one is torn by cares and anxieties; when his body is diseased; when he is deeply immersed in domestic worries; when he is at the mercy of the buffets of sorrow; when he wanders to and fro and finds no home nor hearth where he can rest; even then, if he carries out the meditation of the Lord, he shall attain inner calm and peace.

"But lay up for yourselves treasures in Heaven, where neither moth nor rust doth corrupt, and where thieves do not break, through nor steal: For where your treasure is, there will your heart be also."   B

If meditation is carried out in accordance with the directions of the Master and in a proper way, the devotee achieves wondrous results within. The soul currents that permeate every pore of the body withdraw from the nine apertures and collect at the Tenth Gate, which lies between the eyes. The body then becomes completely numb. The disciple begins to behold scenes in the spiritual regions and sees stars and the sun and the moon.

After the devotee crosses these phenomena, he beholds the radiant form of the Master, who, after that, is ever by the side of the disciple and who guides the soul to the higher regions, ultimately taking it to the Court of the Lord. It is by focusing our attention on this resplendent Form that we make it stay with us.

Meditation banishes fear of death and frees one from the cycle of births and deaths. It removes obstacles and difficulties, and pleasure and pain. Duality is shed; the dross and filth of the mind wear off; and the refulgence of God's Name becomes manifest. The devotee is ever at the feet of the Master. He gains glory in the Court of the Lord and, crossing the ocean of phenomena, he attains everlasting salvation.

The Time Of Elixir

Many Scriptures have described the early morning hours as auspicious and as God's own time. The last three hours of night are known as the time of Elixir, for this pure and serene time was utilized for meditation by the ancient true Yogis and Saints.

"It is the practice of Saints to keep awake at night. Men of the world spend this time in sensual and worldly pleasures. Men of God spend their nights in remembering Him. Both are awake, but the blessed are those who utilize it in the remembrance of the Lord."   A

Shams-i-Tabriz says:

"Night is the time when the Beloved Lord appears. Those who sleep at this time are depriving themselves of a great boon. Day is for work, but night is for love and devotion to the Lord. Therefore, the whole night should be spent in communion with the Lord. The whole world sleeps, but the devotees spend the night in meditation at the Feet of the Lord."

All times are good for meditation, and one should utilize whatever time suits him. But the morning time just before daybreak, and evening time immediately after sunset—are particularly beneficial, because these times unite night and day, and spiritual currents are particularly strong and powerful at such a time. During the day, we are engaged in the affairs of the world. Therefore, only night remains for devotion to the Lord.

No spiritual practice should be undertaken immediately after a heavy meal or on a full stomach, because then the body energies are engaged in the digestive process. It is better to meditate on an empty stomach. In the early morning hours the stomach is empty, as the food taken the evening before is normally digested completely by that time.

Also a man who works during the day naturally feels tired in the evening. For him sleep is essential and it comes automatically to remove the fatigue of the day. Thus, only the latter part of the night remains during which a person can do meditation in complete alertness. The time of Elixir begins from three in the morning. The body and mind are refreshed and calm, and fit for meditation. Therefore, the latter part of the night is considered more beneficial for this purpose.

In the early morning hours there are usually no worries of the world to occupy our minds, and such a time is therefore better for concentration. At the time of Elixir the mind is quite fresh and the day's turmoils have not spread their tentacles over it. In the early morning hours a person is very near God. Concentration attained and meditation done at this time leave their impression on the day's work. And whatever such a person does, he does with a concentrated mind.

The fruit of meditation done in the first part of the night is just like the budding of the trees, but meditation during the latter part of the night is like the tree bearing the ripe fruit. At this time, one gets the Grace of God.

John S. Hayland in his book **The Life Of Christ** has given the undernoted description:

"There is an hour of the Indian night, a little before the first glimmer of the dawn, when the stars are unbelievably clear and closer, shining with radiance beyond our belief in this foggy land. The trees stand silent around one with a friendly presence. As yet there is no sound from awakening birds, but the whole world seems to be intent, alive, listening, eager. At such a moment the veil between the things that are seen and the things that are unseen becomes so thin as to interpose scarcely any barrier at all between the eternal beauty and truth and the soul which would comprehend them."

The world sleeps while men of God are awake in

His remembrance and are dyed in the hues of His love.

"You have spent thousands of nights in endeavoring to fulfill your desires and cravings, but if you do not sleep for the sake of your Beloved, then what harm can befall you? Do you not know that whatever the spiritual kings possess, was obtained by them at night?

"You should remain awake for the sake of that Giver of all gifts, and you should have no fear that sleeplessness will result in mental fatigue, because during that time flows the Fountain of Life, the Nectar of which will make you refreshed and heighten your consciousness. Therefore, do not sleep. Every morning the Voice of the Lord calls you. By listening to it, all your worries and troubles will vanish, and the stains of previous evil impressions on your mind will also be washed away. Do not sleep throughout the night, because at that time thousands of lives receive the sustaining life-force. Like the full moon, the Supreme Lord descends from the highest heavens to bless His disciples with the gifts of Grace and Mercy.

"There is seclusion at night. Our Beloved is within us, and what a gracious time it is! The Sound Currents of Nam are reverberating on all sides and are easily audible in the silence of the night. If you have an intense longing to meet your Lord, you should know that the darkness of the night is like the long black tresses of the Beloved, spread everywhere. And if you continue to sleep at night, then you should be ashamed."   12

In other words, you should tread this Path so that you may meet your Beloved. The lovers of God keep awake in meditation at night, particularly in the early morning hours. They repeat His Name, and are rid of all their sufferings and cares, anxieties and dissensions.

Posture

Posture signifies sitting in a particular position and maintaining it firmly and for a certain length of time. Hatha Yoga describes numerous postures, and of these, eighty-four are well known. The practice of these postures confers many advantages because they are an aid to concentration. They help to eliminate all bodily ailments and weaknesses.

However, Yogis have performed all the eighty-four postures without gaining the ultimate goal. They do not rid the mind of errotic or vicious thoughts. They are primarily for the benefit of the physical body, and do not lead to God-Realization. Obviously, if a medicine does not cure the ailment, it is useless. These postures require sustained effort without much profit. Sant Mat, therefore, depreciates such practices.

We have first to see which is the easiest posture by means of which our soul currents can be brought to the eye center and concentration attained, and, which a child, a young or an old person can adopt with equal ease. It is essential to be alert before starting the spiritual practice. The practitioner should take a bath to get over sloth and drowsiness. If for some reason this is not possible, one should at least wash the hands, feet and face. One should then sit cross-legged, keeping the back straight but neither stiff nor loose. It is essential that the spinal column remains erect. When doing the practice, one should sit on a firm surface. The practitioner should not support his back against a wall or a chair. He should be careful not to fall asleep. If one has to sit for a long period, one can use an arm rest with advantage.

Whatever posture one may adopt for his spiritual practice, he must satisfy himself that it causes no restlessness and that he can easily forget the body. The Saints have adopted a posture that is both easy and natural. They do not regard the different postures of Hatha Yoga to be essential for spiritual uplift. The posture adopted by the Saints is that by which the soul currents can be withdrawn from the nine apertures of the body to the soul's headquarters between the two eyebrows.

One can obtain outstanding results by this posture, for the soul currents, which are scattered into the world through the nine apertures of the body can collect at the eye center and ascend upwards. The soul then contacts Nam or Truth at the Tenth Gate (Daswandwar), and finally it reaches Sach Khand, where ego, attachment, greed, desire, and lust leave it, and the cycle of births and deaths is ended.

Daily Simran

"The power of speach of the tongue should be utilized in simran."

The whole world is engaged in thinking of its own work; or in remembering or thinking about something: the shopkeeper about his shop, the farmer about his land or crops, a person in service about his work, a mother about her child, a friend about his companion, and an enemy about his foe.

No one is free from repetition or remembrance of some kind. It is through this process that the worldly objects enter into every pore of our body, mind and intellect, and man is virtually dyed in the hue of the world. It is because of this that the soul has to be born again and again. "As we think, so we become." If we give up remembrance of the world and instead think of the Lord, we can easily gain the means of Salvation.

Everybody remembers the Lord for the fulfillment of desires. One does so for a wife, another yearns for a son; and still another asks for wealth. Everyone has a motive behind his Simran. But if the objects of desires are achieved, they do not accompany one when he dies. Even his body remains behind. What else can ever go with one at the time of his departure?

The Scriptures tell us that all things in this world are transitory. They are truly shadow shapes that vanish in a moment. Therefore, begging for anything other than God Himself is foolishness. So long as the Simran is done with an ulterior motive, we are asking God for objects of the world, and thus bringing further privations upon ourselves. It is only the selfless Simran that is acceptable to God. A Muslim Saint says: "Do not blacken your heart with useless thoughts. Ask not from God aught else but Him."

So it is necessary that repetition be replaced by Repetition. The simran of the objects of the world must be replaced by the Simran of God, and thoughts of the world by Contemplation of the Master, who is God incarnate. Thus is imprinted on our subconscious mind the impression of God in the form of our Satguru. Where the waves of the world once dominated the scene, there will now be remembrance of the Lord and Contemplation of the Master. The devotee begins to forget the world and its shadow shapes. The mind loses much of its fickleness and a certain amount of concentration is achieved.

What is Simran? In order to understand it properly, one has to pay attention to its true signif- icance. Simran is a Sanskrit word derived from the root 'Smar'. It has several meanings: To protect, to make a mental picture of one's deity in the heart and to contemplate on this form, to remember a certain person or thing to such an extent as to think about it with every breath, to make it a part and parcel of one's life, and ultimately to awaken into and to live in it.

The repetition of any name or names of God is called Simran. Through it an extraordinary current of consciousness enters the body. In the early stages considerable effort has to be made to carry out Simran, but as practice is gained Simran goes on automatically. This practice is both natural and easy.

Everybody thinks of God in adversity, but if one were to think of Him with love at all times, then no pain would ever visit him. Pain is the result of sin. By forgetting God, one moves away from Him. In this way, he falls victim to the endless cycle of births and deaths.

If one were to carry out Simran when in fortunate circumstances, his willpower and mind would grow strong. Even if a calamity should befall him, he would remain indifferent to it. If a person has failed to do Simran during a time of ease, but has taken to it only at the time of a reverse, or on falling ill, or on getting involved in a lawsuit, little can be expected from it. If Simran were to be done ceaselessly, all cares and anxieties would vanish. Then the mind would not give up Simran even for a second.

A person takes three meals a day. This is all

to feed the body, but the food for the soul is Simran and Contemplation of His Form. This food we must tender to the soul. Just as you take food daily to maintain your body, similarly, whether you are at home or traveling, you must provide food for the soul. Never be remiss in this respect.

Repetition of God's Name is an unfailing remedy for all ills. This is a spiritual food for the soul. Christ says:

> "Man shall not live by bread alone, but by every word that proceedeth out of the mouth of God."

If a person were to remember God constantly, he would awaken into super-consciousness. But this is a state which can be achieved only with the Grace and blessing of the Lord. One who gains this state even for a moment, gets life everlasting.

> "The remembrance of God is so amazingly intoxicating that those who attain it do not wish to be separated from the Lord even for a moment, like the swan who cannot do without a pool of water."

Kabir says:

> "Remember the name of the Lord with the same intensity of love as the fish has for water. It does not stand separation from water, and dies."

People perform Simran in a variety of ways and these are:

1. Some do it with the help of beads. This divides the attention, because a part of it is engaged in counting the beads, and the other in reversing the process on reaching the head bead. By this means complete concentration does not come. So long as the attention accompanies the process, some benefit

accrues.   Otherwise, while the fingers rotate the beads, the mind roams about.   Kabir says:

"The true rosary is the rosary of the mind. The rosaries of the world are false. If it were possible to have communion with the Lord by rotating outside beads, then the Persian wheel, round whose neck rotate water-holders, should have been the one to realize God."

Many people use their finger tips instead of a rosary for doing their repetition.   Kabir says:

"If you say the rosary of the mind, you can have communion with the Master. When the mind has not become motionless, of what use is counting on the fingers? You are counting on your fingers with the hand, but your mind is strutting about. This is all futile."

If the hands are busy in rotating the rosary, how can the soul currents collect within? If the soul currents concentrate, the hands cannot rotate the beads. If the soul currents have not withdrawn to the soul's headquarters, nothing can be gained. Therefore, we make a rosary of the mind. There is no need for one of wood.

2.   Some people repeat their prayers with the tongue. This has a certain value as long as the attention is concentrated on the repetition. But like the rotating of the beads, when the repetition with the tongue becomes automatic, the mind involuntarily wanders.

3.   Some people do repetition with their throat. This is beneficial so long as the attention is properly directed; otherwise the mind wanders aimlessly, as it does in the first two methods.

4.   Some carry out repetition in their heart. This suffers from the same shortcomings as the other methods mentioned above.

Repetition by the tongue is better than that with a rosary, and that in the throat is superior to one by the tongue. Similarly, that in the heart is more beneficial than the one in the throat. All types of repetition, when accompanied by one-pointed attention, yield good results. They cleanse the mind and bring some measure of peace. But the soul currents do not collect at the eye center, so there is little gain in spiritual development.

> "The practice where the rosary rotates in the hand, the tongue moves in the mouth, and the mind runs in all the ten directions, is not called Simran."

It is for this reason that the Saints start from the very root of the thing. They advocate repetition by the tongue of the soul. This way we gain the means of making the mind still. Saints call this the Simran of the soul.

By following this method, the mind does not roam about. Here it is not a case that repetition continues and the mind strays out, as happens in the methods described earlier. The Simran of the soul awakens the inner consciousness and enables one to hear Shabd, which brings real peace and bliss.

> "If the rosary of the mind is repeated, then the inner consciousness is awakened and Light appears within. For ages people have rotated beads, but their minds have not changed. Therefore, giving up the counting of beads with the hand, rotate only the bead of the mind."

Many people perform their worldly tasks with their hands and feet. Their minds remain free. Employ your hands and feet in work, and your mind in the remembrance of the Lord. If one is to succeed in this practice, he should carry out Simran at all times whether

awake or asleep, just as the hands of a clock move
ceaslessly.

To do Simran, it is not necessary to give up the
world and its tasks. Carry on your duties and still
keep your attention fixed in Simran. Simran should
be done with every breath—sitting, standing, walking,
eating—one should so remember Him with one-pointed attention that he becomes inseparable from Him
and does not stray away. But special times for Simran
are the night, the midnight and the time of Elixer.
Simran during these periods is highly fruitful.

Simran is a precious practice. It is only through
great good luck that a person takes to Simran. The
secret of Simran one can learn from a True Master
alone.

Repetition by tongue, without understanding the
significance of the words, or parrot-like repeating of
a name without much thought, is a mere show. The
ordinary people who do this type of Simran remain
bereft of any good.

The Saints tell us that we are accustomed to repeat
certain names. How good it would be if we were to
turn our attention to the Name of God! Simran
gives pleasure and removes pain. By doing the Simran
of the Lord, one merges in Him.

What are the names which one should repeat,
and what is their connection with God?

For Simran there are two kinds of names:

1. Personal or subjective names.
2. Attributive or qualitative names.

Generally, people repeat the names describing the
Lord by one attribute or another. Such repetition is
beneficial only up to a limit, for it fails to open the

inner vision and enable one to witness inner phenomena. Saints, therefore, reveal to us the names of the presiding deities of the regions within.   Hence, the names that a Master imparts are the only ones to be repeated; for they alone can lead the way.   These names are also energy-charged and help the transference of spiritual energy to the disciple, with the result that rapid progress follows.   The Negative Power has placed a number of impediments in these regions, with which the soul traversing the Astral and the Causal planes has to contend.   These can be overcome by repeating the holy Names given to us by a True Master.   They also save the devotee from other difficulties and pitfalls. Simran of such holy Names is beneficial both here and beyond.   It is for this reason that Scriptures lay emphasis on repeating only such names.

The Names that are revealed to us by a True Master carry His power, and this comes to the aid of the disciple, enabling him to transcend both death and the Negative Power.   The words of the Master are eternal, and through them we are freed from the cycle of births and deaths.   Therefore, whatever Names are bestowed upon us by a Master are conducive to our greatest good.

Simran At Meditation

Constant Simran during the working day prepares the mind for meditation.   In meditation Simran is a ladder which takes us to the higher regions where we may have communion with the Lord.   Whoever finds pleasure in doing Simran as instructed by the Master, will one day assume or merge into the form of God

Himself. It is for this reason that all Saints have preached and taught the proper methods of doing Simran within.

In meditation we have to concentrate our attention at the Third Eye by means of Simran. In order to concentrate at this center, we have to carry out one-pointedly the Simran of the names of the Lord. Other methods are unnecessary.

By maintaining a convenient posture and by concentrating our attention at the eye center, slightly towards the right, we should repeat the Names with the attention of the mind. In other words, we should fix our attention at the center of the eyebrows but slightly towards the right. One should fix the attention of the mind on the eye center and start Simran as well as Contemplation.

In the beginning, the Repetition of the Names given by the Master should be whispered or uttered semiaudibly. As soon as one is sufficiently advanced in the practice, then the Repetition should be done with the mind only. But one must do it with love and faith.

While doing this, care should be taken not to put any pressure on the forehead or the eyes. Start with a short period, but gradually increase the duration to two or three hours.

Some people close their eyes while doing Repetition, and others do so with open eyes. In the first case, there is a possibility of falling asleep; and in the second, there is a danger of the mind running after the objects of the world. The former is a much better method, but one should start the practice after getting over drowsiness. It is also essential that the practice be done regularly as well as punctually, at the appointed time.

If one feels drowsy during Simran, he should stand up and do the Repetition for about half an hour. Cold water may also be sprinkled on the face.

Simran should not be done in haste. It should be done slowly and with love and devotion, the Names being repeated clearly and correctly. To do it in haste or to regard it as an unwanted task, or to go through it merely as a routine leads nowhere. If the mind becomes lazy while doing Simran, or the attention turns towards sense pleasures, one should repeat the Names audibly for ten or fifteen minutes, so that the minds attention reverts to the proper place.

Repetition should be done with one-pointed attention. By so doing, your hands and feet will become numb and the entire consciousness of the body will collect at the eye center. In due course a stage is reached when Repetition ceases and the Form contemplated upon manifests itself. This is the culmination point of Repetition.

The results of Repetition will be in direct proportion to the love and faith brought to bear upon it. Carry out the Simran of the Lord with love and faith. His Names have a great power. When done with faith one feels intoxicated with joy, with the result that he forgets his body and himself and is aware of the presence of the Lord. How potent and blissful is the Name of God, for it creates in the devotee a fast-flowing current of bliss, peace and soul force, and he gets truly blessed.

"During Simran the longing for God in one's mind should be as intense as that of a lover for the beloved, so that sitting, standing, awake or asleep, the form of the beloved is always in the mind of the lover. He does not forget it even for a second." 4

If you wish to be filled with the Grace of God, then you should banish all else from your mind. Leave everything else aside and cherish the Name of the Lord alone in your heart. As soon as you empty your mind of all thoughts by means of Simran, you will find the way to the Lord's mansion.

This is the only method by which the soul meets its Lord and becomes one with Him. But this state is realized only with the Grace of the Lord. Our own efforts are utterly futile. But by constant Simran one awakens super-consciousness and attains the state of everlasting tranquility and peace.

Tennyson, the Poet Laureate of England, in his memoirs furnishes some hints about the super-conscious state that results from Simran:

"A kind of waking trance I have frequently had, from boyhood onwards, when I have been all alone. This has generally come upon me through repeating my own name two or three times to myself silently till all at once, as it were, out of the intensity of consciousness of individuality, the individuality itself seemed to dissolve and fade away into boundless being, and this is not a confused state, but the clearest of the clearest, the surest of the surest, the wisest of the wisest, utterly beyond words, where death was a laughable impossibility, the loss of personality (if so it were), seemingly but the only true life. I am ashamed of my feeble description. Have I not said the state is utterly beyond words?"

Soul is of the essence of the Lord. You acquire the form you think about and have to return to it. As ye think, so ye become. If the essence thinks of its own source, which is all Consciousess, it will merge in the source and attain the eternal and everlasting state.

A Muslim Saint has very aptly described the greatness of Simran:

> "The soul is the essence and the Lord is the source. When it remembers the Lord one-pointedly, it becomes the Lord."

Contemplation

> "The power of the sight of the eyes should be used in contemplating the form of the Master."

It is a well-known fact that when we think of something, its mental picture appears before our eyes. This is only natural. Everybody contemplates the forms which he thinks about.

Whenever we close our eyes, we behold scenes of the world such as family and children, hearth and home, wealth and possessions; we constantly dwell upon the world and its objects with the result that every cell of our mind is immersed in it. It is for this reason that we are firmly tied to the world. We do not know how to contemplate upon the form of the Lord. The One we have to contemplate upon is beyond the three worlds. So long as we do not meet Him, on whom shall we contemplate?

Some people dwell upon the pictures of ancient Saints. This is contemplation of material and lifeless objects. Both pictures and idols are lifeless. They cannot draw one upward. He alone can draw us to the spiritual regions who frequents them himself. Contemplation on the form of ancient Saints can do us little good. Most of the pictures of such Saints are not true to life and are mere figments of imagina-

tion. Besides, the worship of a lifeless thing is pro-
hibited. The pictures or photographs of a Saint certainly remind us of our Master, but they can give us
nothing more. It is only the living Master who can
bestow His Grace on us.

Therefore, Scriptures emphasize the need of Contemplation upon the form of the living Master who is
one with the Lord. Such a course is conducive to
valuable benefits.

God is manifest in the Master, because the Master
is God in human form. Therefore, the Contemplation of the Master is really that of the Lord, and His
worship is true service to the Lord.

In the initial stages, the Contemplation of the
physical form of the Master is necessary. After that,
the disciple contemplates on the Radiant Form of
the Master, which remains with him in the spiritual
planes. This form subsequently merges in Shabd,
its real Form.

Shut your eyes and you will find nothing but
darkness within. This darkness is even more pro-
nounced than a completely moonless night. When
the soul, withdrawing from without, goes in, there
come into view the stars, the sun and the moon.
Beyond them appears the Radiant Form of the Master.
The Master does not come secretly, but flashes of
light emanate from his Radiant Form in such a manner
that the soul is irresistibly attracted towards it. In
reality, this scene beggars description.

When we see the Radiant Form of the Master
within, the soul is able by concentration to maintain
a stable position, and begins to listen to the inner music.
In this way the Sound current flows and the devotee

remains immersed in its enjoyment. The mind then takes to Shabd with fervor.

The Radiant Form of the Master resides within every true disciple. When the soul withdraws from wihout and goes within, crossing the stars, the sun and the moon, it beholds His refulgent form. It is this radiance that bestows light on both the sun and the moon. Whoever goes within sees His wondrous form.

We are wonder-struck to hear descriptions of the beautiful physical form of the Master, but if we manifest Him within, we will find Him a thousandfold more beautiful. Hafiz, addressing the Lord, says:

> "O Beloved, I have heard many a tale about your wondrous beauty; but now that I have beheld you within, I see that you are really a thousand times more wonderful than the tales depict you."

When the Refulgent Form appears within, the disciple should fix his attention in it, so much so that he completely merges himself in this form and can no longer distinguish between himself and the Master.

> "I have become You, and You me. I have become a body and You have become my soul, my very life, so much so that none can say we have a separate entity."   12

According to the Scriptures dealing with the soul, when the course of Contemplation is complete, the disciple, the discipline, and the Deity all merge into one. The worshiped and the worshiper become one, as the caterpillar becomes a butterfly and loses its own identity.   Such a state is known as merging in the Master. But the Master has already merged in the Lord, with the result that the disciple also merges into Him. Whatever you dwell upon, that you become.

Just as we cannot scale the wall of a fort without the help of a ladder, even so, we cannot reach the Lord without Contemplation of the Master. It is concentration that takes us from the physical to the Astral, from the Astral to the Causal, and beyond the Causal to the Lord.

The Radiant Form of the Master manifests only in pure and sincere hearts. In an impure heart, it simply cannot reside. Hafiz says:

> "Such inner Contemplation is a gift from the Master. But it is obtained only when the Lord wills it. The outer learning and contemplation do not lead to God-Realization, with the consequence that the soul continues to be tied to this world."

The Upanishads say: "Purity of mind and its cleanliness are regarded as essential prerequisites for Contemplation and meditation." The purity must be both inner and outer.

By Repetition and Contemplation the disciple begings to remember the Lord automatically and becomes worthy or witnessing the inner scenes. The lovers of the Master's form get tied to the Master. They become oblivious of the body and also of the world.

The Master is free from birth and death. One whose attention is fixed on the form of the Master, one who loves naught save the Master—who can ever make such a person return to the world?

Contemplation of the Master's Form is wondrously rewarding. Those who think of the Master's Form, gain honor and glory both here and beyond. All their desires are fulfilled. By merging in the Master, they attain God-Realization.

Bhajan

"—and the power of hearing of the ears should be spent in listening to the Sound Current."

When the first two methods of spiritual practice, viz., Repetition and Contemplation, are completed, they lead to the third one which is Bhajan.

Repetition is complete only when Contemplation has been achieved. When Contemplation is complete, the Sound is wakened automatically. This is known as Bhajan in the language of the Saints.

Bhajan simply means listening to the Sound Current, which is also termed by the Saints as the practice of Shabd Yog. This is done by the soul, or by its attention. It is through Surat or Soul that the Divine Melody is heard. The practice awakens the soul that has been slumbering for ages and results in a state of bliss.

Shabd is a royal road to God-Realization. It is by traversing this road that the devotee reaches the Court of the Lord, which is Sach Khand. There he meets with no obstacles. He constantly dwells upon Shabd and remains steeped in it. Both the Negative Power and Maya remain away from Shabd and do not cross the path of a devotee.

The Shabd is really the music of the Lord, and it is listening to it that is greatly stressed in the Scriptures. It is the method of singing the glory of the Lord. It is the unstruck Melody. It is One, and yet it manifests itself in all. The entire universe is sustained by it.

Mind is not amenable to control, even though millions of ordinary methods may be tried. Yogis of the past tried all their techniques and failed; the intellectuals gained nothing from philosophical discussions and critical commentaries; the efforts of anchorites performing penances and austerities proved abortive; the learned used all their knowledge, but with intellect and cleverness alone they failed to subdue the mind. The only remedy for controlling the mind is to listen to the Sound Current. No second way exists.

True knowledge consists of the practice of Simran and Bhajan. The Divine Music ever plays, and it is through listening to it that one begins to love the Lord. This is true worship of the Lord, but it can find a place in our hearts only when the Lord wills it.

It is not possible to obtain this treasure of Shabd by reading Scriptures. The books contain only its description. We may read or hear all the Scriptures, but these can never equal the sweet music of God's Name. So long as the soul does not contact the Sound within, it remains bereft of the Reality. It is like a bird that imitates the songs of others, but does not understand their meaning.

The Inner Melody is resounding ceaselessly. It is eternal. But in spite of its ringing day and night in everybody, we remain poor. We are deprived of this treasure. It lies latent in us, but we quit the scene of life without awakening to it. We never care to dig for the treasure. It is only when we meet a Master and follow his instructions that we become aware of it and open the knot of the material and the conscious.

To be successful in Bhajan it is essential for one to be the disciple of a perfect Master. The Sound manifests itself only in the devotee of a Master. It appears only when the course of Repetition and Con-

templation is completed. When the devotee attunes
to Shabd, he realizes the inexpressible Truth.

Where can we get this Sound? God is our real
Lord. In His Court resounds the Divine Melody.
When a devotee is able to still his wandering mind and,
with the help of a Master, gains access to Daswan
Dwar (the Tenth Door), there he drinks the Elixir of
Life. It is at this place that the Master showers
Ambrosia and the Sound Current resounds. Shabd
then manifests in the body. By listening to it one
subdues the mind, and the temple of the body becomes
sublime.

When the mind listens to the Shabd, it is completely enraptured by the bliss conferred. One who has
joined his consciousness with Shabd goes beyond the
reach of Kal and thus ends the ages-long cycle of birth
and rebirth. God's Name then dwells in the heart,
one is attuned to Him, and the Soul merges in the
Lord.

> "Within our hearts we contemplate the Master, on our tongue
> is His holy Name, in our eyes resides His Form, in our ears
> resounds the Divine Melody. We remain completely en-
> grossed in His remembrance. We become merged in the state
> of ceaselessly dwelling upon Him. Our mind and intellect—
> their very fabric—are completely colored with the dye of His
> constant remembrance. It is such persons who gain honor
> and glory in the Court of the Lord and thus fulfill the great
> destiny of human life."

CHAPTER 3

DEATH AND DYING WHILE LIVING

Everyone has to die some day. Whether man or beast, rich or poor, healthy or diseased, nobody escapes death. All have to pass through its gate. The soul that has taken the physical form has to leave it. "Dust thou art, and to dust returnest." Everybody knows that he has to quit this world some day, but he knows not when.

We lament the death of others. But, actually, we should be concerned with our own end and should prepare ourselves for our own life beyond death.

What kind of country do we have to pass through after death? Whom are we to deal with? We must ponder over these questions. The Scriptures make occasional mention of this subject, but we pay little heed to them, for we always believe them to be either phantasies or fairy tales, or efforts to wean people away from sin, or to induce them to perform good deeds. We have to cross the gates of death. No one can be an exception to this. Saint Paul says: "Death is the last enemy to be conquered." We should not shut our eyes to this subject.

It is our common experience that whenever we have to go to another country, we make preparations for it and carry with us the necessary funds. We make arrangements for the means of transport, be it an automobile, airline or boat. We write a letter to a friend in that country, and also decide about where to stay. We are so careful in these worldly matters that we never undertake a journey without making adequate arrangements. Yet for the journey after death, which hangs over our heads like the sword of Damocles, and which we all must undertake in due course, we care very little. Have we arranged for food, which is Shabd, for this journey? Have we decided upon a guide, or a Master who has personal knowledge and experience to accompany us? Have we ever thought of the place where we are to stay?

We are very clever about our worldly affairs and always make appropriate arrangements for their successful prosecution. But with regard to death, which has no time fixed for it and may come at any time— in childhood, in youth, or in old age—we are completely ignorant of our destination.

What Happens At The Time Of Death And After

To solve this riddle, people have spared no efforts. The intellect fails. The learned and the illiterate are equally helpless in resolving this mystery. The reason is that no one has returned after death to relate to us his knowledge. Again and again the thought crosses our mind, how satisfying it would be if someone had gone to the regions beyond death and had returned to narrate his actual experiences! We merely make guesses, but with no success. No telescope is able to see the regions beyond death, nor are they accessible to the airplane. These instruments and machines can merely tell us a little about the material regions. They are of no value where the higher regions are concerned.

A Master alone knows everything about death. At the time of death, when family and children, our wealth, possessions and body, all leave us, it is the Perfect Master alone who accompanies the disciple. For this reason He is our only true and genuine friend.

The Perfect Master is a true guide in the Astral, Causal and the higher purely spiritual regions. That is why the Scriptures have strongly emphasized the need for us to meet such a Master and to keep constantly dwelling upon him in our mind.

Death is not to be feared. It is only the name given to the phenomenon of the soul leaving the body. After discarding the physical body, the soul ascends to the Astral, Causal, and higher regions. It is merely the withdrawal of the soul from the gross senses, and its entrance into finer regions. It is merely giving up the present garment, namely, the body. It does not mean annihilation. There is life after death, although we may not be able to see it.

The Saints have solved the mystery of death. They leave the human body every day and travel into the Astral and Causal regions. In their company we learn the means by which we too can triumph over death.

This subject has been dealt with at length by the Saints. They have described the method of passing through the Gate of Death and of conquering death. By following this method, a devotee can also pass through the Gate of Death and travel through the regions beyond it. He leaves and returns to his physical body at will. While doing this he is completely conscious, and whatever scenes he witnesses he vividly remembers.

A person whose soul has traversed the upper realms, before death has overtaken him, can alone understand what it is to die while living. Intellect is helpless to comprehend this phenomenon.

Plutarch described the state at the time of death as follows:

> "At the moment of death the soul experiences the same impressions, and passes through the same process as is experienced by those who are initiated into the Great Mysteries."

Those who follow the instructions of a True Master die daily—while living. They go into the regions above, and they come back into the same physical body at will.

One of the benefits of the teachings of the Saints is that a disciple crosses the Gate of Death in a state of happiness and thus conquers it. This is the experience of all disciples who have been blessed with the Grace of the Master. It is not merely talk or a fable taken from some book of holy Scriptures. Death has no fear for a follower of the Path of the Saints. If one learns the art of dying while living, he can forever end the cycle of birth and rebirth. He loses all fear of death, for every day he crosses its gate. Therefore, Saints eulogize the state of dying while living and teach the manner of doing it. Death is sweet if a person can die while living.

The body is an ocean of Spirituality which none can fathom. Only one who dies while living can obtain pearls of super-consciousness from it. Such a one, if he enters the ocean of his own body even once, can recover a treasure of super-consciousness from it. Otherwise, the treasure remains completely hidden.

One who dives deep in the ocean and rises up into the sky will make the higher regions his abode and will realize the jewel of the Lord. So long as we yearn for life (in this world), we can never obtain this precious Jewel. It is through the Grace of the Lord that a rare devotee who dies while living can find this Jewel. If you wish to realize God, you must die while living, for it is impossible to attain Him so long as you do not die. So long as you cherish worldly desires, God-Realization will not come to you.

A person who dies while living lives forever. One who looks upon life in this world and death with the same attitude, is also free from death. This dying while living has nothing to do with being cremated or buried. It is a state or condition in which the Master bestows eternal life on his disciples.

The chief essential in Spirituality is to die while living, because it is after such a death that the soul becomes really alive. Most people in the world are ignorant of this true path, for they are afraid to die while living.

We can never realize true life so long as we do not go beyond the domain of death or, in other words, so long as we are not born into the subtle higher regions.

Christ says:

"Except a man be born again, he cannot see the Kingdom of God."

But such a death, namely, dying while living, can be had only through the Grace of the Master. There is no other way. The lovers of the Lord, by dying while living, ever drink the wine of happiness and bliss. This is the privilege of those to whom the Master Himself offers the 'Wine'.

Dying while living is not accomplished easily. The method can be gained through the Grace of a Master. Only that person can die while living who has subdued his mind and curbed his desires and cravings, and has annihilated his ego. This is not as simple as it may seem. It is not as easy to do as it is to talk about. One achieves it by renouncing all desires for the world. So long as desires assail the body, the soul cannot succeed in leaving it. It is only by detaching oneself from the body and mind that one can die while living. When for the first time the soul leaves the pot of clay (body) during practice, it has to pass through the Gate of Death. Giving up the world and its desires and surrendering completely to the ever-helpful Master, let your soul rise to higher regions. You will experience no trouble.

What really is this dying while living? The headquarters of the soul in the body is at the eye center, and from here the entire body receives its energy currents. In the practice of dying while living, there is no need to stop breathing. Simply collect your full attention at the eye center by doing Simran, thus depriving the senses of their motive energy. The body will then appear as a corpse. In other words, the gross senses should cease to function and the fine ones get awakened, so that the soul can rise to subtle regions and behold their glory.

By Simran all the active energy in the body is concentrated at the eye center; by Contemplation it is fixed there; and by means of the Sound Current it ascends to higher regions. When consciousness separates from the body, it is known as dying while living. The practitioner leaves his body in the same way that the soul leaves it at the time of death. The difference is only this—that his connection with the physical body is not completely broken. There is a silver cord, referred to in the Bible (Ecc. 12:6), by means of which one can leave the body and return to it at will and be at all times connected with the body. In this manner he gets an insight into death while living. He travels in the Astral, the Causal and the higher regions, and becomes fully familiar with them. He is able to meet and talk with the inhabitants of these regions.

Guru Angad gives an apt description of the condition of dying while living. He says:

"You have to see without eyes. You have to hear without ears. You have to walk without feet. You have to work and speak, using neither hands nor tongue. Even while living you have to die, and only then can you hear the 'Word' of God and meet your Beloved."

The condition of dying while living is the result of the Master's Grace, listening to His Satsang, and devoting oneself to Nam. It is only then that one crosses the ocean of life and is acclaimed in the Court of the Lord as having fulfilled the mission of human life.

The disciple or the devotee is the only one who works for everlasting bliss. In other words, he is the one who practises the Shabd that confers this bliss. Such a one knows both life and death, and treats them alike. Such a one is the beloved of the Lord.

Kabir expresses the same thought very aptly:

"Spirituality is a tall tree. Its fruits hang in the sky and only a rare bird can partake of them."

Only those persons who die while living can taste the fruits. Therefore, so long as the soul does not leave the body completely during one's lifetime, births and deaths will continue.

The spiritual regions are the abode of your soul. If a person dies such a death, his soul need not return to this world any more.

The state of dying while living is the state of separating the conscious from the material. This is a highly evolved state. Such a person knows himself and his mind, and comprehends the mysteries of life. This state can be achieved by persons on whom descends the Grace of the Lord through a Master.

> "The whole world keeps dying after death, for no one dies the real death. I have died a death that will make me never die again. So long as you do not know how to die while living, you will not gain freedom from the cycle of birth and death."

THE STAGES OF LOVE

It has been observed that normally, when we hear about something very good, a desire arises in our mind to obtain it. When we keep somebody's company, a connection is made with him, and our mind feels happiness in keeping that company and in seeing that person as much and as often as possible. A certain feeling is produced in connection with that person, and that feeling develops into a current of love.

Love is like a fountain of fragrance in the garden of life. When the connection with our companion becomes strong, our attachment towards him changes into love and the condition of the mind becomes such that we do not like to part company, so much so that even if our reason tries to restrain us from meeting that person, the mind is irresistibly attracted. Then the mind rules the intellect, and as this feeling gradually increases, it becomes so strong that separation from our companion, even for a short period, makes us restless, and the mind is constantly attracted towards him and yearns to be with him. There is, however, still a slight control of the intellect over the mind, but the control is gradually reduced and the feeling then takes the form of intense love. In that state a lover begins to forget himself. He pays no attention to his body or his mind. He feels happy if the beloved is with him. Otherwise, he is like a dead body. He becomes indifferent to everybody, including his own kith and kin, and the entire control of the intellect vanishes.

A lover drinks from the cup of the wine of the beautiful eyes of the beloved and becomes intoxicated. He does not care for the opinion of his friends or relatives. His intellect and mind are completely devoid of the power of discrimination.

The feeling of love is universal. Animals, birds, insects, and even plants and flowers are full of it. The spark of the flame of love intoxicates a human being who is attracted to it. The entire universe sings its praises. There is no heart which is completely devoid of love. All are born into this world gifted with at least a particle of love. We all live on it, but those who do not follow the path rightly are sometimes drowned in it.

Love is a soul quality and is inherent in all of us, but not everyone can avail himself of it. This ocean of all joys is within us, and we need not spend a penny to achieve it. As soon as the soul is freed from the filth and attachments of the world, real love automatically makes its appearance.

Love is to be found in its original form in every human being. God is Love and the soul is a part of Him; therefore, the soul is also Love. But because the soul is concealed under the coverings of the mind, love is also concealed along with it. It is necessary that we remove the covering.

Just as there are regulations and principles laid down for obtaining different types of knowledge, in the same manner there is a definite code of discipline to be followed for admission to the school of love. It is necessary that these principles be followed rigidly: A lover must give up the thoughts of the world, the attractions thereof and of the world beyond, and must then be completely absorbed in contemplation of his Beloved at all times.

"When I looked in, I found within me that which has been sought for ages by all mankind, from one corner of the world to the other. We have been searching for it for many ages here and there, but we have found it only in our heart. Therefore, you should not search for your lost Beloved outside. You will find Him only in the recess of your heart."

Four Things Are Necessary In Love

1. No other idea should creep into the mind except that of the beloved.
2. The question of bargaining or give and take should not arise.
3. All types of fear should be removed.
4. The lover should not be in a state of enmity or hatred with any one.

Such persons are never disappointed or lose hope. Their Beloved (Satguru) is always by their side.

The prayers of a person, who depends on rituals, are said in a specified posture, but the prayers of a lover are always said in a state of self-forgetfulness (rising above the mortal self or ego). A person who says his prayers according to rituals, washes his hands and his face before sitting in prayer; but a lover washes his hands of the world. In other words, so long as you do not remove your thoughts from the world, you cannot remember Him.

Bulleh Shah expresses the same thought in the following beautiful words:

> "Religious customs are our nurse; rituals and ceremonies
> are our mother; but if we wish to achieve something really
> worthwhile, that can be done only by spiritual practice (inner
> method.) Then alone do we realize the real Truth."

All austerities and practices are empty without
love. Knowledge and contemplation in themselves
are also unsuccessful efforts, but all these practices are
performed only to inculcate love. If there is no love,.
then all meditations are dry and useless.

The mind should be cleansed of all thoughts and
desires, and thus become like a highly polished mirror.
So long as one entertains greed and desires in his heart,
the face of love will not be visible. By love alone the
Saints achieve conscious union with the Lord. In
other words, if there is any self-interest, then it is not
true love.

Love knows only how to give. One has to
abandon all desires and to leave all power and fame,
and has to become the slave of someone. Such is
love. To achieve true life is to lose one's self completely in love. One has to awaken in one's Beloved
and completely merge in God. That is love. It is a
work of sacrifice and surrender. To meet the Beloved
is very difficult, because one has to bargain for this
path with one's own head.

> "If you wish to know about Love, go to a Saint and ask
> him. If you want to know how the heart goes out of your
> hands, ask one who has lost his heart." A

Love is first produced in the heart of the Beloved.
If there is no light, the moth will never burn itself.
Love is born in a man through good fortune by the
grace of God, and then only is one able to go into the
company of Saints. Guru Ram Das says:

"Regarding those who possess the wealth of love, you should understand that He Himself has granted this favor to them out of His Grace.   This treasure can be obtained only through a Master.   It is exceedingly difficult to serve Him, but that is also the means of achieving all joy.   This love is bestowed only on such persons on whom God Himself bestows it with His Grace.

Just as electricity exists in a battery in a latent state and when connected in a circuit can brighten a large area, similarly the spark of love is produced in the heart of a seeker by the grace of God or a Master and its force then becomes apparent.

The first essential is to awaken love for God by means of repetition and then by contemplation.   As we repeat the five Holy Names, our attraction and love for Him increase within ourselves.   When a lover remembers Him and becomes fully absorbed in His remembrance, then God turns the lover's attention towards devotion by His divine grace.

The third part of the spiritual practice is listening to the Shabd, Nam or Sound Current.   God is Shabd, and God is also Love.   Therefore, Shabd is Love. As the soul contacts Shabd, Love flows out from within.

This is the path which a seeker has to tread in order to come near the Beloved.   But it sometimes happens that the currents of love irresistibly enter into the heart of a person as the result of just one gaze into the eyes of a true Master.   Even one glance from the Master is enough to create in the seeker a feeling of intense love without passing through the stages of association, intimate connection and emotional attraction.

The path of Love is as sharp and as narrow as the edge of a sword.   There is room for only one to

tread on it.   Here God and the devotee have to become
one, and the least waver or negligence on the part of
the devotee will cause his downfall.   Therefore, only
the strong-willed can follow this path with the support
of God and the Master and by surrendering themselves
at all times into the lap of the Beloved.   Such fortunate
devotees are guided at every step and cannot fall.

Love is the most powerful and effective of all
practices to meet the Lord.   Shamas Tabriz says:

> "If the road is lengthy, you should fly on the wings of love.
> When you unfold the wings of love, you need not ascend by
> means of the steps."

> "You should ride on the steed of Love and go forward without
> fear, because that steed is very swift.   The path may have
> ups and downs, but it will take you to your Goal in no time
> at all."

CHAPTER 5

A LOVER

The status of an ordinary worshiper is better than that of persons attached to the world. The former has meditated, has done good works, and has abstained from evil in order to find a place in heaven and to save himself from the fire of hell. But better than a worshiper is a hermit who tries to avoid all evil actions and desires only communion with God. Such a one has sacrificed the world in his desire for heaven, and is engaged in the worship of God. And better than hermits is the status of lovers, who have ascended the steps towards the love of God and have forgotten this world and the next in their love for Him. They have no fear of hell and no desire for heaven. They want to travel only on the path on which the Beloved takes them.

This world is really a prison house, and the world hereafter is the place of satisfaction of one's desires. A lover does not care to purchase either world even for a farthing.

A lover points out, by his own example, that the real way to love God is not through outer observances. Quarrels and disputes amongst persons of various beliefs are due to narrow-minded intolerance. Those who confine their love to their own countries or nations are also subject to the same narrow-mindedness. But one who places the ideal of love above everything else in his daily life is really following the command of his Lord. He is loved by the Lord.

If a person engages in austerities or rituals without developing the quality of love for the Lord and for His children, then he is like a flower without fragrance, like a well without water, like a lamp without oil, or like eyes without sight. Such persons, even if they sometimes have a spark of spirituality in them, would prefer to keep their interest centered in worldly ties, and they flit from one object to another.

A person who does not follow the path of Love is not honored in the Court of the Lord. Such a one is entangled in the miseries of the world, and whosoever comes in contact with him is also miserable.

"A person in whom there is no love should be considered as a moving statue. He is like the bellows of a blacksmith, which breathes and yet has no life."

Love cannot be gained without devotion to a Master. A worldly man cannot understand it. Only those who have one-pointed attention can share it; that is, those whose mind and heart are one, and who have faith and devotion. A person who is prepared to sell his conscience or, in other words, to deceive himself, cannot drink from the cup of love. To tread the path of love is the work of those resolute souls who will not turn back no matter what may befall them. They alone can meet the Beloved. But those who have only shallow pangs of separation fall down long before they are able to reach the Goal.

Therefore, turn your mind away from the worldly love for your children, for your wife, for your wealth and treasures, for your sovereignty and fame. These are all ephemeral. Instead, we should turn our faces toward the Lord through His manifestation on earth, the Sat Guru.

Once God said to Moses, "I was not well, and how is it that you did not come to inquire about my health?" Moses replied, "O God, you are the King of this world and of the regions above. How can you fall ill?" The reply was: "Moses, a certain very dear devotee of mine was not well and you did not go to him to inquire about his health. If you had visited him at that time, you would have automatically visited me."

This clearly shows that love and service to the devotees of the Lord is love and service to the Lord Himself. Similarly, love and service to the Master and contemplation of His form is, in reality, love and contemplation of God.

To take the path of love is not the work of ordinary people. Only those who are fearless and who are prepared to sacrifice their very lives can do so. Cowards cannot approach it. The Lord of Love is very high and it is not possible for weaklings to gain access to his Court. So long as we do not sacrifice our ego at the altar of our Beloved, we cannot succeed on the path of Love.

"The least condition that love demands is the surrender of one's ego. If you are not able to do this, you should go away and not even talk of love."   3

In love there is no law except the Will of the Beloved. Whatever the Beloved orders or commands, the lover bows his head in obedience.

"If you wish to taste the nectar of Love, you cannot be arrogant. Two swords cannot be contained in one scabbard." 4

One should forget this world in order to get to the world beyond; and he should forget the world beyond in order to divert his attention towards God.

One whose mind is happy in the remembrance of God cannot be satisfied with anything else.

Love is the true austerity which bestows humility, teaches us to remain in the Will of the Beloved, and removes the attention from worldly pleasures and pains. Such a mind does not waver and is always fixed in the Beloved. If such a person were to face difficulties or troubles, he would bear them without complaint, for he remembers only the Beloved in his heart, and he creates a new world of love around himself. He is not attracted by the outer world nor affected by its troubles. In addition to this, the spiritual secrets are disclosed within him and he comes nearer to God-Realization.

Real love will not permit one to follow one's own bent of mind. Real love is another name for implicitly following the desires of the Beloved and desiring only to please Him by remaining in His Will. In such a state one does not consider his own comforts or discomforts, but effaces his own self for the comfort and convenience of the Beloved. He feels a rare and special bliss or happiness, so great even in discomforts, that the people of the world cannot begin to imagine them. Guru Ram Das says:

"When a person has imbibed true love for his Beloved Master, his mind and body both become cheerful by meeting Him, for, a Master who is a manifestation of God has a strong and true attraction for the heart. By having a glimpse of the light of His beauty, one forgets his own self. Such a lover is fully absorbed in that bliss."

"The eyes of a lover are always drowned in love, and they see only God and God's Name."

The surest sign of a lover is that if he loses any worldly or material thing it causes him no pain whatsoever; but if time is lost without meditation, prayer or remembrance of the Beloved, it causes him immense pain.

A true lover is as fond of remembering his Lord as a thirsty man longs for water. The tongue does not speak but the mind is never empty, for the Beloved is always in his remembrance, and is never forgotten even for a moment. Love for the Lord and His lovers is always in his mind. He loves the ones who love Him, and also loves the entire creation.

Who is a true lover? One who has cleansed himself from the dirt of all worldly thoughts and desires by burning them in the fire of devotion and separation. His mind is always restless to meet the Lord, just as thirst makes a man restless for water. The lover's mind and body have been pierced by the arrow of God's Love. His real friend and Beloved is none other than God Almighty.

Real love removes the lover from the worries of pleasure and pain, praise and blame, poverty and wealth, and takes him beyond all such limitations. Love enters every cell of the lover and gives him unlimited power, so that he is never in need of wealth or fame, or honor or name. He has no desire for this world or the next. He is freed from the web of heaven and hell. He is no longer tempted into the snares of rituals or worldly ties.

People misunderstand the meaning of love. The spirit and the meaning of love can be ascertained only from a true lover, and its glow or spark can only be seen on his countenance. If you wish to hear it described, you should ask Mansur or Christ, both of whom went to their death serene and filled with joy.

You might even ask Mirabai, who drank a cup of poison as though it were nectar. You could also ask Guru Arjun Sahib. He sat on hot iron plates, and exclaimed, "Thy Will is sweet."

Lovers do not hate anyone. In their eyes there is nothing but love and more love. They seek love and their thoughts are always concentrated on their Beloved. It is there that they pray, and bow their heads. Where does their Beloved live? The reply is: everywhere, in each one of us. God is Love and Love is another name for God. He is in every thing and His current is flowing everywhere.

"Love is the form of God, just as God is the form of Love. Both of them live as one, like the sun and the sunshine."

A true lover is not confined to any one language or creed. He crosses all such boundaries and loves everybody. Love is the fulfillment of the law. If you love, then you are not doing only a single act but many more without your realizing it. By loving, you send forth the currents of love far and wide in your environment and thus benefit the whole world.

A beloved is loved by the lover, and the lover longs for the beloved. He is the worshiper of his beloved and does not turn his eyes towards anybody else. He is always thirsty for the sight of his beloved and he cannot live without his beloved even for a single moment. You may give him wealth and all other valuable things of the world, but his hunger or longing will not be satisfied, except by meeting his beloved. Love for his beloved is in every cell of his body and his mind. He cannot be sustained by anything other than the sight of his beloved.

Only the Name and praises of his Beloved are on his tongue, nothing else. The repetition of the same Name is never-ceasing, and sighs of separation, when the Beloved is farther away from him, are wrung from his body as well as his heart. He asks for nothing from the Beloved except the Beloved and longs to surrender himself entirely to the wishes of the Beloved. In the ecstasy of his love and in his complete surrender, he considers poverty or wealth, pain or pleasure, health or illness, and whatever else may happen as gifts from the Beloved. He feels no difference between pleasure and pain. By the grace of love he rises above these things and remains above the limitations of the body.

In love there is no other desire, just as nothing remains in a burning fire. The people of the world demand fulfillment of their desires from God. But a lover in whom the fire of love has been kindled demands only God from God. Guru Ram Das says:

"If the precious jewels and treasures of all the seven worlds and the seven oceans were taken and placed before a lover, and someone were to ask him whether he would prefer this wealth or the Beloved, the lover would not even consider the treasures. He asks from God for only the nectar of His Name."

BOOK 4

RELATIONSHIPS TO THE INFINITE

CHAPTER I

THE LORD

God Is Beyond Mind And Intellect

The infinite Universe of universes and worlds is before our eyes. But there is present behind it an indescribable power which is running the entire "show". Even those who do not admit the reality of religion and say that man cannot know God's nature and form, do not deny the existence of this Supreme Power· The well-known philosopher, Herbert Spencer, came to the conclusion that Reality is neither known nor can it be known by anyone. He wanted to discover the Reality through intellect and reasoning. But Reality is beyond the reach of the mind and the senses. His conclusion, therefore, that the Reality is not conceivable by the mind and the senses, was inevitable. Every phenomenon of the world can be explained by reason, but in so far as access to spiritual regions is concerned, reason is useless.

The Lord is beyond time and timelessness, high and separate. All the creation is under His orders, yet He is not the doer. He is beyond form and formlessness. He is omnipresent and the sustainer of all; creator, immovable, all-powerful, imperishable, redeemer of sinners, unknowable, inaccessible, without beginning, eternal and pure consciousness. He is everlasting, invulnerable, a storehouse of knowledge and nectar, without attributes, kind to devotees, self-existent, apart from all, an ocean of sweetness and omnipresent. He is the embodiment of Shabd and His Name sustains all.

The American philosopher Will Durrant, in his book "The Mansions of Philosophy" states:

"In the heart of matter, giving it form and power, is something not material, possessed of its own spontaneity and life; and this subtle, hidden and yet always revealed vitality is the final essence of everything that we know."

What is this essence? This is the omnipotence of the Lord, which is beyond the reach of mind and intellect, as has already been mentioned.

He pervades all and is ever with us. But because we are always engrossed in objects of the world, we cannot see Him. The sun is not to be blamed, if the bats cannot see it. The sun is shining equally for all. The Lord is all-pervading. Then why do we not see Him? The reason for this is that the eyes that can see Him are as yet unawakened. These eyes which can see Him everywhere are different from the physical eyes.

"O Nanak! those eyes that can see Him are different."   A

We can see subtle things only when we ourselves become subtle. The Lord is extremely subtle. Unless we become as subtle as He is, we do not get connected with the Lord. It is a basic principle that the instrument with which we see must be appropriate to the thing to be seen. Our eyes cannot see light that is extremely bright or extremely dim. Similarly, we cannot hear a sound which is either above or below the range of our hearing. Therefore, we have to use various scientific instruments with the help of which we can hear them. Thus, with the help of the instruments we magnify these subtle sounds so that we can hear them. We can see far-off things through a telescope and minute things through a microscope. But this applies only to gross things. To see astral things however it is necessary that our inner eyes become subtle. The Lord is the subtlest of the subtle. To realize Him we have to be equally subtle.

It is impossible to describe the great Lord, who is nameless, ever-existent, the immaculate one, and without attributes. He is beyond mind and speech. He cannot be understood or known by intellect and imagination. He is experienced by the soul only when the mind and intellect are stilled.

The German philosopher Kant became impatient and gave up even thinking about the Unknowable Reality. John Stuart Mill, in "Three Essays on Religion", says that what experience tells us about the First Cause and what we understand by the word 'Cause' is that the primal and immanent essence that pervades all causes is nothing but force. These learned men are of the view that this universe originated from an Indescribable Force and that that Force is eternal and immortal.

In the Upanishad, seers say that "Reality is beyond the reach of any possible description in terms of form and matter, nor can it be described in these terms. Just as it is impossible to extract oil from sand or to quench thirst with wine, similarly it is useless even to conceive that Brahm (the Lord) can be known through learning." In this Upanishad there is a short aphorism "Neti Neti" (Not this, not this). It is repeated four times. Its meaning is that what is described is not Brahm or the Lord. Or in other words, what is beyond name and form is Brahm. As He is without qualities and indescribable, He is not a subject for these eyes, nor can mind and speech have access to Him.

Guru Nanak also says that He is beyond the realm of thoughts:

"He cannot be conceived however hard one may think."

The following quotations are from the Adi Granth:

"You are all-pervading.
What shall I say; hear You my Master.
You are the Great All-Wise."

"You are the great Lord;
You are Unperceivable and Invisible;
In our search we find You unfathomable.
You are yonder of the yond;
And You alone know Yourself."

"He is the Lord of myriads of universes,
The Sustainer of all life.
He takes care of all and supports all;
But the universe acknowledges not His beneficence.

"Sublime and most high is the Lord's Court,
Unfathomable and beyond thought.
Says Nanak, it is through the Lord's Name
That one is blest with glory."

"O, our infinite Lord,
You who are from the beginning of the beginning,
O, our primal Lord, our Immaculate One,
I reflect on how to be attuned to you,
O, embodiment of Truth."

Where Is God

Ignorant persons think that God lives beyond the skies or beneath the depth of the oceans. Great souls realize Him in their hearts, and perfect Saints see Him everywhere, both within and without. Saints and holy men say that He pervades the entire universe and that the universe is in Him. This force is all-pervading and is running the entire great Universe of universes.

"The lovers are many but the Beloved is one.
Religions and creeds are different,
but all have the same object."

In all the religious scriptures He is not described as confined to any one race, religion or community. He is described as "the Lord of all universes". It is stated that all things have emanated from Him. He pervades everywhere. No place or thing whether sentient or insentient is without His light.

"Whither shall I go from Thy spirit?
Whither shall I flee from Thy presence?
If I ascend up into heaven, Thou art there;
If I make my bed in hell, behold, Thou art there,
If I take the wings of the morning, and dwell in the uttermost
. parts of the sea;
Even there shall Thy hand lead me and Thy right hand shall
hold me." B

This universe is His body in which He dwells. He pervades every atom in the same way as the soul pervades every pore of the body and is enabling it to function. The body is reduced to dust when the soul leaves it. Similarly, this universe is destroyed when He withdraws His power from it. The Ether from which this universe is made and the Life Energy which runs it, are powers created by the Lord. He is the Creator, the Sustainer and the Destroyer of the entire universe.

Where is the Lord?   After creating the world, He is not apart from it.   He is the Supreme Being. He dwells in the creation and pervades it.   He is Immortal and Omnipresent.   There is no need to seek Him in wildernesses.   The need is to awaken the inner eye that can see Him.

Without actual personal experience it is difficult to understand this fact.   We can, of course, make out something by using an illustration.   He is for example pervading   and   resounding   everywhere like the waves of a powerful TV station.   Those whose minds have become subtle and who have attuned themselves to Him, hear Him and see His glory.

We are particles of the Lord.   The relationship between us and the Lord is that of a part to the whole. There is no distinction between the ocean and its waves. There is no difference between the sun and its rays. The Lord is never unmindful of us even for a moment. He is always looking after us.   We have never been separated from Him.   He is always with us and always pervades our entire being.

What Is God And What Is
Our Relationship With Him?

The Supreme Lord is the Creator of the universes. In the external world, one makes an article from some material, but He requires no help or aid from any quarter for creating the universe.   He is the Supreme Being of all and is capable of doing everything.   He creates all out of His own Being.   Therefore, He is the real Creator.

The Lord is the great storehouse of consciousness. He is the embodiment of reason and the treasure house of intelligence. He is the repository of love and compassion. We are parts of Him. He is the whole. The essence of which our souls is made, its fountain source is called the Lord. If we are a drop of consciousness, He is the ocean of consciousness. We are a ray of the essence of consciousness and He is the sun of the essence of consciousness. Every particle is a part of the whole. Our real substance is a part of that whole which is called the Lord.

> "The Lord pervades all beings,
> He is the inner-knower of all hearts.
> He who contemplates Him, through the Guru's Word,
> Sees the Lord pervade all beings." A

If we become childlike, the Lord Himself watches over us. But when we grow in our intellect and begin to reason and ruminate, then we feel unhappy. If we turn to Him and hold fast to His garment, live in the world but not let go our hold of Him, as a child does with his mother, we will be happy. Beg of Him, eat and drink and cry out, "O mother! I am yours, whether dutiful or otherwise. I am in your lap. Where else could I go if I left you?" But this should, however, be said with love, truth and simplicity. There should be no cleverness about it. The waywardness of upright children is forgiven. The Lord also relishes love, simplicity and faith.

> "The simple realize the Lord."

Continue to be children of God. Do not surrender the rights of your precious patrimony. Know the Lord as immanent and conscious. Remember

Him as a living entity. Have devotion. He is both with and without qualities and is also beyond them. He who is with form is the formless One also.

The powers that exist in the soul also exist in the Lord. The soul is consciousness and the Lord is the storehouse of consciousness. The soul is capable of thinking, and the Lord is an ocean of thoughts. The soul has intelligence and knowledge, and the Lord is the embodiment of knowledge and the treasure-house of intelligence. The soul is full of love, and the Lord is the source of all love. We are made in His image. Every particle is a part of the whole, and so are we.

He is governing and administering the affairs of the pure spiritual regions as well as of the universes and the lower worlds, according to His will. Is this work, the vastness of which it is impossible to conceive and which bewilders us, any burden to Him? Is He busy thinking about it all the time? No! While doing all this He remains fresh as a blossom and in spite of its onerous nature He remains detached. He is unconcerned, independent and unmoved. After creating the universe and taking care of it He still remains free and ever happy.

The tenth Sikh Guru has sung the praises of the all-pervading Lord in a brilliant way:

"God is in the water, God is on the land.
God is in the heart, God is in the forest.
God is in the mountain, God is in the cave,
God is in the earth, God is in the heavens.
God is here, God is there.
God is in space, God is in time.
God is invisible, God is without creed.
God is without sin, God is without enmity.

God is deathless, God is shelterless.
God is impenetratable, God is indissoluble.
God is not moved by charms or spells;
God has His own light, He cannot be moved by incantations.
God is without caste, God is without lineage.
God is without friends, God has no mother.
God feels no physical or mental suffering.
God is without doubt, God is without Karmas.
God is invincible, God is fearless.
God is unbreakable, God is indissoluble.
God cannot be punished, God is radiant.
God is transcendent, God is inscrutable.
God is unconquerable, God is imperishable.
Repeat God's Name; establish God's Name
In your heart; do penance to God and repeat His Name.
O God, You are in the water, You are on the land.
You are in the river, You are in the sea.
You are in the tree, You are in its leaves.
You are in the earth, You are in the firmament.
Your Name is repeated again and again.
Your Name is fixed in man's heart.
You are space, You are time.
You are the occupant, You are the dwelling.
You are unborn, You are fearless.
You are impalpable, You are indestructible.
You are continence, You are fast.
You are deliverer, You are adviser,
You alone are, You alone are."

SAT NAM—The True Name Of God

A study of ancient history and religious scriptures shows that the ancient people worshiped the forces of nature such as the moon, the sun and so forth in order to strengthen their belief in God. They also coined different names for Him and as a result the world has become entangled in the cobwebs of these names.

Guru Gobind Singh has mentioned more than a thousand names of the Lord in the Jap Sahib. He, however, emphasizes the necessity of understanding the real significance of the names, and advises that one should go beyond them and realize the "Named One" who is the object of all of them.

Sat Nam (True Name of God) is that Truth which does not perish in the three periods of time (past, present and future). It is always true and does not change. It is the personal name of the Lord. The fifth Sikh Guru has said:

"The tongue utters Your definitive name.
Sat Nam is Your age-old original name."

All other names are definitive ones which describe some quality or virtue, as for example He is called the Creator because He creates or the Merciful Lord because He showers mercy.

To understand Sat, commonly translated as Truth, is very difficult. It is different from truth and untruth. Truth and untruth are a pair of opposites and receive light from each other. The Gurus, however, speak of that Sat which is self-luminous and self-sufficient. Both truth and untruth do not exist there. It is that Sat which sustains both the truth and the untruth.

"True, True, True is He,
Nay, not one is separate from True Purush."   A

This Sat is experienced when the mind and senses are stilled and he who gets this experience knows the Creator.

"To him who knows Him all is truth.
O Nanak, He alone is true."

"He who believes in God as Truth in his heart,
Knows the essence of the Creator, the Cause of causes."   A

According to the dictionary the word Nam comes from a Sanskrit root meaning 'known, determenistic and definitive'. The word by which we call a person or thing in order to distinguish him or it from others is called its name. But by Nam the Masters mean that all-pervading power which governs all universes and regions, which is the fountain-head of all knowledge and contemplation, and which sustains all. Guru Arjan sings praises of this Nam as follows:

> "Nam sustains all knowledge and contemplation.
> Nam sustains all skies and underworlds.
> Nam pervades all the worlds."

A

The Lord manifests Himself as Nam. Sat is a wave of that eternal existence. The soul gets connected with It and enjoys Its bliss. The Lord is one; but when It reveals Itself, It is realized as *Satnam* (True Name). The soul experiences It by uniting with Its definite and indivisible existence. This is neither a matter of talk nor of mere imagination. Saints and seers experience It and they admit that they do so. There is no room for doubt in the matter.

God-Realization

These eyes of flesh cannot see Him. The eyes with which He can be seen are different and to see Him they have to be opened or awakened.

One should see the Lord with one's inner eyes and hear Him with one's inner ears.

How can one know Him, the One Being who pervades all? The Sikh scriptures say that only he on whom He showers His grace to make Himself known alone becomes fit to see Him. It is through the Master that the inner eyes that can see the bewitching Lord everywhere are developed and all doubts are banished.

"The Lord is One.
But He manifests in different forms.
He pervades every heart.
O Ravi Das, He is near.
He can be realized if He wills it."   9

People often say that if God-Realization is so difficult, why should we strive for it. The answer to this question is that just as a hungry man cannot live without food, similarly we cannot live without the Lord. St. Augustine has said:

"Thou, O! God, hast made us unto Thyself, and the heart of man is ever restless until it rests in Thee."

As has been mentioned before, correct information about God can only be had from those who have realized Him in the transcendent regions, for their knowledge is not merely a matter of imagination nor has it been gathered from religious scriptures or hearsay. They have seen Him with their own eyes. They have, by expanding and illuminating their consciousness, experienced Him and have made others experience Him. Even today they can make the seekers after God realize Him.

He is not far from us. He abides in the inner recesses of our heart. He is not separate from us. Wherever one looks, one feels His presence.

It is however, a rare devotee who attains this state in his life and thus experiences everlasting bliss.

"He is in the body,
Whether you find Him or not.

The devotee searches for Him within,
And by meeting Him
He gains everlasting peace,
And unites with Him."

A

Love Of God

Everybody knows that love for this world and worldly people and objects is the cause of many miseries, because these things are all temporary and will leave us sooner or later. We shall leave them at our death. Therefore, we should give our love to a being who is beyond death and who will never be separated from us, so that we may never feel the pain of separation.

Such a being is none other than God Himself, or His manifestation whose soul is completely merged in God and who has everlasting life. Therefore, it is God in the form of His Saints who are worthy of our love. God is within each one of us, and consequently He, unlike worldly objects, cannot be separated from us. To love Him will never cause any pain. Therefore, it is only God or His Saints with whom one can be in love constantly throughout eternity. So, if you wish to love and be loved at all times, then your love should be offered to God Himself through His manifestation on this earth, who is no other than the Sat Guru.

The highest and the greatest boon that anyone can have is the love of God; but only those on whom God bestows His grace can be the recipients of this sublime gift.

Generally, people worship God with some ulterior motive, and they ask for worldly blessings. They pray that their children may be healthy, and they ask for the joys of heaven. Such people are either lovers of the world or of the comforts of heaven. Only a rare few worship God for the sake of God alone. Our aim should be to remember God only out of love for Him. We should not blacken our heart by worldly desires, and should ask from Him nothing but love for Him.

How can people who are submerged in worldly attachments know anything about God's Love? So long as they are not free from worldly attachments it will not be possible for them to taste God's Love.

Those who demand things of the world from Him will get their worldly desires fulfilled, but God will not meet them. He knows our every thought, so how can we deceive Him? He knows even the latent desires in our mind. In some places people are engrossed in love for worldly objects. At other places they worship abstract heavenly goals. But here and there we also come across people who have correctly placed their love in the Lord. The love for worldly objects is temporary and transient. The love for a heavenly goal is better; but the noblest and the purest form of love is love for God.

It is extremely difficult to describe true love for God. Some people say that it is impossible to love God, and that love for God simply means that we should follow His commandments. Such people are ignorant of the real Truth.

Some people say that we should love God's creation, so that we may be able to love God. On the surface, this principle appears feasible; but if we go deeper, we shall be able to see that this principle is not entirely correct, for, pure love is free from all attachment to the world of matter and illusion, and is found only in the regions beyond the reach of mind and Maya (matter and illusion).

One who desires to achieve communion with the Almighty Father should first of all wash the dirt from his mind with the water of love. The bandage of ego should be removed from our eyes, because then alone is it possible for us to see the Lord. And this bandage can be removed only by emptying ourselves of everything except the remembrance of the Beloved. No thought of any kind should be allowed to enter between the devotee and the object of his devotion.

People say that love is blind and mad, because a lover does not listen to anyone. But the lover of God is not blind. He has eyes that see the Truth. He sees only that One whom he wishes to see. He accepts only that One and believes in Him. He is not mad. He gives his heart to One alone, and is free from duality. "Love is the Divine Law. It will triumph where reason fails."

God is love. Just as it is impossible to praise Him adequately, it is similarly not possible to define love. Those who have drunk deeply out of the cup of love have become intoxicated by it, and in their ecstasy have sung songs of praise for Him. Below are given a few quotations by way of example:

"Love is God. It is the religion and faith of man."

"Love is a pilgirmage. It is a magnetic power which attracts the hearts and everything good and beautiful in them."

"A heart full of love is contented and sweet."

"Love is the comforter and sustainer of hearts. It is the

hope, the longing for union, and surging emotion in the heart."

"It is a Power. When we love, we learn the lesson of courage and fearlessness."

"It is the shield against which no weapon can be effective."

"It is Truth and Reality. It is faith and sacrifice."

"It is a divine flower, which imparts its perfume to the entire universe. It is a fragrant flower through which man's life is beautified."

"It is a light by which the universe is illuminated."

"It is a silent emotion full of sweetness, in which man forgets himself completely."

"It is a heavenly gift and food for the soul."

"It is the permanent union. Both, the lover and the beloved, are imperishable. It is an indescribable state of their hearts."

"The key to heaven is love, and not intellect."

"Love is not blind. It increases vision."

"Love is stable, imperishable and infinite. In the end all one's ties and connections with the world are broken, but it is impossible for the relationship of love to be destroyed. It is stronger than chains of steel and unbreakable even by death, because it is a part of the soul."

"If love for the Master is in your heart, then rest assured that God also loves you, because the Master is the reflection of God on earth."

CHAPTER 2

THE SOUND CURRENT OR SHABD

Shabd is a Sanskrit word. Its original root is not known. It means sound, letter, voice, name, conscience, word, clarity, declaration, expression, speech, etc. That which can be spoken or that which can reveal secrets, is called Shabd. However, the Gurus and the highest Masters have used it in a very deep and abstruse sense.

Before the creation, the Shabd was unmanifested and nameless. It then existed in itself. In that state it was called indescribable, nameless, invisible, unfathomable, unutterable and inexpressible. When it became manifest it became known as Nam or Shabd.

"When Shabd was unmanifested it had no name.
When Shabd manifested, it became the Name."   E

Prior to its becoming manifest, there was no sun or moon or sky. The Shabd was formless. The Shabd, however, is consciousness. All are under its control. Nothing can manifest without its help. The Shabd is the life, the essence, the root and the quintessence of every created thing. It does not depend on any one for manifestation. On the other hand, all that is manifest or unmanifest is sustained by it.

The Shabd, Sound Current, Word or Holy Spirit is not a subject matter for speech or writing. In order to make it understood, we can only say this much, namely that it is the quintessence of the Lord and that it sustains millions of universes and regions. It is the soul-current of consciousness. It is the Celestial Melody. It is the life-current which originates from the Lord and pervades everything. The Lord creates and sustains the entire universe through this great Current of Power. It gives life to the whole of the creation and can take every living being back to his Original Home or the Lord. The currents of the Lord pervade everywhere, like radio-waves. His divine music fills all space. Unless we are correctly tuned to it we cannot hear this music. As we grow more and more subtle, we begin to hear clearly its melodies. Shabd is a string which connects everyone and everything with the Lord.

The Shabd is the basis of all true religions, for religion means 'that which connects us with the Lord.' All the forces of nature are sustained by the Shabd. The life force is also its manifestation, even though it is working in the regions of Maya. Like electricity, Shabd, whether manifest or unmanifest, pervades everywhere. It is all-powerful and is the Creator of all.

The Shabd Is The Creator

In the scriptures of all religions, Shabd is recognized as the Creator of the universe. According to the Vedas, fourteen regions came into being by the power of the Kalma. In the Gospel of St. John in the Bible, it is said that the world was created by the Word or Logos. St. John says, "In the beginning was the Word....and the Word was God. The same was in the beginning with God. All things....were made by Him." The Sikh scriptures say that all the creation is being sustained by Shabd and that it is the Creator of the entire universe. The earth and sky are made by Shabd, which pervades them and sustains the entire universe:

> "The Word is the life of sky and earth,
> From its refulgence all take birth,
> And all creation sings.
> O Nanak, in all souls that be
> This heavenly power sings."   A

The Shabd is the conscious melody-current of the Lord. It is His form, and It creates and sustains the entire universe. The Shabd is the seed of the entire creation. Whatever is in the seed is also in the tree which springs from it. Everything is within that Eternity. Whatever is manifested in time and space merges in It, and the origin of everything is in the Shabd.

The effect is a form of the cause. The Shabd is the cause. The entire creation is Its effect. What is not in the cause cannot be found in the effect. If a ray of the sun falls on a clean mirror, the entire sun can be seen in it. If our mind is entirely clean and there is not even an iota of egotism in it, then the reflection of the Lord can be seen in it. The rays of the sun emanate from the sun and are not different from it. Cause is always present in its effect. Similarly, the attributes of the Lord are not different from those of the soul.

This Sound or Melody pervades all. It is even inside stones and wood, as these are made up of atoms, and motion is inherent in them. Because of this motion everything constantly undergoes change. The motion itself is the cause of change. In reality, everything is changing. This world changes every hour, every minute and every second.

Whether we know it or not, a stone continues to change. There is motion in it. Sound is a necessary corollary of motion and, therefore, a stone is not free from the Sound. Both the bodies that we see and those we do not see are in motion. There is, therefore Sound in all, and the Sound is the essence of all. Whether full or empty, all are full of His divine Melody.

This Melody pervades all and is the life and sustenance of all. This current of consciousness is very subtle. It requires equally subtle ears to hear it.

The waves of the ocean of Shabd are surging in each one of us. Those who drink of its waters are no longer troubled by thirst or hunger and gain eternal life. This was the water of life that Christ offered to the woman of Sychar at the well so that by drinking it she might quench her thirst for ever. It has also been described as the Bread of Life, by eating which one's hunger is fully satisfied. The Shabd is that medicine which is the panacea for all ills.

This sound is coming from the direction towards which the soul has to go. Without It the soul wanders in the dark.

The Shabd is also referred to in the Scriptures as: TRUTH, NAME or NAM, DIVINE AMBROSIA and NECTAR.

The Sikh Gurus have described Shabd as Truth. This is because it never perishes.

"It is true from the beginning and has been true through the ages. It is true in the present and shall be true hereafter, O Nanak."

The Truth is obtained when one meets a true Master and follows His directions. It can dwell within us only through the grace of the Master. As is taught in the Adi Granth:

"Without the Master all is darkness;
But without the Word we realize it not.
The Master's Word illumines the way;
And one merges in the Truth."

"Through the Master's Word,
Is banished all egoism.
And the Truth abides in the heart."

"The Lord is merciful,
He Himself makes us realize Him.
Through Guru's Word does He dwell in our hearts,
And we are attuned to the Truth."

"Those who serve the True Lord,
Attain the glory of Truth.
Through the Master's grace.

"For him who loves the Truth,
True is the Word and the Melody.
The Name of God dwells in his heart.
He gives up anger and egotism."

"In them is the treasure of the Name.
Through It are they known.
They worship the Name and contemplate on the Name,
Which is the Eternal Truth."

"Truth exists both inside and outside, and is eternal.
Truth rings throughout the four ages.
It proclaims nothing but Truth."

"They merge into the source from which they spring.
The Truth pervades everywhere."

What is the Name or Nam? It is easy to talk of Nam, but its real significance can only be learned from those who have realized it. There is no difference between the Name and the Named. He who obtains the Name realizes the Named One also. Those who have not been initiated into it are millions of miles away from it.

The Name is all in all. Everything emanates from the Name. Those who do not know the Name or have not realized it know nothing. They come empty-handed into the world and like gamblers go away empty-handed wasting their wealth in this world.

The Adi Granth also describes the Shabd as Nectar—the Nectar that makes us immortal. This power is possessed only by the Shabd. The Shabd of the Guru is that Nectar, the drinking of which rids us of all our cravings and merges us in the True Lord.

"The Guru's Word is the Nectar;
He who drinks it quenches his thirst.
The mind is dyed in Truth.
And it merges with the Truth."   A

"I gave up searching for Him without;
For the Guru has revealed Him in my own house;
The Unending Music plays at the Tenth Door;
There I was fed with the Nectar of the Name."   A

"Come, let us go to Sukhman, that land of calm,
Unruffled by passions;
Let us sit there and enjoy a drink of great rarity,
With sweets of knowledge and mahua flowers of meditation,
Brewed in faith with the water of the mind."   4

Sound And Light

Two things, namely Sound and Light, serve as guides in the world. These are the two paths by following which one progresses on the path of Spirituality. Both are fruitful. They are related to the practice of listening to the Inner Sound and seeing the Inner Light. Each has its own place. There is Light inside us and it contains Sound within it. True devotion springs from contact with this Light and Sound:

"When the mind was attuned to the Shabd;
It became detached and dispassionate,
There appeared Light within and from It emanated
The Heavenly Sound which made me a devotee of the
True Lord."

The Sound and the Light, in reality, are one. Vibrations up to a certain extent produce sound; but if their frequency is increased several-fold, they change into light. Spiritual Sound is the real and basic life-force which sustains the entire universe. This is the Light that lights our dark homes or bodies, it is however, imperceptible to the physical eyes.

This Light is within all of us. Christ also mentions that this Light lights all. It does so without any distinction, be one a Hindu, a Muslim or a Christian.

"In Him was life, and the life was the Light of man. And the Light shineth in darkness—that was the true Light, which lighteth every man that cometh into the world."

St. Augustine has also described the appearance of this light within him thus:

"I entered even into my inward self, Thou being my guide, And able I was; for Thou wert become my helper. And I entered and beheld with the eye of my soul (such as it was), above the same eye of my soul above my mind, the light unchangeable. Not this ordinary light which all flesh may look upon, nor as it were a greater of the same kind, as though the brightness of this should be manifold brighter, and with its greatness take up all space. Not such was the Light, but other yea, far other from all these. He that knows the Truth knows what that light is, and he that knows it, knows Eternity."

All the great souls, whether of the East or the West, who went inside and had access to the inner regions, have mentioned the Sound and the Light. The soul is imprisoned in the cage of the mind and the body. Both light and sound are within us. The Sound and Light are related to the two faculties of the soul namely *Surat* (hearing) and *Nirat* (seeing). Surat hears and Nirat sees. In ascending upward through the spiritual regions, Nirat leads and Surat follows.

After the maturing of the Surat (the Soul's power of hearing) and of Nirat (the soul's power of seeing) the soul is freed from the bondage of the body and rises to the higher regions. It then gains freedom from birth and death. Reference is made to this fact in the Sar Bachan.

"I will follow the lead of Nirat and reach Sat Lok."

In the beginning the Sound alone is manifest. The Light appears later. In practice also, we first rely upon the Sound, although we begin with Simran and Dhyan. Their function is to prepare the ground for hearing the Sound. Simran and Dhyan have their own functions, but they merely act as pilots or advance-guards for the bridegroom—the Shabd which alone really counts. Simran is the key to the practice of listening to the Sound. During his practice the seeker comes across regions in which he is surrounded by effulgent light. For crossing the brilliance of this light, the Sound is the guide. There are some regions where it is complete darkness, like Mahasunn (the Great Void). In these regions, the Sound is the only true pathfinder or guide. It is just like a traveler trying to find his way to a habitation when he is lost in a lonely forest and enveloped in thick darkness, by following the

barking of a dog.   The Sound helps the blind seeker
within in similar circumstances.   This is the superiority of the path of the Sound Current.

This Shabd or Sound is really one.   In the lower
parts of the creation, where the proportion of mind and
Maya is greater and the Shabd creates the regions of
subtle and gross matter, its melody or Sound principle
changes.   Since there are five primary regions in the
creation, this one Shabd appears to be five.   There are
two Shabds up to Trikuti; two from Trikuti to Satlok;
and the fifth one is in Satlok.   These five Sounds
become perfect there.   By the practice of listening to
them according to the directions of a perfect Adept,
the soul becomes one with the five Sounds and unites
with the Lord from Whom they emanate.

> "The highest good is gained through the grace of the Master,
> when the Merciful One plays the Five Melodies."   A

The Sound that is heard in each region is made
plain at the time of initiation by the Master.   After
this, as the disciple continues to practise and ascends
through the higher regions, he sees everything himself
with his own inner eye.   It is only as a result of great
good fortune that the Five Melodies play in this body
and such a body is really blessed.

> "In that fortunate home ring the Five Melodies,
> After the Lord has manifested His power."   A

These melodies are not imaginary.   Those who
have practised the path of the Sound Current, in any
Age, have described the Melody in similar terms.
Even today the ignorant children and new seekers who
keep the company of Saints, hear It and bear witness
to its existence as an experienced fact.

There is mention of the melodies of the Shabd in the Upanishads.

"In the beginning of the practice there are loud sounds. They go on increasing and are heard in a subtle form. The sounds in the beginning are those of the sea, thunder clouds, drums, running-water brooks, the bell or the conch-shell horn."

In the book called Bhakti-Sagar, Saint Charandas has mentioned ten different kinds of sounds, such as the chirping of sparrows and the cricket, the tinkling of small bells, the ringing of big bells, the conch shell, the bagpipe, the cymbals, the reed, the small drum, the flute and the roaring of lions.

In the Hathyog Pradeepika, there is also mention of ten similar sounds such as those of the humming of bees, anklet bells, the conch shell, the bell, the cymbals, the flute, the kettle drum, the small drum, the reed and the roaring of lions.

On page ninety-eight of the Sar Bachan, also there is mention of ten sounds heard in Sahansdal Kanwal:

"The sounds of conch shells and bells come aloud.
The wonderful music of the vina and the reed resounds.
The sounds of cymbals, drums and kingri are heard.
The sounds of drums and tambourine rattle,
The nectar rains in thousands of showers;
The skies revolve liké a wheel."

Madam Blavatsky writes in "The Voice of the Silence" as under:

"The first (sound) is like the nightingale's sweet voice, chanting a song of parting to its mate. The second comes as the sound of the silver cymbals of the Dhyanis awaking the twinkling stars. The next is as the plaintive melodies of the ocean spirit imprisoned in its shell. And this is followed by the chant of the Vina. The fifth like the sound of the bamboo

flute, shrills in their ears.   It changes into a trumpet blast.
The last vibrates like the dull rumbling of thunder clouds."

Amir Khusro has also mentioned these sounds,
describing them as follows:

"The first is the humming of bees,
The second the ringing of bells,
The third is the sound of the conch shell.
The fourth that of a big, bell.
The fifth is the sound of the tall bell,
The sixth is the sound of the flute.
The seventh is the sound of the kettle drum,
The eighth the sound of the small drum.
The ninth is the sound of the clarionet,
The tenth is the sound of the roaring of a lion."

The ceaseless music is of ten kinds,

"The Yogi becomes engrossed in them,
And the mind and senses fall away.
When the ceaseless music begins to ring,
The thieves from the body slink away.
The grace of the Master is upon him.
Khusro has merged in the Divine Music."

These are the sounds at the preliminary stages.
The real sounds are those of the bell and conch shell,
which are related to the higher regions.

"Nobody knows where the home of the Beloved is;
But from that region comes the Sound of bells."

"O! listen to the singers in the garden.
How harmoniously they play,
On harp, lute, guitar, pipe, flute and reed."   3

We find that bells are rung in Hindu temples.
They are also tolled in Christian churches.   In the Sikh
Gurdwaras shell horns, conch and bells are used, and
drums are beaten.   By research, it can be l earned that
the outer musical instruments are imitations of the inner

ones. Ponder deeply and you will find that Hindu temples have domes and a bell hangs in the middle. Whoever enters the temple rings the bell. In the human head, which also is like a dome, a devotee hears the Shabd at the seat of the soul. In the same manner, Christian churches have high steeples in which a bell is hung. These are based on the shape of the nose. In the human body at the root of the nose, when the soul is concentrated at a place between the two eyebrows, one hears the sound of the bell.

Bells are also found in Buddhist temples. The ringing of bells, in fact, is mentioned in the scriptures of all the religions. The fact is, when one goes within the body, the temple of the living God, one hears a sound which is like the ringing of a bell. Similarly, various other sounds are heard in the inner regions. Of these, five Sounds are the principal ones. These inner Sounds are inter-related. After receiving instructions from an adept in the Sound-Current technique and carrying out spiritual practices, one can reach the region whence the melody of the Five Sounds is emanating. This is the abode of the Supreme Lord. The musical sounds are, in a way, milestones on the way that leads to the country of our Lord and which tell us how far we have come.

Musical instruments are widely used in spiritual assemblies. All religions give them a special importance. Yogis use them, and so also do Muslims. Music is extensively used by Hindus, Sikhs and Christians. Wherever sadhus gather, they use musical instruments. People sing hymns with instrumental accompaniments and go into ecstasy over their beautiful melodies and harmonies. The mind becomes enraptured with this outer music but it does not become conscious nor is it awakened. The Saints do not accept this form of worship. They point out that outer music does not lead to contemplation. Truth is not realized. Egotism is not lessened even a little bit, and one gets no real or lasting peace.

The time wasted in correcting the tunes and rhythms and in practising them could, with greater profit, be spent on the practice of the Name, according to the directions of the Master.

The outer sound can help one in gathering the scattered attention; but it takes the heart to a center which has no settled place of its own. The outer music is a trap that makes us forget ourselves and the Lord. Beethoven, the great composer, said, "Music is the mediator between the spiritual and sensual life." By listening to the outer music we find ourselves entangled in an imaginary world created by the player or the singer. But the inner attachment to the world is not broken and cravings are not destroyed. The Gurbani throws particular light on this point and tells us that even though we are enchanted by outer sounds and are attracted by them, even though the whole world is enchanted by beautiful outer music, one who listens to it remains within the domain of the three gunas and wastes his life. Without the true and all-pervading inner music one always remains in misery and ever suffers at the hands of the billows of Maya.

However, the divine Music breaks our worldly fetters and we become truly pure. We float like a lotus on the waves of Maya, and like a duck living in water fly away with dry wings.

The human body is the temple of the Lord. The Shabd is inside it and can be easily realized. It is the birthright of all. Whether one is rich or poor, literate or illiterate, belonging to one country or religion or another, all can realize the Shabd by receiving initiation from a perfect Master. After becoming a devotee, we can easily practise listening to the Sound and this practice quickly bears fruit.

> "The Lord's temple is also the Lord's shop,
> Embellished with the Word.
> And therein is sold the Lord's Name
> And it is through the Guru
> That one obtains It."   A

The man of riches is blind and deaf and remains entangled in darkness and doubts, for he does not hear the Shabd.

> "The favored of Mammon are blind and deaf,
> They can never be attuned
> To the Heavenly Harmony."   A

> "Blind is the soul without the Shabd.
> O! where can it go?
> It finds not the door that leads to the Lord's Name.
> And so it wanders to and fro."   4

All the Saints have asserted that this Shabd, which is heard inside, is the means for gaining release from the world. It cannot be had, however, until a seeker is instructed by a holy man who is an adept, and he then withdraws his attention from the nine portals of the body and fixes it on the spot behind the two eyes. This Shabd takes the soul to its Original Home.

The Name has been known and taught since very ancient times. It is God's own Law. Since the beginning of the world the Lord's Name has been known to

Saints and has been responsible for the salvation of mankind. Kabir Sahib, Guru Nanak and the other nine Sikh Gurus, Dadu Sahib, Paltu Sahib, Tulsi Sahib and many other Saints preached this path to their disciples during the last four or five centuries. The Muslim holy men have taught the same Name during the last 1300–1400 years. Prophet Mohammed and other Muslim Saints like Shamas Tabriz, Maulana Rum, Hafiz and others also taught the Lord's Name. St. John and Lord Jesus Christ referred to the Lord's Name some 1900 years ago. Similarly Zoroaster also taught it. Some two thousand five hundred years ago Mahatma Buddha practised the same Name. Gorakh Nath also taught the same Name.

Archaeological excavations in Egypt show that King Ikhnaton, who ruled about 4000 years ago, encouraged its practice. The Name was then called 'Aton'. It was secretly practised in the time of the Upanishads, and there are many references to the Name in them. In the Copper Age, Lord Krishna was familiar with the practice of the Name. There are references relating to the practice of the Name in the Rig Veda, the oldest recognized religious book in the world. In its Vak Devi Sukt, the Name is highly praised.

In the Vedas, the Divine Sound is called Nad (Inner Music) or Akashvani (sound from the sky). In Buddhist scriptures it is referred to as sonorous light.

The ancient Greek philosophers also mention this Shabd. Socrates states that he heard within him a sound which took him to indescribable spiritual regions. Plato also mentions it. Pythagoras called it the "Music of the Spheres". It is called Logos (the Word) in Greek.

The Sound which emanates from the Silence is called the Word. All things manifested from It. In the Chinese scriptures, it is called "Tao", meaning the Way or the Word. The Prophet Zarasthustra of Ancient Persia while mentioning six spiritual powers referred to one other power called Sharosha. This word comes from the Sanskrit root "Sh" which means the power of the Lord which can be heard. It is like the word 'Shabd' which is used by the Saints of India.

In the Zend Avesta, the book of Zarasthustra, there is a prayer which says: "O Mazda (Lord)! Send Sharosha to him whom you love."

Kabir, all the ten Sikh Gurus from Guru Nanak onwards, Dadu Sahib, Jagjiwan Sahib, Tulsi Sahib, Darya Sahib, Baba Lal Das, Paltu Sahib and many other Indian Saints or True Masters have taught the practice of listening to the Shabd. The Christian Bible calls it the Word. It says:

> "In the beginning was the Word and the Word was with God, and the Word was God. The same was in the beginning with God. All things were made by Him; and without Him was not anything made that was made."

> "The grass withereth, the flower fadeth; but the Word of our God shall stand for ever."

Madame Blavatsky, the founder of the Theosophical Society, described the Divine Sound as the Voice of the Silence. In the Masonic Order this Logos is described as the Lost Word, which is sought after by every Masonic Master. But it can be had only from the Saints or True Masters of the Word.

It is mentioned in the Holy Quran that God said, "Be, and it was." In other words the Shabd appeared and the whole of the Universe came into being. The

Persian Sufis have called it Wadan, the Divine Sound. They say:

"If he had not thought of manifesting;
There would have been no sound or world."

In other words, if the unmanifest had not desired to manifest Himself, there would have been no creative Sound or Power and the world would not have come into being.

The Sufi Saint, Hazrat Inayat Khan, who had access to the spiritual regions, describes the Sound as the Divine Music. He says everything manifested from It and is Its manifestation. In the writings of the Indian Saints it is also clear that all Universes and Regions were created by the Shabd. The Udgit or Celestial Song is resounding in all. Hazrat Sahib called it "Sot-e-Sarmadi", or the Voice of God.

There are many references in this context in the writings of Muslim Saints.

"When Mohammed reached the age of 40 years, the signs of his having received the revelation began to appear. According to tradition, he used to hear the Celestial Sound for fifteen years before he received the revelation. He often had divine dreams, and he saw different lights seven years before the revelation. Two years before, he went to the cave at Hara and practised there for a month." 5

"O brave one, bring down the skies to your feet.
Listen to the Voice of Silence from the skies." 5

"The world is filled with the Divine Sound,
Open the portals of your ears;
Listen to the Eternal Sound;
It is beyond the reach of dissolution."

"The Sound is coming from the Divine Home.
Why are you entangled in the snares of the world?" 3

"Take the cotton of doubt out of your ears,
So that you may hear the Celestial Sound.
This is a Divine Message,
What is the Divine Message except hearing
the Heavenly Sound within."   5

"The Prophet said about the Voice of God,
It comes to my ears as do the ordinary sounds.
But God has placed a seal on your ears,
You hear not the Voice of God."

A man obtains a new life through the Shabd.
Jesus Christ refers to the new life given by the Word
or Holy Spirit but this has been forgotten by our
Christian brothers of today.   In this very connection
St. John says:

"That which is born of the flesh is flesh;
But it is the spirit of man which is born of the spirit."

He also clearly speaks about a new life which
begins after hearing the Word.

"The wind bloweth where it listeth (wisheth) and thou hearest
the Sound thereof; but cannot tell whence it cometh nor
whither it goeth; so is everyone that is born of the Spirit."

"Verily, verily, I say unto you, except a man be born again,
he cannot see the Kingdom of Heaven."

"Marvel not that I say unto you, ye must be born again."

Whenever the Saints come to the world, they
emphasize the importance of being born again through
the Shabd.

When the Master, at the time of initiation, connects us with the Shabd, we are born again.

What Is Devotion To The Shabd ?

Devotion to the Shabd consists in turning inward
and listening one-pointedly to its Melody.   The

Sound is subtle, and unless we ourselves become subtle, we cannot hear it. In order to be connected with the Sound, the Soul must be devoid of all worldly coverings.

Why do we not hear this Sound?

This Sound is resounding all the time. Why then do we not hear it? The reason is that waves are constantly arising in our minds and we are full of selfhood and pride. We cannot, therefore, enjoy the Sound nor do we love the Name of God.

"The mind is entrapped in a whirlpool,
The ego is greatly inflated.
Such a one is not attuned to the Shabd.
Nor does he cherish the Lord's Name."   A

Maulana Rum also says that your ears cannot hear the Divine Melody because sins have deadened and defiled the sensitivity of your ears.

This Sound is not within the reach of the physical ears. But everyone has the faculty of hearing it within. For this it is necessary to open the inner ears and this can be done by following the directions of the Master.

Those who have not gone within and who are still engrossed in the worldly sciences are ignorant of this Divine Melody. The physical sciences may not be able to prove it, but whatever has been stated above is a fact and can be actually experienced by practice behind the eyes, by a seeker, by going within the laboratory of the Saints.

If our ears cease to hear the outer sounds and our eyes cease to see the outer sights, then we can hear the call of the Lord. When in this way our thoughts cease to wander out, we begin to hear the inner melodies and to relish the celestial joy. And then the secrets of the Lord begin to be revealed to us.

How Is The Shabd Realized?

(1) Through the grace of the Lord. He alone realizes the Sound on whom the Lord showers His grace. The Shabd then manifests within him.

"When He showers His Grace, the Shabd abides in the heart,
And one is rid of all doubts.
Body, mind and speech become pure.
And the Name dwells in the mind."   A

"He alone realizes Him whom the Lord unites with Himself.
One is then attuned to the True One
Singing day and night the Guru's Word."   A

(2) Through Sat Sang (association with a Saint) and the Satguru. When the Lord is kind, we meet a Master who connects our soul with the Sound.

"By the Lord's grace is the True Guru met.
And then alone He joins our soul with the Word."   A

(3) The Shabd can be had by giving up pride of knowledge, caste and creed, and by sitting at the feet of the Master.

Do not let the feelings of 'I-ness', wealth, knowledge, caste, creed or nobility of family or glory come near you. All these lead to stopping of the Sound. Put on the adornment of humility and listen to the Sound, and obtain bliss from its intoxicating powers and sweetness.

If seed is sown in a field which is not prepared, or if it is sown out of season, it does not bear fruit. Similarly, so long as the mind is not rid of its cravings and has not become pure, it does not cease its wander-

ing or running about. The mind becomes pure
only through devotion to the Shabd. So long as the
mind is divided, there is no success. We neither
realize the Shabd, nor see the Lord. "So long as the
mind is wandering and there is pride and egotism,
the Shabd is not heard and there is no love for Nam."
Therefore, it is far more necessary to rid the mind of
inner uncleanliness than to remove outer impurities.

Worldly people do not know of this Sound. When
one goes within after receiving instructions from a
Master, who is adept in the practice of the Sound,
one hears hundreds of sounds, while those sitting
near him hear nothing:

> "He hears within him hundreds of sounds;
> Those sitting near him do not hear any."   5

There are ten doors of the body.   Nine are outer,
and one is inner.

> "The fort of the body has nine doors.
> The tenth is kept secret.
> The secret door will not open.
> Only the Shabd of the Master can open it."   A

So long as the soul wanders in the outer nine
doors, it is being robbed of its birthright. It is not
able to see the precious inner treasure. There is,
however, the tenth door, where the Heavenly Music
is heard.

> "He who closes the nine doors
> And stills his wandering mind,
> Enters he through the tenth door his Original Home.
> Hears he day and night the unstruck Music
> Through the Guru's instructions."   A

The Guru's Shabd is limitless. It has no end.
It is beyond the reach of Kal.

"You are the Friend, the Wise, the One who unites.
Through the Guru's Word I praise You.
But there is no end to Your praise.
Kal cannot reach where the Lord's Name abides."   A

The Master is Himself the Shabd or the Word made flesh. He alone can manifest the Shabd. The Shabd is a boon from the Master. The Master makes It dwell in our hearts. It is impossible for anyone else to manifest It.

"The Shabd of the Guru can be bestowed only by Him. It cannot be manifested by anyone else."   A

Benefits Of Practice Of The Shabd

The practice of listening to the Shabd brings a number of beneficial results. The Shabd is a store house of power. It is the essence of wisdom. Those who are connected with It and are sustained by It are true sons of the Lord. The Shabd cuts all the bonds of the soul and leads to its salvation. It is the bread of life which descends from Sach Khand (the True and Imperishable Region). Those who partake of It, become immortal and attain everlasting life. Those who engage in the practice of the Shabd need no outer light like that of a lamp or the sun or moon, for the Light of lights appears within them.

By listening to the Sound all worldly bonds and external attractions are removed. The mind gives up its base desire, and one conquers the five enemies—lust, anger, attachment, greed and pride. When the soul gains release from these passions, it soars upward to the spiritual regions.

"The melody of bliss and balance,
Comes from the true Inner Sound.

The mind is attuned to the truth.
And the devotee enshrines in his mind
The unfathomable invisible Nam."   A

Man can attain salvation only by means of the
Shabd.   Through it alone man turns from glass into
gold and is transformed from poison into nectar.

"By listening to the Sound glass turns into gold,
And poison becomes nectar when the Name given by the
Master is practised."   A

The Shabd is the only path that leads us to our
Original Home.   It is the ship that ferries the soul
across the ocean of Existence and takes him in the lap
of the Lord.

The Shabd is conscious and consciousness.   It
is a wave of the ocean of the Lord and a man is a
particle of His Being.   He is related to Him as a part
is related to the whole.   The Lord is the ocean of
superconsciousness, and Shabd is its wave.   The
soul is a drop of this ocean.   The wave of super-
consciousness or Shabd attracts the conscious soul towards it and absorbs it.   Until the soul, with the
help of the Shabd, rises to its Original Home, it
cannot achieve salvation.   The melody of the Shabd
is ringing within us.   When the soul is connected
with it, it becomes fit to rise from the finite towards
the infinite.

The connection between the soul and the Divine
Sound is a natural one.   There is form and melody
in the Shabd and through these the mind becomes still.
The soul then becomes absorbed in the Sound and
merges in the Lord.   The Shabd emanated from the
Supreme Lord and through it the soul realizes the
Lord.

The Supreme Lord, the soul and the Shabd are a holy Trinity. The One Lord exists in all the three forms. The soul has no separate existence from the timeless Being. It is a particle of Him.

A man is never alone when he realizes the Shabd. Whether he is at home or anywhere else, his Lord with His Divine Music is always with him and is calling him back to his original Home. By practising the Shabd all diseases, vices and sins are removed; lust, anger and the other passions do not get a foothold; one becomes very pure and completely detached. Shabd is the support of life and death. The fear of death is banished. At the time of death the devotee discards his body just as one casts aside old clothes. Through the Power of the Shabd one is freed from the cycle of birth and death. The misery caused by Kal and the fear of death end. The difficulties of the inner path are resolved; the karmas of millions of births are destroyed; and one crosses the ocean of worldly existence.

By the practice of the Sound, light appears within and the lotus of the heart blossoms. One realizes his true Self and attains the state of dying while living. He trasncends the domain of the three attributes and time. He goes into trance in the Void, and the tenth door opens. He learns the sign of the Lord's door. He is dyed in the hue of the Lord, and true devotion and divine bliss arise within him. He is honored in the Court of the Lord. He attains salvation and realizes the most blissful state.

CHAPTER 3

THE MASTER OR SAT GURU

What do we understand by the term 'Guru', and who is the Guru?

To know a Master or to understand His real significance or reality is, in fact very difficult. To do this, discerning eyes like His own are necessary. Only a Godman can know a Godman. How can a person, who is confined in the case of the body, realize the Lord's glory? Unless we are as great as He is, we cannot understand Him.

> "He who is as high as He is,
> He alone can know the One on high."   A

Only a swan flying with other swans can know them. How can the doves and crows know from which country the swans come and to what land they go? The Guru does His work on the earth, and then takes flight and returns to the skies.

Although the Masters have assumed human forms similar to our own and live amongst us, yet they live with the Lord of all regions and universes. They appear to be bound to earth because of their bodies, but they live beyond the seven skies.

> "Their bodies are in the world, but their souls are with the Lord of the world;
> Their bodies are tied to earth, but their souls are beyond the seven skies."

It is impossible to praise the Supreme Lord adequately. The perfect Master is His manifestation and it is therefore also impossible to praise Him adequately. He is like the Lord, beyond the reach of thought, imagination, inference, guess, theory and reasoning. He cannot be seen, heard or described. Book after book can be written and the whole of one's life may be spent in writing, but still one would not be able to describe even one letter relating to His personality.

> "You are beyond inference, imagination, probabilities or intellect.
> You are beyond what I have seen, heard or read.
> The book is finished and life has drawn to a close.
> We are still only at the first letter."

If we were to attempt to describe the Lord, we could only describe Him according to our intellect. If a buffalo were to describe Him, it would describe Him as a great buffalo.

If a small child were to stand before his mother and say, "Mother, I know you," how imperfect would his understanding of his mother be? Similarly, how can we sing the praises of the Guru? Our praises would be so imperfect.

Millions of people visit a Master and see him. They hear his discourses and describe him according to their own respective understanding. They call him a kindly gentleman or a philosopher or a learned man or a wise moralist. They comfort themselves by so describing him. But there are a few amongst them who see the Lord in him. Everyone praises him according to his own degree of undrstanding. If the Master were only a man, he could give us nothing more than human virtues. But in fact he is more than human. One who is not developed inwardly, fails to recognize him. He reveals himself only to those who are sufficiently developed. He whose eye is not trained cannot recognize him. How can a blind man see or recognize another person by his face? Unless the Lord or the True Being is Himself kind to a person, that person will not recognize the Guru as Guru. Unless the perfect Master, who is Truth incarnate, reveals himself, one cannot recognize him. Even if the Master should live next door, an undeveloped person would not know him. Very often, the members of a perfect Master's own family fail to recognize his stature.

The Word is the Master of the entire universe, and the soul the disciple, which, having merged in It, becomes indistinguishable from It. In the sphere of unity and oneness, He in the form of the Word is the Guru of all the universe, but in the sphere of plurality, it is the person in whom the Word is manifest and who is granted the status of a Master that acts as a Guru.

Is There One Guru Or Are There Many?

There can be many Saints, but the Lord only rarely nominates any one as a perfect Master or Guru authorized to initiate. All perfect Masters are Saints, but all Saints are not Gurus. There are many graduates or holders of the Master of Arts degree, but only a few of them are professors. Similarly, all those who seek spirituality do not become Gurus. Actually, it is only rarely that one becomes a Guru.

The perfect Masters or Saints, also called Gurus, are regents or viceroys of the Supreme Lord. They are of two kinds. First, there are Sant Sat Gurus

in their own right.   They are born Saints who come
direct from the highest spiritual region, such as Kabir
Sahib, Guru Nanak Sahib and others, all of whom
taught the true spiritual Path from an early age. They
always remain connected with the Lord.   Whenever
such Saints come into the world they start a wave of
spirituality.   Then there are others who succeed them
and continue their teachings.   After some generations
this work slowly decreases and dies out.   Then another
Saint comes and starts the wave again.   These Saints
may come anywhere and in any nation.

The second kind of Saints are those who are not
born as Saints but who have practised spiritual meditation in this world and, by this means, have attained
the stage of Anami (Nameless).   They have the necessary ability, and have been commissioned by the
Lord, to do the work of a Guru.   Even they are not
brought up to mastership here. They come here
already perfected.   For name's sake only, they appear
to attain completeness and perfection in this life.

The first kind of Saint gets an order from the Supreme Lord to go forth as a Guru, and He then takes
birth; while the second kind receives the order to act
as a Guru after he has been born.   There is no difference in their spiritual powers or work.   Both kinds
of Saints possess full powers and use them when
necessary.

Besides these two kinds of perfect Masters or
Gurus, all others, who work as gurus, are merely
imposters.   Many of them are selfish and proud and
are worshipers of Maya. They use their knowledge
as a tool and use the seekers after spirituality as their
beasts of burden.   Narrow-mindedness and religious

prejudices are the results of their teachings. Gurus of this kind are dangerous. By their willful and harmful actions, they give a bad name to the institution of a 'perfect Guru'—the glorious, unimpeachable and spotless Power.

Bread is for the hungry, and water is for the thirsty. Nature provided milk for a child born five hundred years ago and also for one born two thousand years ago. Nature is also providing milk for children being born today. The law of nature is immutable. It is against the law of nature to say that no help was available for one seeking the spiritual path before Jesus Christ, or that no help is available for a seeker born after Jesus Christ's time. It is not correct to say that True Gurus visited this earth for a period of two or three centuries only and that the world has been without them both before and after. It is not correct to say that the 'law of supply and demand' operated for this period alone.

The teachings of the Saints are for all the world and for all times. They are not confined to two or three hundred years only.

"At all times throughout the ages,
The Gurus did exist.
Throughout all the ages the Masters exist,
And men of faith who follow Nam."
                                                                        A

Both Kabir Sahib and Guru Nanak Sahib were Great Masters. According to history, Kabir Sahib was born in 1398 A.D. on a full moon day near Banaras and his light merged in the eternal light in 1518 A.D. Guru Nanak Sahib incarnated in 1469 A.D. at Talwandi in the Punjab and his light merged in the eaternal light in 1539 A.D. at Kartarpur. This means

that Kabir Sahib manifested 71 years before Guru
Nanak Sahib and that they were contemporaries from
1469 A.D. to 1518 A.D. Both of them taught the true
spiritual path of Surat Shabd Yoga.

Similarly, Shams-i-Tabriz and Maulvi Rum were
contemporaries in Persia from 1207 A.D. to 1247
A.D. Guru Arjan Sahib and Dharam Das, were also
contemporaries from 1561 A.D. to 1606 A.D. It can
be seen, therefore, that there can be several perfect
Gurus functioning at the same time. But for a person
who wishes to become a Gurmukh or a beloved disciple, he must have one Guru only.

His Way Of Life

The Master's way of life is of a particular kind,
and it distinguishes him from others.

You may ask what is special about this perfect
man; whence and where from has he come after traversing the various regions? Where is he living? What
does he do here? The answer to these questions is that
he comes from Satlok (the True Region). He has come
to this land of death and lives here. He is manifesting
the glory of the Highest Reality. The influences and
virtues of the various higher regions are found in him.

(1) The Master is bountiful. He is never a
beggar. He does not hanker after anything. He
earns his own living. He is a burden on no one.
He maintains himself, and helps the helpless and the
suffering.

"He is no Master,
Who begs from door to door.
Do not bow to such a one.

He who labors and gives in charity,
O Nanak, he is on the right path."   A

(2) He charges no fees and does not accept any donations for his teachings. He imparts them free of charge. His teachings are free, like the other bounties of nature such as air, water, sunlight and so forth.

(3) His ornaments are prayer and humility. Despite the fact that he is all-powerful, he does not boast that he can do anything out of the ordinary. He always says that it is the Lord who does something, or that it is being done by his Sat Guru. Truly, a fruit-laden branch bends humbly.

"He who is humble is truly great."   A

(4) He is not opposed to anybody and does not complain about the conduct of anyone. Even if someone bears him ill-will, he forgives him. He does not criticize anybody, and he does not slander anyone. He loves everybody, including his enemies. He believes and lives up to the precept: "Love thy enemies."

(5) He is the radiant sun of purity, universal wisdom, truth and spirituality. He is spiritual, and seekers after spirituality gather round him like moths and make their lives fruitful by obtaining spiritual benefit.

(6) He does not dress in any particular manner and does not torture his body for controlling the mind. His method is quite different. It is easy and natural.

(7) He does not perform miracles like a juggler to please his audience. Although he is all-powerful, he keeps his powers hidden. But he does sometimes use them if he is so disposed. His disciples are always benefited by his grace.

The Character Of A Perfect Master And The Influence Of His Company

(1) By sitting near a perfect Master and contemplating on him the mind is inclined to get under control and is stilled to some extent.

Rays of purity constantly radiate from him. He is full of wonderful light and kindness. He has an indescribable influence on others. He has magnetic attraction. By his words, which are full of mystical meaning, he pulls the soul upwards. He produces an experience of bliss which defies description.

(2) One finds a strange radiance and attraction in his eyes and in his forehead when one gazes at them, even for a moment. He feels a pull, and his attention gathers together and seems to ascend to the higher subtle regions from the gross regions. His consciousness expands and is elevated.

(3) There is peace and evenness within a perfect Master. As a result of being in his company, a current of bliss runs through us. We feel happy on meeting him. All our doubts are removed and we feel certain that our ultimate destination will be attained.

"Such a one is the Sat Guru,
   On seeing him one feels happy;
   That the doubts of the mind are banished,
   And the abode of the Lord is attained."   A

(4) He is full of the elixir of life. His face is bright and radiant. His voice is attractive and the light in his eyes is both alluring and piercing. Powerful currents of life-energy emanate from a Saint and surcharge the surrounding atmosphere. His words have a strange influence. They penetrate the hearts of

the listeners. The mere presence of a Saint awakens souls and redeems them.

(5) A perfect Master can, with a single glance, find out one's inner condition. He then instructs us according to our condition. When anyone visits him he can see the visitor's inner condition as if that person were encased in transparent glass, but he keeps it a secret. Bees rush to flowers for their fragrance and honey; similarly, the seekers go to the perfect Master to partake of his wealth of spirituality and righteousness. No one returns empty handed from the bountiful Master. They bring back with them the seed of Nam which, sooner or later, fructifies and gives release to the soul. When one begins to visit a perfect Master, his good days begin.

(6) The Sant Sat Guru is the true son of the Lord. To him all religions, castes, faiths and sects are alike. He sees the same Lord in all living beings.

Without partiality to any religion or caste, he imparts the same message to all the world. To him, all are the children of God, and he looks upon them with the same eye.

He does not ask anyone to give up his religion and adopt a new one. He is concerned only with the soul. He does not mind what religion you belong to. But it is necessary that you should have a desire for spiritual progress.

(7) The perfect Master is an incarnation of the Lord. Just as the Lord communicates His teachings to the Saints without the agency of speech, similarly, the Saints impart their messages to their disciples by means of internal experiences, and without the use of speech.

The teachings of the Saints are imparted in an unspoken language, the language of the soul, which one soul conveys to another soul.   The soul is a particle of God and His great mystery.   It speaks without tongue or throat.   It can function and act without the aid of any senses.

> "He sees without eyes;
> He hears without ears;
> He walks without legs;
> He works without hands;
> He speaks without a tongue;
> He dies while living.
> O Nanak, he knows His law;
> He is one with Him."   A

(8)   With perfect Masters it often happens that seekers after Truth have no need to put questions during discourses.   They get answers to their questions without asking them.

(9)   Whenever the Saints manifest themselves, they preach the practice of Nam or the Yoga of Surat Shabd and clearly say that the Lord has never been and will never be realized by formal religious practices. He is inside your heart.   Your heart is the true temple of God.   You must search for Him there.   The Lord can be realized only by going within.

Those who search for Him outside the body are fools. Out of ignorance they wander in solitudes and wastes. Whatever is in the macrocosm is in the microcosm. You must search for Him inside your own self. We are mistaken when we search for Him in brooks, streams, hills, man-made temples and other places. We will not find Him there. If we know the secret of the path, we will find Him. We cannot, however, go inside without a true Master.

"Know ye by the grace of the Master,
The temple of the Lord is within you."   A

(10) The teachings of the perfect Masters are wholly true and scientific. They are natural and practical. They are not merely the result of imagination and intellect. Whatever they teach, they teach with absolute conviction, for their teachings are not the result of mere reading or learning. They are based on their own personal inner experiences, and these experiences are common to all holy men. Their spiritual experiences tally with the experiences of other holy men. They do not ask people to have blind faith. They have themselves seen the Lord.

(11) Whenever Saints and holy men appear, they sometimes create an atmosphere which is not liked by the worldly-minded people. They do so, so that the slaves of the world and worshipers of mammon, who often gather round them like flies, may leave them, and the real seekers may not suffer. They intentionally provide some cause for criticism so that only the deserving will come to them.

"Should there be no keeper at the gates of the Master?
There should be one so that worldly dogs may not crowd in.
Slander acts as the Masters' doorkeeper,
So that no underserving soul may approach them."

Guru Nanak said that whenever Saints would incarnate, many imposters, who followed the formalities of religion, would criticize them. A few would follow the Saints, but they, too, would be criticized by the so-called diciples of the so-called gurus. People would forget the Yoga of the Sound Current and would read the written words and say prayers while kneeling. The path of the unending Music would be forgotten. Men would repeat other holy names and would not know about the path of inner devotion. When the Yoga of the Sound Current would not be practised, I will appear in the garb of Saints. When the practice of Shabd commences, one could know that I was there.

(12) When a Saint appears on the earth, there is a flood of spirituality. The true seekers gather round him from all sides. All benefit from his teachings— the simple as well as the righteous, for they find a true satisfaction in the teachings. It even happens that some thieves, robbers and other sinners also come to the Saints, benefit by their teachings and become holy men. The Masters act like a washerman and wash away the dirt of our sins. They are living examples of selflessness and sacrifice. They rule the hearts of the people. Spirituality is preached by them on a grand scale. People throng around them by the thousands, and the world is wonder-struck by this demonstration of spirituality and devotion.

(13) The perfect Masters or Saints are powerful personalities. They look after their disciples whether they be near at hand or far away. This naturally creates confidence in the hearts of their disciples. Their hand is no less strong than that of the Lord. Their reach is so great as to transcend the seven skies. As the disciple's contact with his Master increases, he receives fresh benefits and sees new miracles.

When one goes inside, he sees the light-form of the Master and this form speaks to the disciple. It replies to his questions and remains with him constantly.

"Surrender body and mind to him,
Who has no desires;
Who has given up all consideration for the self,
And who attunes you to the Lord.
Surrender of the mind means surrender of all,
For the body goes with the mind.
What else is left with you to give?
Kabir has said:
Surrender of body and mind is for your good;
The burden is then removed from your own head.
If a man asserts that he has done this by his own efforts,
He is quite in the wrong.
Surrender of body and mind means nothing,
If the underlying desires are not given up.
Kabir says to that seeker:
How can the mind be controlled?
When the body and mind are truly surrendered,
The desires should go with them.
Kabir says that he is without fear,
For his mind is with the Master.
His innermost thoughts are also surrendered,
At the lotus feet.
O Kabir, these feet are those of the Master,
I see naught else."   4

The Work Of The Guru

A Master is a donor, and not a beggar. His
benevolence is for all, whether rich or poor. He feels
happy in rescuing souls from physical bondage.
The Saints may be in any garb; but they work only
for the good of the soul and for its spiritual evolution.
They do not believe in blind faith, and they do not
ask anybody to believe blindly. They speak of a
faith that can be tested right here and now, on the
counter, as it were. They do not promise release or
emancipation after death only. All that they say is

meant for all and is open to inquiry—it is the message
of the wide, open road.

"Unless I see with my own eyes,
I believe not in the words of the Master."   14

It is true that we have to rely on the Master to
enable us to experiment; but when we realize the
truth of his teachings through our own experience,
we become steadfast in the faith which cannot be shaken even by the opposition of the whole world.   One
sees the sun rise.   If hundreds of bats should swear
that there is no sun, one's belief would not be disturbed,
because he has seen the sun rise with his own eyes.
Those whose inner eye has not opened remain
deprived of this truth.

There is a great difference between our coming
and the Masters' coming into the world.   The convicts
and the doctor, who looks after their health, both visit
the prison.   The former go there to undergo imprison-
ment for their misdeeds, while the latter goes there to
treat them.   We come here to work out the consequences of our karmas, or good and bad acts, but the
Masters come here to redeem us.

There are many kinds of good deeds done by
people that are of help to others; but the good deed
done by the Master is of the highest degree.   He
takes us out of the prison of Kal and the deceit of
Maya, and unites us with the Lord.

A social worker takes pity on the prisoners and
serves them with milk.   That is a good deed, and
they are pleased for the moment.   Another kind person
brings them sweets to eat.   They are again pleased and
are happy for a short while.   A third person supplies
them well-made clothes, and their bodies are properly

clothed for some time. In spite of all these good
deeds, they however, still continue to remain prisoners. Another person, the Guru, comes along with a
bunch of keys in his hand. He opens the door,
releases the prisoners and sends them home. All
of these helpful persons did good acts, but the best
act is the one done by the last person.

There are many kinds of good actions in this
world, but in spite of them all we are not freed from
the cage of the body and the mind. The Master comes
to the world, which is a prison with eighty-four lakh
cells. He sets us free and takes us home. His act
is the best, the really helpful act. His purpose is to
give life and to free souls from the prison of eighty-
four lakh cells and take them to the Lord.

The perfect Masters are those who have indistin-
guishably become one with the Lord. They are born
in human form according to the wishes of the Lord,
so that they may take souls from the lower regions
and unite them with the Lord. They connect with
the Lord those who follow their instructions, and make
them like themselves.

Are Saints the rivals of God? No, never. Actually, the Lord is captivated by the Saints, for they
hold Him in bondage by their love for Him. Whatever
the Lord wishes to do, He does through His Saints.
In this universe, the Saints are His agents or officers
and do His work. Paltu Sahib says that in His
household there are no other managers. All Saints
are lovers of the Name. Whatever they wish come
to pass.

The Masters are one with the Lord. They come
here simply to redeem the souls. In the hymns of

all the holy men it is said that the Masters come to the world with the mission of redeeming the souls. Shams-i-Tabriz says:

"You do not know what kind of birds we are,
Or what we are reciting silently.
We are apparently beggars in this world;
Find the Reality and you will see that we are kings.
We appear to be poor,
But if you look into our hearts you will find what treasures we have.
Since we are kings in our own land,
What does it matter if we are in prison here for a while?
How can we live forever in this house?
All of us are guests in this house.
We have made promises to our king;
And we shall not go back on our promises.
As long as we are wearing this mantle (of human body),
We do not grieve, nor cause grief to anyone.
We are full of light and blessing as in Heaven
We eat, make merry and laugh."

Guru Gobind Singh similarly says, "From duality we merged into One. I had no desire to come into this world, but the Lord so willed it and sent me here."

"From two we became one.
I did not like to come;
The Lord willed it,
And sent me to this world."

The primary duty of the Guru is to prepare the disciple and then to take him to the court of the Lord. The Master takes the responsibility for those who take shelter with him. To take care of spiritual seekers, Masters come to this world again and again and show them the spiritual path.

It is immaterial whether the disciple is near to, or far away from the Master. He has a long reach, for his hand is the hand of God. His hands wield the power of God.

The Master does not let the disciple face situations that are too difficult for him. Just as a child is ignorant and the mother saves him from impending catastrophies, similarly, the Master protects the disciple from sufferings and difficulties without even telling him anything about them. The sufferings ordained by fate are lightened. He gives strength to the disciple, which enables him to regard the worldly sufferings as insignificant.

The Master helps the disciple to overcome difficulties in both the worlds—the physical and the spiritual. There is no helper other than he.

All this care is given to the disciple while he is in this world. But the Master himself comes and stands by the disciple at the time of his death, which is the time of utmost anxiety. He takes the soul of the disciple with him. He is also present to help the disciple at the time of final reckoning.

The company and friendship of worldly people is transitory and evanescent. Some leave us when we face difficulties; while others desert us in the end. But the Master is the true protector and helper of the disciple. He is always with him at the time of need or difficulty. He does not leave him alone at the time of death or even later.

The relationship between the Master and the disciple is that of pure love. He is very kind. He gives us instructions regarding how to return to our home, and then prays to the Lord to forgive us and free us from bondage.

The Lord resides in his heart. The Guru mani-

fests in his being the virtues and personality of the
Lord. In this worthy man, perfection of personality
and perfection of virtues have met at one place.
The virtues of Divinity are manifested in him. If
you wish to see God, you should see the Guru.

"He has hidden a sun in man."   5

When the inner eye is opened, one realizes that
the Master is the one before whom all should prostrate
themselves. He is the life of the universe. He is
Truth personified, or Reality in human form. He
is of the Truth and reflects the Truth. He is the top
of creation. There is no one better than him. There
is no one greater than him here or hereafter. All the
good qualities to be found in the astral and causal
regions find a place in him. All virtues are centered
in him. He who has seen him has seen the Lord
in human form. All the virtues of the Lord are
reflected in him. He is the image of the Lord in this
world. He is His viceroy and does His work in this
world. His intellect and wisdom are unique, and
his judgment is sound and unquestionable. He may
not have received an education in any school or college,
but he is nevertheless the fountain-head of all learning. He understands its meaning.

Even if you look at him from the human point
of view, he is the most perfect man. He is the source
of all virtues. He does not belong to any particular
country or nation. He belongs to all countries and
nations. He serves all and teaches all. He has love
for all. His teachings are for the entire world. He
is a citizen of the world. He lives in this world radiat-
ing love, and has come here to spread the light of the

Lord as His messenger.

The Guru lives like an ordinary human being. He lives in the world but remains unaffected by it. He treats every one lovingly and sympathetically. His love and care is many times greater than that of a mother. He is a perfect man and has no defects. He takes pity on us despite our faults.

In outward form he is a human being. He is, however, a superman. He is beyond good and evil, and is the most exalted of men. He is the Lord Himself in human form. He is a mixture of morality and spirituality. He shows himself powerless, even though he is all-powerful. He is humble in spite of his greatness. The blending of power with solicitude and humility, and of wisdom with love—the ideal which has been placed before the world by Plato and other philosophers, is to be found in a Sat Guru only.

In actual fact, the Guru is more than a superman because his reach extends beyond human limits. He works in regions which are not perceptible to our senses. He has access to subtle and causal regions and even beyond. These cannot be perceived by our senses, even with the help of external instruments. The scientists are unable to see these regions, since it is not possible for them to travel beyond the material universe. They confine their activities to the world of the mind and intellect. They have experimented a great deal and will continue to do so. But there are subtle regions and worlds beyond the reach of the mind, and the regions of pure consciousness lie still higher. The Master travels through these regions every day.

The Master Is The Manifestation Of The Lord

The Lord is unfathomable and unknowable, but He is manifested in the Master. The Master manifests His glory. The Lord has locked the inner door in our body and is sitting behind it. He Himself takes on the form of a man and carries the key to open the door. The form which He takes is particularly loved by us, and this form should be worshiped by us. The glory of the Lord shines through the Master. He takes the human form outwardly and lives amongst us. Having a body like us he undergoes pain and pleasure like us. Therefore the visible form of the Lord, seen by our eyes, is dearer to us than the original and invisible form of the Lord.

The Master is not distinguishable from the Lord. He is one with Him. How, then, can one be greater than the other? In fact, Saints and the Lord are not different. Maulvi Rum says:

"When you accept the Master, realize that in his person are included the Lord and the Prophet. Do not consider them to be different. Do not look at them as different beings, and do not talk of them as being separate. Consider the Master as one who is merged in the Lord. If you have a defect in your eye, the Master and the Lord will appear to be different; and you will lose both yourself and the reality of spirituality. He who regards the Lord and the Master as separate is a dead body, and not a disciple."

In the Bible it is written:

Philip saith to him, "Lord, show us the Father, and it is enough for us." Jesus saith to him, "Have I been so long a time with you; and yet hast thou not known me, Philip? He that hath seen me, hath seen the Father also. How sayest thou, show us the Father? Believest thou not that I am in the Father and the Father is in me?"

Jesus also said:

"I and the Father are one. He that seeth me hath seen the Father. This that I tell you I do not say of my own, but the Father abiding in me doth His works. Believe me that I am in the Father and the Father is in me."

The body of a Master walks on this earth, but his soul soars to the seven skies. He is human in outer form, but God speaks through him. He is in reality God. He is God plus man, that is, a God-man. He is the string that connects us with God. The Master is the Shabd personified, but he has to take a human form so that he may make us understand him.

It is said that the King of Russia, Peter the Great, went to Holland to learn the art of ship-building. He disguised himself as a workman.   There were many Russians who had fled from his tyrannical rule there, and he talked to them of Russia and advised them to return to their homes. They also felt like returning. They said, however, that the king had turned them out and that therefore they could not return. Peter told them that the king was his friend, that he would recommend them to him, and that the king would agree. When Peter, after learning the art of ship-building, made ready to return home, those who believed his words accompanied him. When Peter entered the country, everyone bowed down and showed him great respect. This encouraged his companions to believe that he would make the king feel favorably disposed towards them and would give them permission to live in Russia. When they reached the capital, Peter left his companions and asked them to see the king in his court. When they went there, they were wonder-struck at seeing him sitting on the king's throne. They had believed him to be a loborer like themselves, and did not know that he was the king. They then felt grateful that the king had brought them home in the guise of a laborer.

The position of a Master is similar. He takes on human form to take human beings to their original home. Outwardly, he appears to be a prisoner amongst other prisoners; but in reality he is the king of all regions and universes. He is not a prisoner. He is, no doubt, in the guise of a prisoner; but he is here for redeeming the prisoners and has come here to free them from their bondage.

When a blackbird is being taught to speak, a mirror is placed before it and a man hides behind it and speaks. The blackbird looks at his own reflection in the mirror and thinks that someone of his species is sitting there before him and speaking. Similarly, the Lord is hiding behind the garb of the Saints and speaks through them. The Lord is indescribable and wonderful. He has to take a human form to manifest Himself to the human beings. How can He communicate with human beings without a body Kabir Sahib says that God speaks under the cover of body and cannot speak without it. How can one see a personality who has no attributes unless it takes a form like us?

Because he has a certain form, he belongs to a particular country, but he is free from the bondage of body. He can travel in the higher regions at his pleasure. He is a Master and a manifestation of the Shabd. He belongs to all. He is one with the Lord. He is present everywhere. He remains constantly with the disciple and helps him. He reveals himself within the disciple.

The perfect Guru does not reveal all his competence on the first day. As the ability of the disciple increases, the Guru also reveals more and more. At first, he appears merely as an elderly person, but gradually he reveals himself as a perfect Guru. He does not stop there. He shows the disciple that he is merged in the Lord and that there is no difference between him and the Lord.

St John described the light-form thus in the Bible:

"I was in the spirit on the Lord's day, and heard behind me a great voice, as of a trumpet."

"And I turned to see the voice that spoke with me. And being turned, I saw seven golden candlesticks: And in the midst of seven golden candlesticks one like to the Son of man, clothed with a garment down to the feet, and girt about the paps with a golden girdle. And his head and his hairs were white, like wool, as white as snow, and his eyes were a flame of fire. And his feet like unto fine brass, as in a burning furnace. And his voice as the sound of many waters."

"After these things I looked, and behold a door was opened in heaven and the first voice which I heard, as it were, of a trumpet speaking with me, said: come up hither, and I will show thee the things which must be done hereafter."

The Shabd or divine Music is the perfect Master. The Shabd is indistinguishable from the Supreme Lord. It is a conscious current of that great power which created the universe and which fully pervades it. All the universe emanated from this Shabd.

"Know the Shabd to be the Guru;
Your Guru will reveal this.
Become the beloved disciple.
The soul will f o llow the Melody."

A

He alone is a Saint or perfect Master who can initiate others. The Shabd is a manifestation of the Supreme Lord, and it is revealed to the Saints or perfect Masters. They are indistinguishable from the Lord.

"I churned the sea of the body,
And saw a wonderful sight.
The Lord is the Guru and the Guru is the Lord;
O Nanak, there is no difference between the two."   A

"In their own spheres,
All are great holy men.
But he who has realized the Shabd,
He is the greatest of all.
There are various Gurus,
And there are differences in their approach.
Worship that Guru alone,
Who connects you to the Shabd."   4

The perfect Master or Guru is similarly described in the Sar Bachan:

"He alone is the Guru
Who loves the Shabd.
He who knows it not
Is not a perfect Guru.
He who practises the Shabd
Is a perfect Guru.
Bow before such a Guru.
Become the dust of His feet."

The perfect Master or Sat Guru is the true physician, for He has the life-giving herb of the Name or Shabd.

All human beings make mistakes. It is a part of their nature. But the Master is human in form only. Inwardly he is one with the Lord. Like the Lord, he is faultless.

In reality, the Guru is not the name of a man. He is a power which is manifested in this body temporarily. He is our true ideal in the light of which true spiritual progress is made. He is full of radiant light, like an electric bulb. While He shines, the thought of the structure of the bulb does not enter the mind. The seekers after spirituality sacrifice themselves like moths over this divine light.

The Master is not a creature of this world and is not in the bondage of this body. He goes beyond all the lower worlds and regions, the mind and the intellect, and lives and moves in the spiritual regions. And he, in his mercy, gives eyes to thousands of persons to see inner sights and cross these regions.

The living Master is one with the Lord. He is the true manifestation of the Lord in this world. He has been given the duty of working for the salvation of its creatures. He is the source of love. He is the incarnation of bliss and peace. Only man can guide man. This is the law of nature. The Master assumes human form according to this law, so that he may persuade people and unite them with the Lord through his own strength. He can every day, or whenever he likes, enjoy the bliss of the innermost and highest regions of light and life.

> "Powerful is the Master's hand;
> It is not less strong than that of the Lord;
> His hand is the power of God.
> One should believe in its greatness
> For it extends to the highest heaven.
> In his palm flows the eternal current;
> The Lord is without rival or partner in His grandeur.
> He has hidden a sun in man.
> Know the Master as He is."

5

The Supreme Lord comes to us in the form of a Master. He knows and feels our sufferings and loves us. Where is the Lord? We can see Him in the radiant and glorious form of the Master and nowhere else. Unless we reach the regions of pure consciousness beyond the reach of the mind, senses and intellect, we cannot see the Lord. In this world, the Lord is merely an idea for us; we are simply clinging to a mental idea of Him. But this becomes manifest in the Master. He lives amongst us and we can see Him.

In this physical universe, the Saints are the redeemers of human beings. The living Guru is the hope of the people, the light of the world and the savior of man kind. Because of the grace of the Shabd, the Saint or perfect Master is free from all limitations and bondage. He takes souls out of the stormy sea of birth and death and takes them to the immortal regions. The Shabd and the perfect Guru are indistinguishable. The Guru, in His outward form, has a human body. He teaches and persuades those who come to hear Him. But when you go to the subtle regions, He assumes a subtle form and accompanies you in that form. If you reach the causal region, He assumes a causal form and in that form He helps you there. He has traveled through all the stages of the journey to the highest regions and can help you in those regions also. He does not rest until He merges you in His real form, the Shabd.

CHAPTER 4

THE SHELTER OF THE MASTER

To take shelter with the Master means to subordinate one's will to the will of the Master and unreservedly surrender oneself to him. This is an easy means of gaining release from the cycle of birth and death. The disciple should implicitly rely on the Master and should give himself up to him in the same way as one confides in a surgeon and trusts his life in his hands. Similarly, one follows the instructions of a guide when one is lost in a wilderness and is sick and tired, and cannot himself find the way. The Master's task is not only to teach, but to help the disciple in overcoming his difficulties. He alone is a true friend who not only advises us regarding what to do in difficulties, but also helps us in freeing ourselves from them.

Prostrating oneself at the feet of the Master simply means meeting Him and taking shelter with Him. Similarly, one is often advised to bow at the feet of a servant of the Lord or a holy man or Master, and to think of His feet or to be a sacrifice unto them.

"They advise us to bow to the feet of the living Master.
For spiritual progress a living Guru is very necessary.
No one can find the Lord without a Master,
Even though he may go on making millions of efforts." A

"Become the dust of the holy men's feet,
And give up egotism;
Give up all cleverness and prostrate yourself
At the feet of the Master." A

The object of having Guru as an ideal is purely spiritual. It is not a doctrine of man-worship. By the Guru, we mean not only the Master in human form, but also in the form of the Shabd. The body is like a robe which has to be cast aside both by the disciple and the Master. But blessed is the body in which He works! We respect it and it should be worshiped. It is also called Guru. We have a body and we can be taught only by one having a body. Those who describe the sitting at the feet of a Master as man-worship do not know the Reality. Even if this criticism is taken as true, it is far better than book-worship or idol-worship. Man is a conscious being, and only a conscious being can teach another conscious being.

When one is reborn in the house of the Master, that is, when one takes shelter with him, it is the duty of the disciple to follow the path taught him by the Master. Whatever he does in obedience to the wishes of the Master is giving devotion to him. If a passenger follows the directions of the boatman while in his boat, he gets across the river. He should therefore obey the directions without any objection. His welfare depends upon his doing so.

The Master is responsible for his disciple in all matters. The disciple should therefore lovingly carry out the orders of the Master, and not let his own whims interfere with them, even though the Master's orders may sometimes appear a trifle strange at the first glance. The Master is all-powerful. There may be something which we do not understand.

To take shelter means to have full confidence in the Master and to be guided by him. One should follow his orders without considering their so-called propriety. Whatever the Master directs us to do is for our good, although at the time it may not appear to be proper or beneficial for us. The disciple should obey him in word, deed and spirit.

It is absolutely essential to obey the Master and act within his will. The salvation of the disciple depends upon this. Everyone may see the Master. But it is very necessary to obey his words and practise the Shabd imparted by him.

> "All the world can see the Master,
> But this does not lead to salvation
> Unless one practises the Shabd." A

It is easier to practise meditation than to surrender unconditionally to the Master. When one takes shelter with the Master, one must be like a child. He must give up his own will and conform to the will of the Master. He must surrender himself to the Master in word, deed and spirit. This is difficult, but if owing to good fortune one gets shelter, then all his desires will be fulfilled. He will merge in the form of the Guru.

The words of the Master bear fruit in accordance with the extent to which you act upon them.

> "The Master is always merciful.
> We get nothing but what we deserve.
> He looks after all with the same kindness;
> And we receive his grace according to the measure of our
>   love." A

When the disciple surrenders himself to the Master for good, the Master looks after him in every way. Just as a mother brings up her child, so the Master looks after his disciple. As the disciple becomes purified, the Master gives him spiritual wealth. The child who sits in the lap of his mother need not worry, because all his worries are hers. He is care-free and happy. Similarly, the disciple, after taking shelter with the Master, becomes care-free and happy.

The relationship between the disciple and the Master is very abstruse and cannot be fully or adequately described. The Saints have, however, tried to explain it so that we may comprehend it to some extent. All worldly relationships, they point out, are based on self-interest. The relationship between the Master and the disciple, however, is pure. It is selfless. We can understand it to some extent by comparing it with the relationship between the mother and her child. The mother cares very deeply for the newborn child. She shares its pains and pleasures. The child has no power of discrimination. He cannot, for example, distinguish cleanliness from dirt. If the child is unhappy, the mother is very anxious and tries to remove the cause of its suffering and even passes the night without sleeping. When the child is happy and smiles, the mother is happy both mentally and physically.

When the child is small, it is ignorant of language and of its home. The mother looks at the child and the child looks at the mother. She prattles to the child and teaches it to speak. She looks after the child in all matters. She sees to it that it does not put its hand in the fire, she feeds it and keeps it clean. She carefully instructs the child until it grows up into an adult.

Similarly, when a disciple is reborn, so to say, in the family of the Master, he is ignorant of spiritual matters. His thoughts and cares are always entangled in low desires. But the Master stills the mind and the senses of the disciple and purifies him. For spiritual progress, control of the mind and the senses by stilling them is necessary. While the Master in his mercy lends help to still the mind of the disciple, he at the same time enables him to understand and to speak that language which is unspoken. The Master is always careful about the progress of the disciple. He does everything possible to make a disciple clean, devoid of all dirt, and pure. He removes all his defects.

"I have no friend but Thee, O Lord;
I take refuge with the Master.
I find the Lord there;
O fellow traveling merchant of small worldly wares,
Come, seek a Master and gather the everlasting wealth." A

This universe is an ocean. The Master is a ship and He Himself is its captain. No one can cross over without the Master. It is only through His grace that we can meet the Lord. No one gets release without this.

"Guru is the ship, Guru is the captain.
No one has crossed over without a Guru.
One meets the Lord through the Guru's grace.
One cannot get release without a Guru." A

"The Master gave the incomparable gift;
He made the name of the Lord dwell in my heart.
When the merciful One is kind,
He gives us shelter with the Master." A

Maulvi Rum says that we should sit at the feet of a person who knows our heart, who can understand our difficulties and sufferings, who can share our sadness and who can remove it. We should sit in the shade of a tree bearing fresh flowers and fruit, which will refresh our mind and heart, and from which we will get the fruit of spiritual life to eat. We should not aimlessly wander around in the streets of this world like vagabonds, but should sit at some place where we can have the Lord's nectar. The Masters are the keepers of this nectar, and they can share this wealth with anyone. They are agents of the Lord through whom the Lord distributes His wealth.

"If God is kind, it is good;
If not, it matters not.
But if the Master is not kind and gracious
My mind will be completely wrecked."

"I would give up Rama, but not the Master.
I do not consider God equal to the Master.
God sent me to this world,
But the Master freed me from birth and death.
God set five thieves after me,
But the Master saved my lonely soul.
God ensnared me with family ties,
But the Master removed my attachment.
God involved me in disease and suffering;
The Master made me a yogi and freed me from them.
God involved me in meritorious acts and deeds;
The Master showed me my real self.
God hid Himself from me;
The Master gave me a lamp and showed God to me.
God involved me in bondage and release;
The Master removed all my doubts about them.
I sacrifice myself to Charandas;
I will give up the Lord, but not the Master."　　10

Love For The Master And Its Advantages

How can one become the recipient of this wonderful gift of love for the Lord? It is impossible to obtain it without following the instructions of a Master. It can be bestowed only on one who possesses a noble heart, and through the special grace of God.

We have not seen the Lord, and we do not know how to love Him. But a Master is the manifestation of His Love and to love the Master is to lose one's own identity completely in the Master and thereby merge into the Lord.

The maker of a lover is the Beloved, and it is the internal attraction of the Beloved that creates love. It is through His grace that the love remains alive. Otherwise, it is entirely useless. A lover should always consider his Beloved to be the Emperor of Emperors. If the Beloved yields to the obstinacy of the lover, it is His grace. The greatness of the Beloved does not suffer thereby. His commands are the orders of an Emperor and the commands of God. You should constantly obey Him. Never utter words of disrespect under the influence of arrogance or the pride of your intellect or strength. Never should an idea of equality or disrespect enter your mind.

Saints are surging oceans of God's Love, and they act as light-houses in our life's journey in this world. Christ, Guru Nanak, Guru Amar Das, Guru Ram Das, Kabir Sahib, Swami Ji, Ram Krishna, Shamas Tabriz, Hafiz and many other Saints have left their footprints on the sands of time for our guidance. Their lives were oceans of Love. By studying their writings, love for spirituality will be awakened in our minds.

But above all, we should meet a Master who is the manifestation of God, so that we may receive guidance and be able to obtain within ourselves the nectar of love.

God is infinite. He has no form nor name. He is free from all limitations and qualities. But we have a physical form, and a lover's heart naturally prays that his Beloved should also similarly appear before his eyes so that he may behold Him. The lover's eyes long to see Him, his hands long to touch Him, his ears long to hear His sweet voice, and he wishes to embrace his Beloved. He desires to express his love, and therefore he wants to clothe the spiritual with a material form.

We love saintly persons because they are merged in His love. To meet them and to be in their presence is to meet God and to be in His presence. Jesus Christ says: "He who has seen me has seen the Father."

Saints are an ocean of Love, because they are already merged into the Lord, and the Lord is Love. The currents of Love emanating from the Saints spread out and influence every nook and corner of the world. By receiving such currents, one's heart is inclined to meet the Lord.

Saints always teach only love, because love and God are one. God is Love, and God's reflection is Love. The only difference between the Saints and other people is in the quality of their love. Saints are Love incarnate and bestow the gift of love on others. They love the evil people as well as the good ones, and their love is of the highest type. Love is the true religion and real guide.

By loving the Master we inculcate love for the Lord within ourselves, and a desire is created in us to meet Him. This creates a sense of contentment within and at the same time the mind is controlled by keeping it busy in repeating His Name.

Guru Arjun says:

"One cannot achieve Love without a Master. You should bear it in mind, that God is Love, and He is manifested in the Master, and it is the Master who enables one to meet the Lord."

A person in whose heart love for the Master has been bestowed by God is really fortunate, because love for the Master is the method by which we come to love God. To love the Sat Guru only for his own sake is better than any other type of love, because the inner beauty in him is indestructible. God's beauty is everlasting, and He shines through a Sat Guru; therefore, love for the Master is free from all defects. But one must remember that in order to love God or the Master, it is necessary to create true longing.

As long as a person is absorbed in enjoyment of the sensual pleasures, real longing for God will not come. Saints have therefore taught us to avoid the expression of physical love and have directed us to love our Sat Guru instead of loving worldly forms, for the Masters are free from all worldly dross, and love for them will not entangle us in the ties of this world. And love for the Master is necessary, because his love reminds us of God. Such a state has been described by the Saints as merging oneself into the Sat Guru. As the Sat Guru himself is merged in the Lord, one who merges himself into the Sat Guru automatically achieves the next step, which is to merge oneself into the Lord.   Thus one attains God-Realization.

Nearness to God is achieved and felt in two different ways: outwardly and inwardly.   Outwardly, it is done by keeping the company of Saints; but inwardly one cannot attain it unless heart is connected with heart.   And to create the path of contact from one heart to the other it is necessary to inculcate in one's self the highest form of love.   When love and affection are firmly established in one's heart, then contemplation of the Beloved is easily achieved, because in the hearts of lovers the form of their Beloved is always present.

It is easy to boast about one's love for the Master but it is extremely difficult to be a true lover.   A disciple should gradually increase his love for the Master. As a result, that love will eventually turn into true ecstasy and His Form will then imprint itself in the mind of the disciple.   Without Dhyan it is not possible to strengthen the bond of love for the Master, nor will the Dhyan be complete; that is, it will not be possible for the disciple to hold the form of the Master within himself.

Therefore, lovers of God remember Him by repetition of His Name and contemplation on the form of their Master.   They are then able to benefit by contemplation outwardly as well as inwardly.

A Master is a lover of God.   In Him there are boundless currents of true love.   He is the physical form of that love.   To love Him is to find the most important medium for developing love for God, because he is a manifestation of God, and his heart is full of love for Him.   His face shines with the light

and energy of God.   By seeing him, love and longing
for God increases.   To love such a person is to love
God Himself, because by loving him we always remember our Lord.

Sometimes the Master appears indifferent and by
other similar signs tries to eliminate ego and arrogance
from the mind of his devotee.   Sometimes the Master's
love for the disciple is apparent and he thereby streng-
thens the love in the disciple, as a result of which the
soul rises higher.

> "It causes no pain or anguish if God is displeased with a true
> devotee, because he has the support of his Master; but if the
> Master is displeased with him, then he has no place to go in
> this world or beyond."   4

A Master possesses the unique magnetic power
of love which draws a devotee towards him and creates
within him a feeling of indifference towards worldly
attractions.   This magnetic power is an inherent
quality of the Master and emanates from his every
action and movement.   Everything that radiates from
the Master—the light of his beautiful face, the lines
on his forehead, even his indifference when he is
displeased with the devotee, the luster round him when
he speaks smilingly—all pierce the heart of the devotee
and thus attract him to his Master.   Through the
luster of the Master's face shines the luster of God,
and one sees God in his Master.

Whenever a Master appears in this world, seekers
for the real truth are attracted towards him like moths,
and like bees they hover round that living flower of
spirituality and enjoy its taste.   They cannot endure
separation even for a moment.   Because of the divine
power of the Master, souls are attracted towards him,

and the fire of steadfast love and devotion is awakened in them. This love and devotion is the means of making the disciple a recipient of the Lord's mercy and of taking him to the Original Home.

The Master sees only the inner condition, and not the external condition, religion or nationality of the disciples. Whomsoever he deems fit he initiates in the inner path, and declines others whom he finds unprepared. What touchstone he uses for the purpose is known to him alone. But he can see the seekers' sanskaras (effects of past karmas) as clearly as one can see pickles or jam in a glass jar.

The Master, through his divine powers, imparts teachings to the seekers after truth, whether they be near or far, and can reveal himself to them without writing or speaking to them. Whoever is taken by the Saints under their protection is stamped with the seal of the Lord's mercy. He is saved from Kal and his hard reckoning. He is free of Kal's demands on his upward journey.

"The Master is the philosopher's stone.
The rusted, iron-like mind
Turned into gold after meeting him."   A

The Gurus have mentioned various benefits that flow from taking shelter at the feet of the Master. Pains, worries and calamities are removed. Lust, greed and other defects disappear. Both the body and the mind become pure, and one gains peace. All troubles are forgotten and the fear of death is banished. The devotee crosses the ocean of worldly existence. He has constant devotion for the Name. The lotus of the heart flowers into full bloom. The disciple awakens. The Lord dwells in his mind and is seen everywhere. The devotee gets peace and bliss and reaches the Supreme Abode. There are many hymns containing prayers that one may reach the feet of the Master in order to obtain these benefits.

The living Master is not confined to his body. He also has access to the higher regions of the universe. Contemplation on His inner form is the second step in spiritual progress. When the soul by means of repetition rises to higher regions, it can stay there only with the help of contemplation of the Master's inner form. The Gurus, therefore, say with great emphasis that the feet of the Master should dwell within our 'hearts'.

"Let the feet of the Master dwell in the heart;
Then the deepest aspirations of the mind shall be fulfilled."

"Let the feet of the Master dwell in the heart;
All your sufferings will then be ended."

"Let the feet of the Master dwell in the heart;
Meditating on Him, cross the sea of fire."   A

The Master is the physician who gives us sight. The Lord is inside us. All the world is blind and works in darkness. If one meets a Master, he can then see the Lord inside himself with his own eyes.

"He who reflects on the self,
Recognizes the diamond.
The perfect Master gives a single glance,
And thereby redeems the disciple.
The disciple accepts the Master;
And his mind is stilled.
Such is our Master, of royal state,
And a perfect connoisseur of jewels,
That at a single loving glance.
He discerns the jewel within us and redeems it."   A

A Master is the manifestation of God. To ask for worldly benefits from Him is to ask for farthings from an Emperor. A lover of a Master does not even demand salvation or Sat Nam. His love is for the sake of love and he gets everything without asking for it. Above all, He bestows the highest treasure of love through which peace, concentration, blissful life and inner awakening are produced. The lover's devotion is for Him alone.

All true devotees get the Shabd, which is real life, from the perfect Guru. He is life in himself, and since He is free from ego, the Shabd speaks through Him. He has transcended the valley of death. He has realized the life of the Lord, which works through the Sound, and he himself can give that life or spiritual awakening to his disciples.

When one, who has real love for the Master, is in the Master's presence, his condition is unique, and due to the burning of the fire of love caused by the Master's Darshan he appears to be an entirely different person.

By looking at the Master the remembrance of the Lord automatically comes into one's mind, and by being absorbed into it the soul soars into the higher regions and is in a state of indescribable bliss.

The inner secrets cannot be expressed in words, either spoken or written. They can be explained only by the perfect Master of the time. He accompanies a disciple on his spiritual ascent and takes him across all the difficult stages of the journey.

This form remains with the soul in all the regions and universes. It takes on the form of the Shabd in the region of Brahm. It takes the soul to the ultimate Home or Sach Khand. When this form appears within, all doubts are destroyed, the service of the devotee is approved and half of the task of the disciple is then accomplished. Thenceforth the devotee has to do nothing. The light-form is responsible for taking the soul to the ultimate Home.

The attitude of the disciple towards his Master and God should be like that of a moth for the flame, and he should burn in the fire of his love for Him, because by such an immolation one does not die but attains everlasting life. The lovers that forget themselves completely in love for their Master drink from the fountain of the Elixir of Life and attain eternal bliss.

This does not mean that it is the lover only who suffers.

The Beloved suffers much more for the sake of the lover.

THE MOTH BURNS ONLY ONCE AND IS FREE FROM ALL PAIN, BUT THE FLAME BURNS ALL THE TIME.

CHAPTER 5

THE LORD'S WILL AND FREE WILL

Do such deeds as please the Lord. Perform the actions with which He is pleased. Whatever is liked by the Lord should be desired by us also. Therefore, "surrender to His Will" means that we should be happy in His Will. The Muslim Saints describe it as "submission to His Will". Such a person always says, "O Lord, whatever you like is good". A Persian Saint has said:

"The work that did not succeed according to our desire.
It was good that it did not succeed."

Whatever one does should be done to please the Lord, so that we may become dear to Him. The key to obtaining His pleasure lies in acting according to His Will.

"I bow my head before the wishes of the Beloved."

We should consider what we should do when we wish to please someone. The main thing would be to obey him implicitly. We should not transgress his directions even by a hair-breadth. Look at the animals. A dog that understands the command of its master and does not even remotely transgress it, is liked and patted by its master. An obedient son gives great satisfaction and pleasure to his parents. An obedient wife is loved by her husband. An obedient servant is pleasing to his master. The law-abiding and good citizens are a source of delight to their government. Wherever you may look, you will find this same principle in action. That is, if you wish to please anyone, carry out his commands. Be content with what he wills. This is the way to remain happy and in his will.

All deeds and duties should be performed with a view to pleasing the Lord. Guru Nanak has considered the various methods customarily used to realize the Lord. He says that the Lord is not within the reach of the intellect or reason. He cannot be realized by practising austerities, by keeping fasts, by observing silence and so on. He is not to be found by wisdom or cunning. How are we, then, to proceed in order to gain access to His door and to see Him after tearing away the curtain of Maya? Guru Nanak says that the Lord cannot be realized by any other method except that of obeying and following His Will. This is the most fundamental principle.

> "He cannot be conceived however hard we may think.
> He cannot be reached by observing silence however long.
> Nor can contentment be bought by all the wealth of the world.
> Of a myriad clevernesses, not one works,
> How can we be true?
> How can the curtain of falsehood be rent asunder?
> By following the Divine Will.
> It is so written in our fate, O Nanak."   A

Divine dispensation, divine law and divine Will are three different aspects of the same reality, namely, the Lord's Will. The Lord's dispensation is the result of the Lord's Will and so are happiness and pleasure. It is through this that His Law operates. The divine law is the materialized form of divine dispensation. It is the Shabd, Name or Word.

He who submits himself to the Will of the Lord merges in Him. This is the highest praise of the Will.

"He who accepts your Will
Unites with You.
He who is pleased with Your Will
Merges in You.
Glorious is submission to God's Will,
But rare is the one who submits to it."   A

A man conceives thousands of plans and puts some of them into effect, but fate sits by his side and laughs at him. Effort is the outcome of the Will of the Lord. What can the will of man do against the Will of the Lord? It has no chance whatever.

"However hard one may try,
It is to no purpose.
That only happens,
Which is ordained by the Lord."

We come together or separate according to our fate karmas and His Will. Whatever He wills, happens. No one can interfere with His supreme Will.

Rabia Basri once met two holy men. She asked them to tell her something about the Lord's Will. One holy man said, "Whatever pain and suffering one receives from the Lord, one should bear them." Rabia Basri said, "There is egotism in the idea." The other holy man said, "Whatever sufferings come from the Lord, they should be accepted cheerfully." Rabia said, "This also smacks of egotism." Rabia then added, "One should lose the faculty of distinction between the pleasure and pain that comes from the Lord and regard both of them as His gifts."

We may be rich or poor, healthy or diseased, happy or unhappy. All these states are boons from Him, a result of our own karmas. Accept them cheerfully. Be happy with His Will. Try to act as you are directed by the Master, and thus free yourself from the shackles of karmas and death, through the Name of the Lord. His Will is His greatest gift. Nothing else excels it. It is only if He wills it that we obey Him. We can meet a Master if it is so willed by Him. We can attune ourselves to Truth and then share the bliss, only if He wills it. But only those for whom it is ordained can obtain it.

"I obey as He wills.
I get bliss as He wills.
He wills and I meet a Master.
He wills and I contemplate on Truth.
No boon is greater than His Will.
Verily this is the truth.
I take refuge with the Creator."   A

"When You are with me, O Lord,
I attain everything.
When You abide within me,
I am at peace.
When You dwell within me,
I am blessed.
By Your Will You make me a king;
By Your Will a beggar.
By Your Will flow rivers in the desert;
By Your Will bloom flowers in the sky.

By Your Will we cross the sea of life;
By Your Will are we drowned midstream.
By Your Will we love the Lord,
And are dyed in His hue.   A

The sign of being united with the Lord is that one recognizes His Law. He is always in the same state;

he is always satisfied and he is always in blissful enjoyment of His Will.

> "This is the sign of union with the Lord;
> The mind recognizes the one true Divine Law.
> He loves according to the Will of the Lord.
> He always enjoys contentment and satisfaction."   A

Since there is no escape from the arrow of fate, a man can do nothing but submit to his karma. It is our everyday experience that howsoever much we may try, success or failure is not within our hands. Of course, it is our duty to make an effort. Lord Krishna gave the same advice to his disciple Arjun, to do his duty but to leave its fruit to the Lord, since he had no control over the fruit of his actions.

An old story says that one day an Arab said to Prophet Mohammad, "O Prophet of God! The Lord is constantly watching over us. What if I do not tie the legs of my camel in the night and thus leave my camel's wanderings to Him, relying on His Will? Would it do any harm?" Maulana Rum has described the reply given by the Prophet in the following words:

> "In a loud voice the Prophet said:
> Tie the legs of the camel.
> And then rely on God."

The Prophet said authoritatively that it was the man's duty to tie the legs of his camel. Perform your duty. Then remain content with the will of God and leave the result to Him. Try your best and leave the rest to God.

Those who act in accordance with the Divine Law or Will are conscious co-workers with it and act according to its provisions. This does not mean that one should sit idle and do nothing. He alone is a doer who performs actions.

The problem of the relationship between fate and self-effort is very knotty. There is a Persian saying:

"Man proposes; God disposes."

Man is free to a certain extent. He is bound beyond that. We can make this clear by an illustration. A boy is flying a kite. His father has given him a hundred or two hundred yards of string. The boy is free to fly the kite to the extent of the string that is with him, and no more. Similarly, we should try to act as best we can according to our strength and then leave the rest to the Lord. We should make use of our effort and intelligence to the extent that we can and then bow before the Will of God, accepting It as sweet and welcome.

"Live by making an earnest effort.
Thus earn and abide in happiness.
Contemplating the Lord meet Him
And dispel all care and anxiety."   A

The Lord's Will and man's free will are mentioned many times in the writings of the Gurus. If by the Lord's Will, it is meant that everything that happens is bound to happen and that man's efforts are of no avail whatever, then what was the use of the Gurus, incarnating themselves again and again, giving out their teachings, taking pains to hold spiritual discourses and putting out scriptural writings? The Gurus say that it is necessary for us to make our own efforts, but these should be in accordance with the Will of the Lord.

The Master's Will Is The Will Of The Lord

We cannot see the Lord and are, therefore, not fit to understand His Will. But the Guru is the manifested form of the Lord. It is necessary, therefore, to act in accordance with His Will, since He accepts the Will of the Lord and is His incarnation.

"The virtues loved by the Lord,
Are taught to us by the Master.
Submit to the Master's Will,
And then you will be blessed.
I worship the Master."   A

His Will is the Will of the Lord. We can see the Master and we can also enquire from Him regarding the True Path. Whoever follows the Will of the Master is the recipient of the Lord's grace.

"He is kind to those
Who accept the Will of the Master.
The Lord knows the secret of their hearts;
They act as He wills."   A

He who accepts the Master's Will accepts the Will of the Lord as well. He easily obtains the fruits that accrue by living in accordance with the Will of the Lord.

There is nectar in the Will of the Lord. The Guru's Will is permeating the Lord's Will. There is, therefore, nectar in the Will of the Master also. When the Lord so wills it, the devotee by contemplating on the Name can drink that nectar. He can then attain the Truth.

When by following the directions of a perfect Master, one understands it, he becomes the administrator of His Will. Whatever he does, he does on behalf of the Lord. The Lord works through him. His will becomes one with the Lord's Will.

Man's will and intellect, being finite, are weak, deficient and incomplete. If we make them one with the eternal Will and the perfect wisdom of the Lord they will also become infinite. Since the law of harmony is in tune with His Will, the echo of the Divine Melody is felt within man. The deficient will of man then awakens in the perfect Will of the Lord and takes its form. He begins to truly understand and follow His Will. He is no longer obliged to grope in the dark. He sees everything in a clear-cut manner. He is rid of all delusions.

The divine virtues that are dear to the Lord are known and achieved through the Master. The True Master is indistinguishable from the Lord, and the Will of the Lord is dear to Him.

> "He alone is a devotee of the Master
> Who is content with the Lord's Will.
> Within him ring unstruck Melodies of bliss
> And the Lord Himself embraces him."   A

The Master is the Lord's Will personified or made flesh. It is by following the will of the Master that the Will of the Lord is known. But this can be known from a perfect Master only.

> "O Lord, keep me ever in your Will
> And bless me with the glory of your Name.
> It is through the perfect Master
> That Your Will is known
> And one merges in Equipoise."   A

Mention of these things is made in many religious scriptures. Ponder over them while sitting in the company of a realized soul. The most important things is to take refuge with a perfect Master and then follow without hesitation the path that he enjoins.

His utterances are those of God Himself and his orders are God's orders.

He who serves the Master and merges his light in his Master's light is acceptable at the door of the Lord. He who enshrines the Will of the Lord in his inner consciousness, is like the Lord Himself. He assumes His form. There is no doubt about it.

> "They who serve the true Master
> Are approved of by God.
> They merge their light in the Flame.
> He alone is the servant of God
> Who submits to His Will."   A

Those who walk in the Will of the Lord are very fortunate. They easily board the ship of the Name.

> "The Master is the boatman;
> The Lord's Name is the boat.
> How can one get into the boat?
> By submitting to the Master's Will,
> One finds himself ferried across.
> Blessed indeed is he;
> Whom the Master unites with the Lord."   A

Shams-i-Tabriz has made a pointed reference concerning the disciple and the Will of his Master. He says, "I asked my Master, O my dear Lord! How long do you intend to keep me entangled in this world and make me miserable?" The Master replied, "I will take you where I like; I will keep you where I like. You should remain silent and obey."

He says in the end, "O Master! Whatever you will that alone I know. Whatever You make me see, that alone I see. If You keep me like this, I will so remain. If you keep me in some other condition, I will live like that." In this reply of the disciple there is a complete absence of egotism and complete resignation to His Will.

"Except what You wish me to know, what do I know?
Except what You show me, what can I see?
I will live like this, if You wish it.
If you keep me in some other state, I will live like that."

Does the Master leave the seeker alone in this struggle? No, never. He gives support from within, and slaps from outside, so that the disciple may be purged of all impurities. The pot is thus completely made ready to contain the immortal and everlasting treasure.

"Only when the True Lord wills it,
Can we worship Him
With His Will enshrined in our hearts.
It is a true devotee alone
Who knows that worship is
Living utterly in His Will.
O Saints, he who accepts God's Will
Is in bliss.
In the end it is His Name alone
That keeps one company."   A

"If You give me happiness, I praise You.
If You give me sufferings, I contemplate on You.
If You give me hunger, I am content.
In pain, I feel pleasure.
If You keep me close to You
I dwell upon You.
If You beat and drive me out,
I call on You.
If people praise me,
It is Your glory.
If they slander me,
I do not leave You."   A

By practising the Name given by the Master, the feeling of egotism is banished, and a devotee begins to understand the working of the Divine Law. He bows to it and sees it at work in all. He constantly observes it and ultimately merges in the Lord.

To observe the Law is the most noble of all actions. Such a person meets no obstruction on the way to Sach Khand.

"He who observes the Law enters His court.
Having the password of Truth, he is not held up."   A

Various benefits of living according to the Law are mentioned in the writings of the Gurus. Doubts and worries are removed. One becomes pure and gains salvation. Shabd or Name or Truth is realized and egotism is destroyed. Death and birth cease. Eternal bliss is obtained and the real abode is attained. One merges in the Lord.

CHAPTER 6

PRAYER

A materialist considers this life to be a machine, the parts of which are being run by the blind forces of cause and effect, and he does not admit that there is an ultimate Being who is directing it. But one who knows the reality, while agreeing that the law of cause and effect is working, further knows that this is being done under the orders and directions of a Supreme Being. He, therefore, while keeping an eye on the causes and their effects, appeals to the Lord, the Supreme Cause, for help, and surrenders gladly to His will and pleasure. The Lord may do whatever is good for him, for it is only the Lord who knows what is good for him. If the result is in accordance with his wishes, he is thankful. If it is not, he submits to it cheerfully, because he knows that whatever is happening is in accordance with the order and will of the Lord. He asks for the Lord's help at every step, because he knows that there is always something that is beyond the reach of his own efforts. Crying for help in this way is called prayer.

Prayer is a universal feeling, which a person feels when discomforts, trouble, disease, danger or calamity visits him and he wishes to avoid these things; or when he wishes to satisfy some bodily need or obtain spiritual gain; or when he wants strength to face some difficulties because he does not find sufficient power in himself; or when the wants the help of a powerful

being.   We see every day that we are often obliged to
ask some stronger or more capable person to help us.
When a student cannot solve a problem, he seeks the
aid of his teacher.   Similarly, in the case of illness,
we ask a physician to treat us.   A subordinate asks
his officer to help him.   These are examples of a kind
of prayer.

When we face any difficulty or an enemy
pursues us and we find no refuge, we ask for help
from the powerful Lord of the universe or from
persons in whom He is manifest. This is called
prayer.

It is natural to ask a more powerful or more able
person to help us, and it is all the more natural to turn
for help to that Supreme Power who is the Lord of
all regions and universes and is their Creator, or to
one who is one with Him.   The fact is that we cannot
help praying to Him.

All the religions say that supplication to the Lord
or to the Master is the way to obtain grace of every
kind.   It is only through prayer that spiritual advance-
ment can be achieved.   Prayer is the most natural,
direct and easy means of connecting individuals with
the Creator, and connecting the slave with the Lord.
Every seeker needs prayer from the beginning to the
end, until he realizes the Lord and merges in Him.
Through prayer, all bodily, religious, national and
social needs are fulfilled.   The ailments of mind and
body are eliminated, and prayer ultimately becomes the
means of bringing about the union of the soul with
the Lord.

"What things soever ye desire, when ye pray,
    believe that ye receive them, and ye shall have them."   B

It is again stated,

> "Ask and it shall be given you; seek and ye shall find; knock and it shall be opened unto you; for every one that asketh, receiveth; and he that seeketh, findeth; and to him that knocketh, it shall be opened."

It is seen, however, that people ask for thousands of things and all of their prayers are not granted. Then what is the meaning of the above words? Let us see which kind of prayer is granted, and why every prayer cannot be granted.

The problem is that we do not know the mercy of the Lord, and ask for things that are not for our real good. That Power wants our evolution and progress. When that Power finds that what is asked for would involve the devotee further in the world, He does not grant it. If the Lord does not grant us the things we ask for, in order to save us from sinning, this is for our good. In the Christian scriptures, it is said:

> "Ye ask, and receive not, because ye ask amiss, that ye may consume it upon your lusts."

We are entangled in bodily and sensual pleasures. Our vision does not rise above them. If we were to receive all we ask for, we would certainly be involved in more sensual pleasures and our sins would increase. Also in this connection it should be understood that man is merely one part in the machine of the universe, and is related to all other parts. Our vision being limited, we cannot see beyond ourselves and our surroundings. But the Lord or the Master can see the whole of the universe. He knows everything from the beginning to the end. He knows the devotee's genuine needs also. For example, the residents of a city which is being oppressed by unbearable heat may pray for rain, while the farmers are praying for more sunshine to ripen their crops. The human intellect is limited and an individual does not know whether what he is asking for would, in the long run be for his good. He simply looks to the immediate circumstances and is unaware of the future. Relying on his limited intelligence, he often prays for something that would harm him. In his haste, he demands many things and then realizes his mistake and is thankful that his prayer was not granted, for otherwise he would have suffered a great loss.

The Lord or the Master knows our past, present and future. He knows when a thing asked for is not for our good, and therefore does not grant it. It often happens that a seeker asks for something which is not to his real advantage. He presses for it, and a promise may be made, but the thing is not given to him. A child may ask his mother for poison. Owing to his insistence the mother may make a promise, but she will never give the poison to the child, even though she may outwardly consent to do so. It is not for the good of the child, but he does not know owing to his ignorance. The Saints, therefore, tell us that we should always pray to the Lord :—

> "O Lord! I know nothing. I have been sold into the hands of the mind and Maya"   9

Nizami says :

> "O my Well-Wisher, lead me to that which is for my good. Show me the path that leads to Your pleasure and to my salvation."

The Lord and the Master are omniscient and know fully well what is for our good and what would do us harm. It is said in the holy Quran,

"O Lord, give us in this world that which will help us hereafter
also, and save us from the sufferings of hell."

A peculiarity of human life is the love that knows
how to give, but not how to take.

Hafiz says:

"Your daily duty is to pray before the Lord. This is your
real work. Never ponder whether or not your prayer has
been heard in the Court of the Lord. That is His prerogative."

Our prayers should be in harmony with the will
of the Lord and the Master, and we should feel happy
in whatever He wills.

To pray effectively, it is necessary that we should conduct our life as desired by the Master, and that we should
experience happiness in the remembrance of the Lord.

The prayer that can redeem sinners and cure
physical, mental and spiritual diseases must be made
with full faith in the Lord and the conviction that He
is all-powerful. Our feelings which have not found
utterance are not hidden from Him. He is cognizant
of every feeling and thought. He knows the sufferings
of both the good and the evil persons.

The welling up of a strong desire is in reality the
making of a prayer. If we should surrender our
desires or acts to the Lord before expressing them, then
there would be no obstacle in the way of success.

That prayer is right which is full of yearning and
pangs. It should be made with patience and full
confidence, and with a loving heart, in all humility
and submission.

"O mind! stand in awe of the Lord.
However low, even the lowest of the low,
He calls him to Him.

A

Prayers should be made according to the directions of the Master and in order to reform one's life. When you pray in this way, you express gratitude for favors received. Gratitude cannot be expressed by mere words that have no connection with our conduct. Since the Master is the Shabd and the Shabd is His form, He is in the Shabd. He who makes the Shabd a part of his life becomes dear and acceptable to the Master. He says, "If you love me, do as I say."

Christ said, "If ye love me, keep my commandments." In order that the prayer may be acceptable, it is necessary that the disciple should be devoted to the Master and His words should dwell in the heart. He can then ask for anything and it will be given to him. Feel happy in remembering the Lord and he will fulfill your desires. Christ says:

"If ye abide in me, and my words abide in you, ye shall ask what ye will, and it shall be done unto you."

"Delight thyself also in the Lord; and He shall give thee the desires of thine heart."

Ceaseless effort to make our life pure and truthful is true prayer. This draws to us the mercy of the Lord, and His grace and limitless blessings then fulfill the sincere and pure desires of our heart. By merely asking of the Lord or the Master that we may love Him, we do not, as a matter of fact, begin to love Him. But if we consciously pray for a truthful and pure life and try to elevate our life, we will then be moulded as He wills and will begin to realize His presence and to share His love.

Is It Necessary To Pray To The Lord?

Many would like to know why we should pray, when the Lord knows all our needs. If we are to be given only after asking, then it seems possible that we might not be given something owing to our lack of knowledge or comprehension. It is also possible that we might ask for something which would be to our disadvantage. We know from experience that we somtimes pray for things and get them, but when they turn out to our disadvantage, we are sorry that we prayed for them. Just as a father knows what is good and essential for his child, similarly, our heavenly Father also knows what we really need and what will be to our advantage. Saints, knowing that the Lord knows our needs, advise us to pray with this in mind.

"Your Father knoweth what things ye have need of, before ye ask Him." B

Prayers for selfish gain and for spiritual progress are very different. As compared to spiritual prayer, the other prayer is of no consequence.

To confess our sins in prayer and to think that they are thereby washed away or removed is a mistake. This kind of mistake keeps us away from true spirituality. Our sins will only be forgiven when the Lord or the Master forgives them. Actually, such prayers may become the cause of evil. A man may offer such prayers and then keep on committing sins without hesitation. And all the while he goes on praying under the false impression that his sins will be forgiven as a result of his prayers.

The Master comes to persuade men to give up sin and to unite them with the Lord. Our duty is to act in accordance with his wishes and to give up all evil deeds which are worldly. We may thus save ourselves from sins and by the practice of Nam and remembrance, unite ourselves with the Lord. Love for the Lord and the Master reforms us, and makes us follow the path of the Lord. Man may forgive, but it is the all-pervading power of the Master which ultimately reforms a sinner.

To think that His mercy is dependent on requests made through prayer is a mistake. He does not forgive or punish as a result of whether or not we ask for forgiveness. This is to make prayer an instrument to permit the committing of sins. The Master acts with great circumspection and consideration. On the one hand he forgives sins; and on the other he restrains the disciple from committing them in future so that he may become clean and pure.

Prayers cannot make any change in the current of mercy. It is what it is. But prayers can bring us into harmony with this current. It is not necessary to beg for our needs. This often becomes an obstruction. Of course, by praying in humility and faith, we can take more advantage of that current of mercy. But he does not stand in need of vocal prayers, for He knows our hidden feelings.

The Lord is love. Is it proper for us to ask Him to be more loving? Is it necessary to pray to Him for more mercy when He is already giving us more than we deserve? By not voicing our feelings, we come nearer to His presence and grace. He is eternal. He is the same in the beginning, the present and the end.

The Lord is the embodiment of truth. Truth emanates from Him continually without His being reminded of it. How can man with his limited intellect advise Him? The current of His mercy is flowing everywhere. It is taking care of us of itself. It knows what is for our good. It is present everywhere. It perceives our feelings and hears us. Where then is the necessity to pray before Him?

"Wherever I look, I see You dwelling there;
To whom should I pray? The Lord hears all." A

It is our duty to be in harmony with Him and thus to derive the utmost benefit. It is very necessary that we should meditate on Him in our heart, so that His reflection may shine within us. The soul is a particle and an image of Him and shares His wonderful qualities. To learn to understand the Lord is a continuous process and to succeed in it, we should surrender all our thoughts, powers and desires at His feet. It is strange that while we say that the Lord is present everywhere and is eternal, we try to tell Him about ourselves. Are we thankful to the Lord for all the gifts and mercies shown to us? If we are sincerely thankful, we become deserving of more grace even without asking for it.

Prayer cannot change the principle of Truth, nor can it enable one to understand it. It is through the attraction of inner love and yearning and obeying the directions of the Master that we are led to the Truth. Our prayers to understand the Truth need not be said loudly. Such prayers can be made mentally or by living properly and in His will.

The purpose of prayer is to lead us to act according to the wishes of the Lord. We are weak and feeble. We wish to reach the Lord with the aid of the mercy and strength of the Master. Even though we may fall at every step, that power helps us. It is a law of spirituality that if a disciple takes one step on the path indicated by the Master, the Master takes a hundred steps to meet him. He is the bestower of all benefits. He is beyond praise or comprehension. He is immortal and limitless.

> "If you take one step to take refuge in the Master, the Master meets you on the way by taking hundreds of steps. If you remember the Master just once, the Master remembers you again and again.
> Even if your devotion is as small as a fragment of a cowrie shell,
> The Master showers all benefits on you.
> The Master is all merciful, His praise is beyond understanding; I bow again and again to the one and incomprehensible Master."   2

Fruits Of Prayer

The purpose of prayer is to connect one's inner self with the Lord, and to become absorbed in Him. Prayer is the essence of spirituality; through it we begin to realize Him.

Prayer is the best relaxation and recreation. The soul, mind and body gain blissful rest and happiness, which cannot be obtained by any other means. Even with the minimum of sleep, no harm is caused to the mind or body

We find that in prayer one's inner stability increases, fearlessness is augmented, and inner purity is obtained. Diseases can also be cured in oneself and in others. At times of need and danger unexpected help is received. These experiences show that it is necessary to pray to the Divine Power. When no human efforts can avail, an appeal to the Lord and the Master brings the needed help.

"Where all human efforts fail, there prayer succeeds."

A deep impression is created on the human mind by prayer. Even if one's fate is not changed by prayer, we are certainly changed. Our whole attitude towards meeting a calamity or affliction changes. The power of the mind to strive for salvation is strengthened. When the angle of vision changes, the whole world changes. The earth and the sky take on a different color. A man feels very much perturbed when a calamity comes, but when the angle of vision is changed, he bears the calamity cheerfully.

It is usually the case, that a man calls for the help of the Lord when he is helpless or in poverty. But when he attains affluence, he no longer feels the need of prayer and thinks that his own strength and social forces will suffice for the future. He thus makes a bad mistake.

Man should pray under any and all conditions. When in difficulty he should pray for the solution of his problems, and when there is no solution, for strength to bear them or to keep up his courage. When, as a result of his efforts, he sees prospects of success, he should pray for the mercy and grace of the Lord, in order to avoid relying on his own efforts and his egotism. Unless His grace and mercy join with our own efforts, no real success can be achieved. When the heart's desire has been obtained then sacrifice all in thankfulness and gratitude to Him.

In reality, prayer is the gathering and stilling of the waves of the mind at the inner center. When some desire springs up in the mind or one is worried by some worldly affliction, he thinks in his heart of the power of the Lord and looks to it for inspiration. The heart of man is the dwelling place of the Lord. The Lord is the great storehouse of power. He is the true and complete ideal. By contemplating on Him a man gains peace within himself and becomes powerful. When he gets this power, he is able to think of ways of getting out of his troubles. The mind gets power to put forth effort. By offering prayers, the mind gets one-pointed. A patience-giving current of thoughts is generated which makes a man alert and active. He develops habits of patience, contentment and forbearance, and acquires courage and strength with which to face difficulties. These are the fruits of prayer.

The highest form of prayer does not consist in the actual act of praying, but in awakening in the Lord. When this state is reached, diseases disappear, sins are destroyed, and death becomes non-existent. True prayer consists in increasing love in the inner self for the Master, and merging in Him. When we are in communion with Him, then by coming in contact with the Lord the inner powers of our soul are awakened.

Prayer And Effort

Should effort be given up when praying? It should be remembered that until man becomes a conscious coworker with and under His will, he should not give up effort. It is not the purpose of prayer or grace that you should make no effort, except to go on praying. This can be made clear by an

illustration. A boy is late for school. What would
you think of him if he were to sit down and pray,
"O Lord! let me not be late." It would be proper
for the boy that, while praying, he should also rely
on his own effort and should walk quickly in order
to reduce the delay.

While making an effort, also extend the hands
in prayer. This is the chief cause of success.
A sincere desire for anything and a sincere effort for
it is true prayer. This is praying in the right way.
All too often we pray with our lips and act otherwise.
Such a prayer is not granted. When a man makes a
sincere effort for something from his heart, that prayer
issues from the very pores of his cells, even though he
may not utter a syllable. Whenever necessity arises
or a calamity comes, then make an effort with firmness
and confidence and pray to the Lord to remove the
defects due to imperfections and weakness in you.
Do not lose courage in the face of calamity. Only he
loses courage who has no refuge. The Lord and His
human form, the Master, is your everlasting refuge.
If in spite of effort you fail, take it to be His Will.
If one loses while trying, take it to be His Will.

Place Of Worship

It is not necessary to offer prayer in a religious
place. What is necessary is an inner urge only.
Sufficient solitude is necessary so that there may be
no obstruction or interference. It may be in the home
or outside of it. Any place where solitude can be had
is suitable. You can use your bedroom for the
purpose. There may be religious books or pictures

there to remind you of holy men whom you revere. If there is no room available, a particular portion of a room may be used. If this is not available, then any place such as a temple, satsang hall, mosque or church can be used. If this is not available, pray while walking alone, whether on the plains or in the hills, in a forest or on the bank of a stream. Concentrate in the forehead, on the Lord or the Master, and place your inner feelings before Him. These places have some influence on prayers, but in reality no particular place or temple is required. All this world is the temple of the Lord.

When you pray, enter the closet of the body and shut the outer doors. Do not let the attention wander outside. Open your heart to the Lord within. He will listen to the prayer made in this secret spot. Christ said,

> "But when thou shalt pray, enter into thy chamber, and having shut the door, pray to thy Father in secret, and thy Father who seeth in secret will repay thee."

Three Methods Of Prayer

Prayer is performed in three ways — with the tongue, with the mind, with the soul. The first is audible, in which we say prayers with our tongue. Ordinary people repeat certain prescribed passages from religious scriptures or recite prayers composed by some Saint. Some think that these are not very beneficial, since they represent the feelings of the Saints, while true prayer is an inner cry from the individual's own heart. Unless our prayer represents the inmost feelings of our heart, we do not derive benefit from it. Reciting other people's prayers is like wearing the clothes of others, which do not fit us. The prayers of Saints and holy men serve us as a model in as much as similar feelings may arise in our own minds, and in this way the reciting of such prayers may help us.

In praying before the public we exaggerate our feelings. If we pray for a thing without desiring it in our heart or hearts, that is, if our head and heart do not wish earnestly for a thing, our prayer is nothing but a public and futile repetition of words. But if our prayers are sincere, and we wish for a thing from our heart, then the Lord, on hearing our prayers, grants it. Can the recital of prayers in public, which have no relation to the feelings of the heart, bear any fruit? Can the words we utter reach that omnipotent Lord more rapidly than our inner feelings? No, never. Audible prayers become mere formalities. They do not arouse our feelings, nor do we become absorbed in them. The prayers that spring from the heart of someone else cannot by repetition achieve their object unless they come from our hearts also. These cannot be beneficial and cannot change our lives for good. The arrow which is shot without the bow being drawn to the breast cannot hit the target. Similarly, words which are not spoken from the heart do not reach the Lord. He knows our real needs even before we speak.

The Vedas, the holy Quran and other religious scriptures all insist on congregational prayers for the good of all. Can such prayers be of any benefit? Yes, certainly. If a number of persons offer prayers for the common good in humility and with sincere hearts, they get the grace of the Lord and the prayers are never in vain. To wish for the common good is to live within the Will of the Lord. Many benefits come from it. It is a good way of keeping nations and societies awakened.

Does praying aloud affect us? Yes. It makes us serious for a time and elevates the thoughts. But if the matter is considered deeply, we will realize that when we do not know the Reality, praying loudly holds us back from preparing the spiritual ground, and the thought of gaining praise from others sometimes enters our mind. There is danger of our becoming impostors by praying aloud. Such prayers, which contain no truth and do not come from the heart, are simply meant to please others. Physical sensations produce in us mental or emotional happiness. and joy. If we were to make some spiritual progress, then we might gain some higher experience from such emotional happiness. But until we are acquainted with the secret of the soul, we cannot gain it. Human passions cannot influence the Lord. It is not necessary to cry loudly to enable our prayers to reach Him. He is not far off. His unseen ears are everywhere. He knows the secrets of every heart and mind, and He can fulfill every desire. Spiritual wealth cannot be gained by praying aloud.

There should be no egotism or showiness. There is no need to stand on high platforms and to cry loudly. One should offer silent prayers with the tongue of the soul, and should pray that he may always act according to the Will of the Lord.

The second method of praying is mental, in which the tongue does not come into play. In this kind of prayer, concentration is necessary. Before doing so, one feels the presence of the Lord who pervades everywhere, and prays for His help and becomes absorbed in His contemplation. While so absorbed, pray. For this, concentration is necessary. The mind should be withdrawn from everything outside and should be focussed on the presence of the Lord or the Master. Then give vent to the feelings of your heart with devotion and gratitude; confess your weaknesses and ask for help. Open your heart to the Lord. For doing this successfully, patience and firm determination are necessary. It cannot be done in a hurry. It is like learning to play a violin or some other instrument, which requires patience and determined practice.

In inner praying, a seeker sometimes meets with difficulties due to receiving no apparent response to his prayers. He may then begin to feel that there is no truth behind it. Not feeling the presence of the Lord, the seeker feels as if he is praying in a void. Some seekers rely on the fact that though they do not see the Lord, He sees them. But this state does not last for long. On closing the eyes, we see a vast expanse of darkness and see nothing beyond it. We take this silence as a response to our prayers. The senses cannot function in this silence, and the seeker feels in this state of unconsciousness that he has lost the way. He wishes to walk further on the strength of faith, but he falls again and again. It is a very delicate stage and requires the guidance of a Master. In addition, a certain amount of dryness enters our mind. It does not want to pray. If it is forcibly made to pray, the desire to do so fades away. A seeker has to spend a long time in this stage of dryness and darkness, and many a time his efforts proved fruitless and he does not find the abode of the Lord. These illusions of Maya and Kal mislead a seeker. The method of removing them is to be steady in contemplating on the inner image of the Master and in trying to achieve one-pointedness.

Until the mind is stilled at some center, both the seekers and the followers of the inner path weep at the antics of the mind. When we withdraw our thoughts from the external world and try to focus them on a center in the invisible world, our pent-up thoughts and fears due to our sins in the past come to the surface of themselves. They should either be eliminated by calm and cool reasoning or removed by praying. The best way to remove these difficulties is to conjure up the Master inside ourselves and to lose ourselves in contemplation of him. It is this kind of constant contemplation which opens the way to the Lord and makes us fit for His mercy.

Slowly and slowly, with remembrance of the Lord and contemplation of the Guru, the mind becomes still and success is achieved. When a seeker makes a little progress by means of audible and mental prayers, he should wait for a while for His mercy and Grace. When this practice is perfected, he will perceive after praying the flow of peace and bliss in his soul and the mind will become joyful. After tasting this joy, the mind does not wander. These are signs of the descent of the mercy of the Lord and the Master.

One's prayers should come from the heart. Our heart, head and tongue should agree. Pray in such a manner that your inner feelings are aroused, every pore begins to weep, and all the veins become like the strings of a violin. The feeling of love should pour forth and you should become absorbed in your prayer. Your discrimination should awaken. Consider the Lord to be present and a witness. Present your inner feelings to Him. There should be nothing whatever between you and the Lord. Ask for His help in all humility.

He accepts whatever men say when they pray, even if it is poorly expressed, when it comes from the heart. The feelings of the heart are the real thing; the words merely express them. He wants real longing from the heart. Generate yearning within yourself. Kindle the fire of love which burns away all thoughts and languages.

Ordinary people consider this to be all. A seeker, however, should be thankful and should all the more desire for union with the Lord through prayer with the soul. In such a union a seeker rises above the bondage of the body and reaches the presence of the Lord and the Master, from whom all blessings originate. He then sees in operation the invisible hands which cannot be described. The seeker feels that he is no longer in his body and that he has entered a new kingdom. He floats in spiritual regions and becomes a dweller in them in this very life. He sees the Lord face to face, and enjoys this supreme happiness. Because of the power of the Lord's attraction, the seeker's heart, mind and soul become dyed in the color of the Lord. This can be called mystical prayer. It has been described by many Saints who have experienced it. This kind of prayer can be found even today. But this kind of prayer can be achieved only through the special mercy and grace of the Lord. The effort of the seeker does not count. Such an experience, even for a moment, leads to faith in the Lord and the Master, and produces confidence in spiritual progress and experience. All sins, selfishness and fears vanish. We progress and become the recipients of the inner grace of the Saints.

While praying, keep yourself in the presence of the Lord and give up all thoughts about the body. If you think on the one hand of the Lord and on the other of the body, your thoughts will be divided. You should go into His presence with the coverings of the mind and body removed. You alone, in your humility, should be there. Then only you and your Lord will be there. To remain always with the Lord is to carry out His orders. A wonderful love for the Lord will then awaken in you.

The relationship between ourselves and the Lord is that of a particle and the whole. When we are fully united with Him, then no thought of the body will remain and egotism will disappear. The conscious current of the Lord will in this way give us a new life, and all calamities and afflictions will be removed. Under these conditions, when we give up bodily actions in remembrance of God, a new life-giving current of the Lord enters us, and our material and spiritual deficiencies are removed.

An essential condition for praying is that there should be a being to whom prayers are offered. One should have full faith in the Lord or in His form, the Master, in whom He is manifested. When there is no faith or belief in His power, there can be no true prayer. We have read about the Lord in books or heard about Him from the Saints. He is manifested in the Saints. He who has seen a Saint has seen the Lord.

"He that hath seen me hath seen the Father." B

We have our Master to pray to, and a disciple should ask him for his aid at every step. There should be full faith in his powers, and full love, confidence and humility. The prayer should be pure in thoughts and offered in humility, free from selfishness, filled with love and full of confidence. There should be no doubt or disbelief. Such a prayer made in humility does not go in vain. With a humble mind, surrender all to his merciful grace.

When you pray, pray to the Lord or to his manifested form, the Master, who can give you all.

Whatsoever you shall ask the Father in my name, He will give it to you." B

There can be no doubt that just like asking for help in worldly affairs from one who is powerful, the asking for aid from the Power who is the fountain of all powers and wealth, is a true and effective prayer. But to sigh while praying, considering Him to be separate from us, is ignorance. He is a pure and infinite Being, but in His mercy He dwells within and illumines our soul. Therefore to pray for help to that Power which is seated in our soul is the key to success. To pray to Him as a Being apart from us is not true prayer, for we are then praying to a Being whose existence we doubt, and there is still a feeling of egotism or separateness. Some doubt still persists as to whether or not we will receive His grace, and there is not complete faith and confidence.

Those who think that the Lord is on high and directs the affairs of the world from there seldom receive a response to their prayers. The Lord is with you and within you and not far away from you. The Lord is inside you. He is none other than the spirit of your soul. Pray to Him and praise Him inside, and ask for His help.

"Praise the One and repeat His Name;
Remember the One, and keep the One in mind.
Sing never-ending praises of the One,
With body and mind meditate on the Lord;
He is One and One alone.
The only Lord pervades everywhere
The One has become many;
By praying to the One sin departs;
The One Lord pervades the body and the mind;
By the Master's grace Nanak knows that One."   A

When you go to the door of the Lord or the Master, go as a beggar. There is no one else before whom one should bow. He is the only one who can listen to the prayer of one who is caught in the whirlpool of Maya. He is the only one who can put healing ointment on the heart that is bleeding from attachment and greed. It is only He who can revive lost hopes. All these qualities exist only in the Lord, or in His other form, the Master. He heals bleeding hearts by sending them the current of His inner consciousness.

To ask of the Guru is to ask of the Lord. He is in every way powerful. If you wish to pray to Him who is able to give life or take it away, call upon Him who is the living God and have confidence and faith in Him. Do not turn to any earthly refuge. Turn your inner attention to Him. No thought of receiving help from anyone else should ever enter the mind. The atten-

tion should be directed to Him alone. Your cries for
help will reach Him.   Even if a disciple is on one side
of the ocean and the Master on the other, the disciple
should turn his attention to the Master. The Master
will then make all his efforts successful. The Master
is the king of kings. Everything is within His
power.

Ask for the Lord Himself of the Lord. To ask
for anything else is to ask for trouble on one's head.
O Lord! Give us Your Name, so that we may gain
peace and our hunger may be removed.

We, due to our short-sightedness, ask the Lord
and the Master for various boons, and these may often
increase our sufferings. Instead of asking for boons
from the Bountiful Lord, ask for Himself. Then
how can there be any lack of anything? To ask for
boons is to display a feeling of inferiority and a lack of
respect.

We should pray to the Lord and the Master to
give us the opportunity to see them, to seek refuge
with them, to get from them the Name, to have their
help in escaping from the snares of the sense pleasures,
and to aid us in crossing the ocean of the world.
They are all-powerful and can grant us anything they
wish.

In addition, the devotee should ask them that he
may live as they wish him to. We are without virtues,
unwise, uninformed and ignorant. We do not know
what to do. O Lord! have mercy, make us sing Your
praises, so that we may live according to Your will.

"Virtueless, unwise, uninformed ignorant are we, and we know
not what to do. Have mercy on Nanak, so that he may
sing Your praises."   A

In the end, after attaining joy in surrendering to the Lord's Will, the seeker gives up praying. He knows that the Lord knows all. He remains happy in the state ordained by the Lord; he loves all actions of the Lord.

In this state the devotee feels that the Lord is always with him. He hands over all his sufferings and worries to Him, and is unmoved by either pain or pleasure. He is convinced that the Lord is thousands of times more intelligent, wise, strong and merciful than himself, and that He looks after His devotee and is his greatest well-wisher. He hands over his worries and his intellect to Him, and remains content with His Will. His intellect becomes keen, and his prayers become perfect. He surrenders everything to the Lord and says, "O Lord! You are the refuge of all living beings. You came here for the sake of all. Whatever You will is good for me. This is my only prayer."

Examples Of Prayer

If you crave forgiveness for your sins, you should first forgive others and then pray. Christ says:

> "When ye stand praying, forgive, if ye have ought against any; that your Father also which is in heaven may forgive you your trespasses." B

I commit faults every moment. I cannot get free of this world because of my actions. You are the forgiver. Forgive me, and take me across this ocean. I make innumerable mistakes and am a great sinner. O Lord! please forgive me. We have committed as many sins as there are drops of water in the ocean.

We are stones, and will be drowned. Have mercy and compassion, and save us from drowning.

Jesus Christ prayed,

"Our Father which art in heaven, hallowed be Thy name. Thy kingdom come. Thy will be done on earth as it is in heaven. Give us this day our daily bread. And forgive us our debts, as we forgive our debtors. And lead us not into temptation, but deliver us from evil; for Thine is the kingdom, the power and the glory for ever and ever."

I pray earnestly, O Beloved, I am ready to sacrifice my all for union with you even for a moment. Alas! How should I plead, that I may make You hear? I am tormented with restlessness because of my hunger and thirst to see You. The Lord can be realized by the Word of the Master. O Lord, I beg of You to enable me to realize the truth.

"Unite me with Yourself; I am lying at Your door;
O Savior, save me, for I am tired of wanderings;
O Lord, redeem me, for You always help Your devotees;
No one can help me except Yourself;
Take my hand, and lead me across the ocean of the universe." A

O Thou eternal Great One! You are the fault-less sustainer. I pray to You. Man lives in igno-rance and does not remember the Lord, and in this way, wastes his life. Your creature always forgets. You, however, keep the honor of Your innate nature. O Helper of the worthless! How can I recite Your virtues? What wisdom can an ignorant slave possess? This life and body are Your gifts. As we have taken refuge with You, You have saved us from the great fire of this world by taking us out of it. We rely and lean in confidence on You, and have given up all other hopes. You are unknowable and limitless and unutterable. You cannot be described in words. O Lord! I have taken refuge with you, and You can protect me. I surrender my life and body to You. This is all Your kindness; otherwise who would know me? Whatever I have to say, I say to you. To whom else can I pray? O Lord! You will not find anyone more helpless than I, and none is more merciful than Yourself. We profess to be Yours, but are so in name only. Make us perfect.

A Prayer From Sar Bachan

O Master, open the door of the heart.
The mind has tried and tried and failed; not once has it succeeded.
You are all-powrful and lacking nothing; why do You delay?
I am tossed between pain and pleasure; why have I not yet had a chance?
Have mercy, O bountiful One! Take my mind and attention to the skies.
The mind asks for false comforts, and does not know the reality.
It hankers after worldly pleasures, and does not taste the nectar of the Sound.
What should I tell the mind, and how should I persuade it?
It does not take to heart the words of the Master.
The mind is strangely made; it does not love and care for the Shabd.
How can it escape the cycle of eighty-four? It does not repeat the Name of the Master.
I will be buffetted in this world, and will be dragged headlong to the regions of death.
I have borne these sufferings for a long time. The mind does not heed and has forgotten.
You are the moving spirit in all hearts, O Master, why do You not call this sufferer to You?
Except for You I have no other; You alone can take me to the eternal abode.

Have mercy, O Radha Soami, and take me to the other shore.
I may now commit an unwise action,
I am a stranger in a strange land.
Set me on the right path in this life,
I bow at Your feet every day.
I repeat and feel remorse in my mind,
How am I to join my Lord?
I live on earth while my Lord is in the skies,
Without my Beloved I remain depressed.
O Master, hear my prayer,
Kal has entangled me in his meshes.
I am helpless and wretched and cry to You,
O Master, hear my prayer.
You are merciful and provide for everyone.
I am the only unfortunate one who is full of sufferings.
What can I say about my pains?
It is as if I were peirced by the point of an arrow.
You, O Master, have now given me hope,
That I may fly in the sky with the wings of love.
By Your mercy I have met my Lord,
All pain is gone and my heart is free of troubles.
O Master, hear my prayer,
I pray again and again.
Remove my evil thoughts.
Give me shelter at Your feet.
Take me across the ocean of this universe,
My boat is in the middle of the stream.
There is no support but You.
Make me Your own and support me.
I am cunning and a hypocrite but Yours.
You are the limitless bountiful Lord.
I am helpless and extremely wretched.
Pray, free me whenever You please.
I kneel and beg before You,
I surrender my mind and body and soul to You,
And have now found a great support.
I am lowly, uninformed and unskilled,
You have placed the secret of the Sound in the heart.

The immoral mind did not find it tasteful,
I have been deluded by pleasure and pain,
I hanker after worldly honor.
How can I reverse the actions of the mind
Without help given by You, my Master?
O Radha Soami, draw up the mind,
I make this earnest plea to You.

CHAPTER 7

SATSANG

The basic meaning of Satsang is True Companionship. 'Sat' means truth, and 'Sang' means company. Sat (truth) is another name for God. It abides in the Saints and their gatherings, so also God resides where His devotees live. There rise the waves of love and devotion. There bliss and grace confer peace upon all.

Satsang may be of three kinds:

1. Outer Satsang conducted by, or with the presence of, a Saint.
2. Outer Satsang conducted with only the spiritual presence of a Saint.
3. Inner Satsang, by means of which the soul unites with the Lord and merges in Him.

For those who have the great good fortune to attend the first kind of Satsang, the fresh air of His invigorating Spirituality will bestow upon you the same spiritual health and freshness, and in a short time you will become good yourself. Then the qualities of virtue will manifest themselves within you. Listening to the Satsang with your mind and heart, and relishing it, you will easily gain control over your senses, and your soul will become steady in the company of Saints and Sadhus.

Where a Satguru lives, the entire environment is spiritualized by his body, mind, intellect and the mode of his life. His very presence greatly influences the people around him. When a Satguru speaks or makes a movement of the hands or confers a gracious look, a special current of attention emanates from him and creates a powerful influence on the minds of the audience. This is subject to the condition that those in the audience are not entirely devoid of loving devotion or, like pieces of flint, are not incapable of understanding or accepting it. Such a current of attention helps the soul to ascend, and the person listening to such spiritual discourses greatly expands his esoteric knowledge.

Together with the thought-currents, the waves of spirituality that emanate from the Master during His discourse help to make the subject matter clear, so that everyone can comprehend it thoroughly. In this way the dirt of evil thoughts gets washed away, the gloom of ignorance vanishes, and in its place emerges the light of knowledge.

Satsang is a unique boon which the Master distributes free to both the learned and the ignorant. His over-powering grandeur, His refulgence and magnetic force attract each person according to his merit, with the result that they become oblivious of the world and its objects and completely lose track of time and the manner of its passage.

Again Bhai Gur Das says:

"A disciple becomes a Saint in the company of Saints, just as water thrown into a river loses its identity and becomes the same as the water of the river. A river flows into the ocean and becomes the fathomless ocean itself. Similarly, the ocean-like company of a Saint makes His disciples become like Him. Just as the sweet fragrance of flowers gives serenity and peace to the mind, similarly the sight or Darshan of a Saint brings peace and calmness. Just as the Shabd is the bestower of all gifts, similarly the company of the virtuous, transforms even a man of utter ignorance into one of high spiritual consciousness".

For those who do not live where it is possible to have the physical presence of their Guru, it is possible to have Satsang of the second kind.

Christ also said: "For where two or three are gathered together in my name, there am I in the midst of them." B

Where two or more satsangis are gathered to discuss Sant Mat, the Satguru is there also. For the meeting to be Satsang, with the benefits of Satsang, it must be devoted to the subject of Sant Mat. The gathering of wordly-minded people is not termed Satsang.

Satsang needs no formality since form may detract from the spiritual purpose. There is no need for a church or temple or special place to meet since the true temple or place of worship is internal, not external.

Satsang must meet two needs, first create an atmosphere of love and devotion to Master, second instruct both seekers and initiates in the science of Sant Mat. There may be discussion or a discourse based on the words of a Master, but it is not Satsang unless those who lead the discussion or give the discourse think of themselves only as a channel for Master's teaching and Master's love. Master is the only leader.

Those who attend Satsang, automatically listen, ponder over, and visualize the form of the Satguru. They do not need to read any outside books, because Satsang deals with them in a practical way. It is not the books alone that are a medium for attaining knowledge. Knowledge can be gained by listening to Satsang.

Look at a blind man. By listening alone he has become learned. By intently listening we can imbibe new knowledge. When a particular subject is discussed in Satsang all the listeners think of the same subject simultaneously, with the result that the entire environment is saturated with their thought currents. The entire audience benefits thereby, and the subject leaves an indelible impression on the minds of those present.

The mind is a wonderful thing. It takes on the color of the company it keeps. It imbibes the attributes of what it dwells upon. If it keeps the company of wordly people, it also becomes wordly. On the other hand, if it lives among spiritual people it acquires spiritual tendencies. Therefore, if one is keen to gather spiritual tendencies and knowledge, he must keep the company of those who are spiritually advanced and must keep his mind fixed on them.

The third kind of Satsang may be explained thus: outer Satsang is an effort to kindle a fire, while the inner Satsang is like sitting near the fire and escaping from the cold while also accomplishing many other tasks. One who associates with a Saint has his soul awakened by the spiritual currents emanating from Him. But the inner Satsang is supremely superior. Although even a glimpse of a Saint is productive of great benefit, it is also essential for the disciples to render physical service, to obey implicitly the Saint's instructions, and to carry out fully the spiritual discipline taught by Him.

Satsang is a powerful spiritual school or college, where practical lessons are imparted in Spirituality and Love. Satsang is a wonderful workshop where the tangles of the mind are set straight, and one is so chiseled that he can realize himself and God.

The following advantages accrue from Satsang:

1. By listening to God's Name and His attributes, one gains happiness and longs for union with Him.

2. By thinking of the Lord and reciting His Name, one begins to lose worldly attachments, gives up desires and sense pleasures, and earnestly longs for meeting the Lord.

3. Our mind is rid of lust and anger, and we become fearless.

4. Our mind is filled with the Love of the Lord and His creation. In the company of the Saints, none remains alien to us, none is our enemy. We become one with the universe.

5. By constant devotion and practice we become worthy of union with the Lord, and begin to perceive His presence everywhere—both within and without.

6. An ocean of happiness, bliss and love wells up in our hearts.

There is no more complete and useful a machine for transforming evil thoughts into noble ones than Satsang. In the company of virtuous, one imbibes virtue and becomes free of all blemishes and sins. Spiritually evolved souls always fill the environment in which they live with currents of purity. Even the worst of sinners cannot escape their influence but turn noble; and in the company of Saints, one is dyed in the hue of the Lord.

CHAPTER 8

SERVICE

It is written in Scriptures that we should serve Him who has created the entire world and who has given life to us, because through His service alone can we derive true benefit and gain honor in the Court of the Lord. Therefore, we should serve only the one Lord who has no equal, who provides us with food and shelter, who gives us father and mother, family and children, who is present in water, on land and everywhere, and who grants livelihood to all. We should sacrifice everything in favor of His service, because by serving Him we shall be free from the cycle of births and deaths.

Except for the Lord, all pilgrimages, prayers, recitals, penances, and other types of worship are meaningless. If you serve other beings, you serve with some ulterior motive, but real service to God is not for material or other gains. Therefore, we should serve God out of sheer love for and devotion to Him. Otherwise, it is just like drinking a cup of poison while descarding the cup filled with Ambrosia, and putting ourselves to all kinds of difficulties and privations. All other kinds of service lead nowhere and are without any profit or purpose.

Man should, therefore, search for a Perfect Master who is able to give him the gift of Initiation, the greatest of all gifts, because by this gift we are freed from the shackles of coming and going.

And we should have, as our aim of service, only the love of God and His Saints, who are God Incarnate.

The house that is devoid of such service is like a cemetery. But the service of the Saints is possible only through the abundant Grace of the Lord. And those who perform this service without ego, recieve all the blessings of the Lord as well as of the Master, who is the embodiment of the Lord.

By serving the Master we serve our Lord. The scriptures go so far as to say that if you wish to serve your Lord, you should worship your Master, because by doing so you worship the Lord.

Without service to the Master, it is not possible to give devotion to the Lord. Nor can the mind reap the fruits of concentration. Man becomes eligible to get a human body in his next birth by service and devotion to the Master. Those who serve the Master are invariably sustained by Him at the time of their death, while those who do not serve the Master, waste their life in vain.

Everybody serves a Master in his own way. But what kind of service is gainful and deserving of merit? Guru Ram Das says:

"Only such service as is acceptable and pleasing to the Master is rewarding. And if He is pleased, all our evil karmas are obliterated. Indeed, by serving the Master we achieve God-Realization. But if a person serves the Master for his own personal gain, that service goes unrewarded".

How do we know that our service to the Master has been rewarded? Any service which helps us in listening to the Sound Current within is a real and rewarding service.

Holy Scriptures enumerate various advantages which accrue from service to the Master:

1. Peace and bliss are achieved.
2. The mind is steeped in the dye of Nam and becomes conscious of His immanence.
3. Liberation from Kal and his punishment.
4. Various bad karmas and their effects are erased.
5. All desires are fulfilled.
6. In the end, one attains freedom from birth and death.

Service has many rewards, but the unique one is that a person imbibes the qualities of the person whom he serves.

We should worship the Master and thereby throw all responsibility for our Salvation on His shoulders. Truly speaking, the Master is God-Incarnate, and by worshiping the Master, we worship the Lord.

Who Can Serve The Master And The Lord?

Only such a one is in a position to serve the Master as has abundant Grace of the Lord, because this service is imprinted on the individual's forehead and was preordained as the result of his previous life's actions or karmas.

He is fortunate indeed who devotes himself to the service of his Master, because the Lord Himself is manifest in Him. And only that person can serve the Master whom the Lord ordains.

Those who have crooked natures, who are fraudulent or have bad or ulterior motives are unworthy or unfit to serve the Master.

A disciple should serve his Master without arrogance and without any idea of reward, and always with the aim of pleasing the Master. By this method his mind will always be contemplating the Master. And if you contemplate on a person intensely, you will one day imbibe the qualities of that person.

A person who destroys his ego, implicitly obeys his Master and worships the Lord with focused attention, is always dear to Him.

Actually a true desciple is one who serves his Master and works according to the wishes of his Master. And it is in him that Shabd becomes manifest. All the difficulties of such a person are automatically resolved and his desires are fulfilled. However, it is very difficult to attain such a state because it can only come with the unbounded Grace of the Master.

Method Of Service To The Master

One should serve the Master by withdrawing oneself completely from the ego, and thus attaining humility. Such service alone is pure, and only he can perform it who himself is pure in heart and mind. Guru Arjun says:

> "We should worship God day and night. In this there should be no lethargy or negligence. And the way to worship the Lord is through worship of the Master with love and devotion, having abjured pride and obduracy".

The service should be incessant and not spasmodic. One cannot calculate its worth in terms of money; and if thus calculated or done with any ulterior motive, it is worthless and merits no reward.

Service should be performed with devotion and reverence. When there is love in the heart and reverence in the eyes, then God-Realization becomes easy to achieve.

According to the teachings of the Saints, there are four kinds of service:

1. Physical or manual service—that rendered with the body.
2. Service with wealth.
3. Service rendered by mind.
4. Service rendered by soul.

Physical Service

What type of service should be performed? Guru Amar Das has said that one should render service in the same manner as does an elephant which obeys the directions of the goad of his mahout. In other words, we should consider the command of the Guru as a goad on our head. We should place our forehead at the feet of the Master and render service to Him with love and devotion, and without hesitation or murmur. Guru Ram Das says:

"This is my only prayer to Thee, O Lord: That Thy servants (Saints) may be the recipients of my service. I should be happy even to offer my mind and body at the altar of the Saints. In other words, I should rejoice to get rid of pride and arrogance. Whatever I receive from the Saints, I regard as nectar. O Lord, I am ever prepared to sacrifice myself to my Master and to fall at His Feet, for I am poor and helpless and am constantly pining for Thy Darshan, that only the help and grace of a Master can bestow."

A true desciple is ever eager to have the Darshan of his Master and adopts all possible means to be in

His presence. Even if it is bitter cold and snowing heavily, he is not deterred; for the pull of his Guru (for His Darshan) is so strong that he will go just to have a glimpse of Him. He constantly longs to meet Him and to have His Darshan day and night. Guru Arjan says:

> "Whatever service is possible for you to do with your hands for the Master, you should do it, because it is the Master who gives us the protection of His Hands and saves us from the fire of transmigration. You should work for Him, because through Him you will know the Lord. You should ceaselessly serve the Master, because it is by His Grace alone that all foes are transformed into friends."

We are elated by such types of service as are described above. It is a unique joy that cannot be achieved by power and pelf. It is therefore necessary that we should not hanker after worldly pleasures.

Service By Means Of Wealth And Mind

Service to the Master will be rewarded only if it is performed with one-pointed attention, because then we achieve concentration of mind. By serving the Master, our heart attains unison with His Heart. Thus Nam will become manifest in us and we shall be able to meet the Lord without much further effort. All our desires will be fulfilled because we shall have no desires left.

Who can serve a Master? In other words, who can attain God-Realization? Only such persons can do so who sacrifice their mind and their wealth for the service of their Master.

"You should therefore serve such a person who perceives the great devotion and the inner longing of your heart. Such a one is none other than a True Master. You should make an offering of your mind at the altar of your Guru, and worship Him because He is the incarnation of that Deathless One".   1

He achieves everything who lives near the Master (is ever conscious of His Presence within), who obeys Him with selfless devotion and without pride, who subdues his mind's reasoning and surrenders himself to his Master.

Service By Soul

This service consists in withdrawing one's soul current from every pore of the body, and connecting it with Shabd. By doing this, all practices (devotion, repetition, penances, austerities, etc.) are automatically accomplished and the ego is destroyed. The aim of all such practices is realized when one surrenders himself to the True Master, who is really God Incarnate. And one can truly surrender only through His Grace and by means of the spiritual practice, which consists in listening to the Inner Shabd.

We are by now aware of various types of service by the soul. But the soul can render service only through the Grace of God. In order to win His Grace, we should pray to the Saints who are God Incarnate. Thus, it is with the Grace of the Master that the soul is able to render service.

The ability to merge oneself with the Shabd is beyond the comprehension of the intellect. It is therefore only through the Grace of a Master that the soul can render service. And the Master's Grace is invoked when, by means of devotion, the disciple completely renounces his ego.

How can we achieve this? It is possible only when the soul, by means of repetition of the holy Names given by the Master, goes within by withdrawing itself from the nine outlets of the body, pierces through a star, the sun and the moon, and beholds the Radiant Form of the Master. It then merges in the Shabd and gradually rises by stages till it reaches its final Goal. That is the true service by soul.

Physical and monetary service is easy to perform, and hundreds of people can afford to do so. Mental service is difficult to perform, and there are very few people who are capable of performing it. But service by the soul is much more difficult to perform and rare to achieve.

All these types of service can actually be performed only if carried out in accordance with the instructions of a Master. The mind is rendered pure by service and then becomes worthy of devotion to Him. Everybody is busy in service of the world. We serve the world, our family, our community and our country. All this is good so far as it goes and should be performed as a duty, but it cannot help in attaining Salvation. On the other hand, if we are attached to these ties, they become the cause of our coming back to this earth again and again.

The highest service is that of the Guru, and it is also the purest. The Guru is free from all ties and attachments. He is an ocean full of the Surging Waves of Love. By serving Him we become free from ties and attachments to the ephemeral world. Then intense love of God is awakened in us.

One who loves the Lord also loves His creation. Thus the Fatherhood of God and the Brotherhood of man are realized, and in this manner love is developed in us not only for God but also for His creation.

CHAPTER 9

DEVOTION

Devotion is an age-old and innate quality of dedication, religious fervor and ardent attachment in man. It is a quality by which the soul rises upwards and attains communion with God. Thus God is attracted downwards towards His devotee and comes and dwells within him.

Devotion to the Lord is a strong magnetic power by which the attention is removed from wordly objects and becomes fully concentrated in the Lord. There is thus no interference by one's intellect or power of reasoning. Devotion is the act of withdrawing our attachment from all directions and fixing it only in the Lord. Shandlya Rishi says:

> "Devotion consists in withdrawing one's love, ideas and thoughts from worldly objects and in thinking of the Lord alone, and in keeping oneself wholly engrossed in this thought. It leads to lasting communion or contact with the Lord, by withdrawing one's attention from the objects of the world".

We have not seen God. How can we worship Him or offer our devotion to Him? Under these circumstances, whom should we worship? Who is the being in whom God has manifested, and who is able to create the right conditions for devotion and for helping us to increase our love for Him? Such a person is no other than a real Master. In him there is the spark of Truth. He is a living example of the beauty of Truth and Spirituality and is able to guide his disciples on the right path by drawing their minds in the right direction.

The best and the highest method of meeting God is to love the Master and to remain at His Feet. This is the first step of the ladder towards God-Realization. Devotion to the Master is to love Him. It is to live according to His orders and directions—physically as well as mentally. In other words, one should give away his heart to his Master.

It is essential that we give our heart to our Master, for, when we give away our heart, we automatically give our whole body and put our entire life in the hands of the Master. If our life and our body are not ours because they have been surrendered to the Master, then where are our religious beliefs? They too are all merged in the Master.

This body, mind and life—and even our religion, all bind us to this world. As soon as they are surrendered at the Feet of the Master, we become detached and shall not be born again. Then nothing remains in the way of the progress of the soul towards God-Realization, and our running about in this world is finished. This is only a small fraction of the benefits resulting from devotion to the Master. Actually, the advantages are so great and so numerous that they are beyond description.

Devotion consists in fixing the form of the Master in our heart. Then love is awakened in the heart of the disciple. So long as love is not of that type, the effort to create conditions for such a love should be continued. Once devotion of this high type is established in a human heart, the soul automatically starts rising upward and is able to catch hold of the Sound Current.

Those who try to listen to the Sound Current without having true devotion for their Master are ignorant, because one listens to the Sound Current only by the grace and mercy of a true Master. The magnetic power of his love and our devotion attract the soul towards higher regions.

Devotion is a spontaneous magnetic current which attracts one towards one's Beloved. Love consists in merging oneself onto one's Beloved. It is one-pointed attention and attachment to the Lord. In other words, it is the culmination of devotion.

This type of devotion is not material. It brooks no interference. It is a strong magnetic current which attracts the soul towards God and connects it with its Beloved. A tiny glimpse or idea of such a love is partially portrayed in some of the rare types of true love in this world, because the principle underlying wordly love and spiritual devotion is the same. The only difference is that wordly love is transitory and is subject to dissolution. It cannot give us the same high degree of happiness and eternal bliss as does spiritual love and devotion.

Physical sentiment or love always aims at the lover's own happiness. In other words, he makes the object of his love an instrument for his own comfort and enjoyment. On the other hand, devotion is a type of love which comes from the soul and includes currents of respect and veneration. In such a state of love, one tries to provide comfort and convenience for the object of his devotion. He is prepared to suffer all types of inconveniences, and is happy only when the object of his devotion is pleased and in comfort. For his Beloved he scrifices his body, his mind, his wealth,

his beauty, his intellect and even his life. All these
are surrendered at the feet of the Lord as the material
of worship. The devotee eliminates his ego completely.

> "This devotion is a path of action and not of intellect. There-
> fore, do not talk but practise devotion, for then you will achieve
> something."   4

> "Just as water cannot enter a stone, even if the stone is
> immersed in it for a long time, similarly, those who are
> without devotion are as impregnable as the stone."   A

The Principles Of Devotion

The first principle underlying devotion is that God
is the Creator of all and is omniscient. He is pure,
flawless and whole. He is omnipresent. Human
beings, the lower species of life, and in fact the entire
universe are a sign of His existence. We are all His
children. Hence there is a natural mutual affinity
between ourselves and all others. For this reason we
should respect our elders, be kind to those who are
younger, be friendly with our equals, and we should
also love our enemies.

The second principle is that this universe is His
creation, and everything is right according to His plan.
Each one, of course, looks at this world according to the
state or condition of his own mind.

The third principle is that one should be happy
in the Will of God, and should always remain contented and grateful for whatever happens to him. Whatever is being done is for our own good. This is beyond
any shadow of doubt. What we may consider as
trouble, has actually come in order to elevate the
condition of our mind. As is well known, gold becomes

purer and brighter when it is put into fire. Therefore, one should never complain.

The fourth principle is that one should consider it to be the greatest sin to hurt the feelings of others. To provide comfort and happiness to others, should be considered the highest obligation, because non-violence or non-hatred in thought, word and deed is the highest form of religious duty.

The fifth principle is that one should become a devotee by taking support from his Guru or Master, so that by being in contact with such a higher being one may also eventually attain the same stage.

Devotion to the Master is intense love for him. If we love anybody, we serve him. We are prepared to sacrifice everything for him. Love knows no burden and no compulsion. A devotee gives away everything for the sake of his Beloved—his body, wealth, mind and soul; in fact, everything is surrendered at the altar of the Master. To serve the Guru is to be devoted to him.

Why should we love the Master? It is done chiefly so that we may imbibe the nature and ideals of the Master. By loving the Master, his consciousness brings light within us and we forget everything about the mundane world.

The purpose of our love for him is that our love may be detached from all other objects and centered around Him. If a stream of water has nine outlets, and if it were allowed to flow through only one of the outlets—all the others being closed—its pressure would be so strong that the water would pour out in a flood, even if the opening is a tiny one. When our love is detached from everything else and is attached only to the Guru, then we are free from all the evil ties and attachments of the world, and we contact God.

We can offer devotion only to someone who is superior to ourselves, and we are able to imbibe his qualities only to the extent of our love for and faith in him. A Master is full of spiritual qualities and powers, to the extent of our love and devotion to him.

Types Of Devotees

There are five different types of devotees:

1. Imitators. People of this type have no real desire for devotion, but when they see genuine devotees they imitate them and thus come into the company of Saints. Naturally, it takes a very long time for them to reach the stage of true devotion.

2. The troubled. Those who become restless because of wordly troubles, as a result of which they seek the protection of the Lord. They believe God to be everything. This devotion is of two kinds. One is of a lower order, and the other is of a very high order. The devotion of a lower order is like that of a sheep dog for his master. Even if the shepherd is very poor or of a low status, to the dog he is the king of kings, and nothing can shake the dog from his devotion to his master. Such devotion is simple and ordinary. But gradually it becomes of a very high order, and in due course such a person desires nothing but love for God to be present in him. Such a devotee does not see the faults or weaknesses of the object of his devotion.

3. Seekers. A seeker is one who wants to know something about God. What he is able to learn,

creates belief and then faith in Him. Then the feeling of devotion is naturally aroused. In the beginning, however, he tries to thwart his own ideal by reasoning. But gradually all his doubts are removed and he subsequently loves not only God but His creation also.

4. Selfish persons. This is a person who has some wordly or religious purpose in mind, and indulges in devotion for an ulterior motive such as wealth, fame, power, and so forth. But when his selfish motives are fulfilled, he does not leave devotion. Naturally his love for and faith in the Lord, as a result of which he satisfied his ulterior motives, does not diminish. In the beginning he loves the devotees of the Lord and hates others, but gradually this is removed and in due course he loves all the creatures of the Lord.

5. Intellectual persons. This is a different type of devotion from the other four types, because such a person, having knowledge, knows about action and reaction, about religion and spiritual matters, and he then becomes a devotee of the Lord with faith and love. Such a man is ready to make progress, and as soon as he has an opportunity to meet a Master, he is immediately successful on the Path.

A devotee must have faith. Firm belief is a prerequisite. When that belief takes the form of faith it turns into devotion, and eventually it culminates in love. Wordly attractions or pleasures do not interest such a devotee. Only love for the Lord remains.

If a person who is under the influence of wordly desires, finds anything lacking in his devotion or in the satisfaction of his desires, he, in his ignorance, blames his Master.

"O Kabir! Devotion to a Guru brings unbounded happiness in the mind of a devotee, but if one does not cleanse his mind of low desires, he cannot enjoy its bliss. So long as devotion is not desireless, any service rendered is useless. O Kabir, how can one attain God, who is selfless and desireless? The people of the world follow the path of devotion because they see others doing so and for the statisfaction of their own ego. People of this kind blame the object of their devotion whenever, in their ignorance, they find any defects." 4

Action, knowledge and discipline are practices for attaining communion with God. But devotion is both a practice and the reward of such a practice. For the path of knowledge and for the path of Yoga, one must have certain qualifications to be able to make any progress. But devotion can be performed by the weak, the sick, or even by one who is of low intellect. It is easier than the path of knowledge, because one does not fall or waver once he has taken up this path.

"Knowledge is very difficult, but Devotion is easier. And a devotee is always happy, because in his path there are no obstacles".

Obstacles In The Path Of Devotion

We should avoid bad company. Wealth and lust are two difficult obstacles, which cause destruction, if one is engrossed in them. By intimate contact with bad company one becomes lost. Likewise, we should not associate with persons whose behavior turns our minds away from our object of devotion, because association with them will lead us astray, will make us arrogant, and will tempt us into many other vices.

Talking about wealth creates a feeling of greed. Listening to talk about the wealthy position of others or dwelling on the subject, also creates a desire to get rich and naturally leads one away from the path of devotion.

Atheists are those who do not believe in the existence of God. By associating with them, doubt or lack of faith is created in one's mind and this becomes the cause of one's downfall, for the foundation of devotion is pure and true faith.

By listening to talk about one's enemies a feeling of anger is produced in the mind, and that is also an obstacle in the path of devotion, because love and anger cannot blend.

Of all these obstacles, the worst one is pride in one's own wealth, power, offspring, knowledge, intellect caste, creed, family status, good character, beauty, and so forth.

The best ornament that adorns a devotee is humility. On the path of devotion one has to discard all useless ideas and attach his mind to the thought of his Beloved alone. Only then come the grace and mercy of the Lord.

Another obstacle in the way of devotion is hypocrisy. To pretend to be virtuous, religious, a devotee an ascetic or a truthful man—all these are forms of hypocrisy. Just as a clean cloth takes a dye easily, a pure heart imbibes the Light of God more easily. On this path one has to become as innocent as a child, because only the innocent enter the Kingdom of Heaven.

"Verily I say unto you, except ye become as little children, ye shall not enter into the kingdom of heaven." B

Requisites For Devotion

In order to be truly devoted it is necessary to believe in the omnipresence of the Lord. True˙ devotees are always welcome at the Gates of God. They give their devotion to God through the Saints, because it is only through them that they are able to see God everywhere and are thus devoted to Him.

Devotion is a natural attribute of the heart. But this quality can be developed only through the grace of a True Master who is himself dyed in devotion to the Lord.

The first condition is to have only one object in mind, for devotion should be offered to one only. The rays of the sun are able to burn a piece of cloth if they are concentrated through a magnifying glass, but if they are spread over a large area they are unable to do so. Similarly, if the currents of devotion coming from one's mind are concentrated on one's beloved, then the fruit of devotion increases.

So long as devotion is not one-pointed, the idea of duality will be in one's mind, and consequently, there will be no concentration. Therefore, for true devotion, one-pointedness is most essential.

The second essential condition is Satsang. We should stay in the company of persons who have devotion fully established in their minds. If we are in the company of Saints, we shall also be dyed in the hue of their devotion.

The third essential condition is a proper diet. Our food should be that which produces tranquility and pure thoughts. This includes rice, wheat, pulses, milk and curd. Food conditions our mind, so our ideas will have the same qualities as the type of food we eat. If we take food which produces restlessness and anger, like meat, fat, and so forth, the mind will be restless. If we take food which produces sluggishness, like fish, wine and other heavy and pungent things, we shall be prone to laziness.

The study of scriptures, maintaining a good character, the practice of simran, attending statsang, the habit of non-violence, kindness, purity of body and mind, faith, prayer, seeing God in everything—all these factors help us in our devotion to Him. One should forget himself and everything else while engrossed in love for the Lord.

Devotion To The Master Is The Path Of Surrender Of Self Or Ego

Because the path of devotion has many advantages, a seeker of Truth is always happy and eager to follow it. But so long as a human being is not able to purify his mind of all the low desires of the senses, he cannot enjoy its fruit. If a person puts on an outward show of humility, it is of no use. If service is rendered for any selfish motive, one can receive no real benefit.

"O Kabir! You should show your devotion to your Guru by discarding all the pleasures of the world, which are like poison eating into a man, because this human form cannot be obtained every time."

"True Devotion is extremely difficult. It is like walking on the edge of a sword, and is not the work of a coward. On this path one has to walk with his head on his palms, i.e. one must destroy his ego. In devotion one has to efface himself completely by merging in his Beloved Master. This is to be done daily, and those who cannot do this are busy in eating, drinking and enjoying life (worldly pleasures)." 4

One should never talk of I-ness. One should talk only of Him, so that in due course there will be nothing but Him. The highest aim of devotion is described in the following lines by Kabir:

"I have been saying 'Thou, Thou' and I have become Thou, myself having completely vanished. I am grateful for Thy Name, because by speaking it I see 'Thou' everywhere I look. To talk in terms of self is a very great evil. If you can be relieved of it, try to do so, because, O Kabir! a piece of cotton cannot escape from the clutches of fire if it is brought into contact with it. You are in me and I am in you. How can I see any difference? And, whenever I wish to discover a difference, leaving you aside, I meet with trouble. When you are, I am not, because I have experienced this from all aspects. Whenever I see you, nothing remains of me. The rope of 'mine and thine' is completely tied around the people of the world, but this humble Kabir is not bound by it because he has the support of the Lord."

Devotion is superior to outward observances, the path of knowledge and yogic practices. By knowledge and by religious observances one develops a touch of arrogance. In devotion one becomes submissive and develops the quality of humility. It is for this reason that knowledge and outward observances cannot attract the grace of God. Those who are humble, surrender themselves completely, and rely on the grace and mercy of the Lord. They attract His grace towards them. The love for the Lord is thus awakened in their hearts.

The path of devotion is achieved only through a Master and by those on whom God has bestowed His grace. Then only are their minds inclined towards devotion to Him. Even angels are yearning for devotion to Him, but it cannot be obtained without a Master. We cannot become devotees merely by reading holy scriptures.

The sight of a true devotee becomes so keen that he sees his Beloved in every place and in everything. His thoughts, his contemplation and the intoxication of his love occupy his mind at all times, and his longing becomes intense. He loses all contact with this world and the next, because he has given himself up completely to his Beloved. How can he look at anything else, and what interest can he have in the world?

Fruits Of Devotion

By devotion all the desires of a person are sublimated, resulting in contentment; and he is therefore freed from the cycle of birth and death. His mind has no desires, because all his desires are fulfilled in remembrance of God. He loves everybody, sin' he loves God and thinks all as His sons.

Hatred and enmity vanish by means of Devotion. One remains intoxicated in devotion to the Lord, because the elixir-like sweetness of devotion keeps him indifferent to all pleasures and pains of the world. On meeting the Lord, one gets everything and therefore does not run after the world. He remains happy at the Feet of his Lord.

"Nothing appears sweet to a devotee except the Name of the Lord. I have discovered that all tastes are insipid compared to His remembrance."

"You should sing the praises of One. You should do Simran with a one-pointed mind. How can I praise the qualities of that state in which mind and body are both joined in being devoted to one object of love!"　　　A

A devotee sees the Lord here, there and everywhere. He sacrifices himself to the Lord, and all his actions and religious observances are surrendered at His Feet. The goal of his life is confined to devotion to the Lord only. By such devotion all sins and bad actions are annihilated and the mind becomes pure.

By devotion to the Guru we are able to get rid of the worldly attachments. The gross attachments can be cut off only by means of Guru Bhakti (devotion to the Master), and the finer attachments of the mind will be sublimated by means of Nam Bhakti (devotion to Nam). Nam Bhakti can be obtained from no one but a Guru. So long as we do not meet a Guru, we cannot get Nam; and so long as we do not obtain Nam, the ties or cords binding our mind to the world cannot be cut. Christ describes Guru Bhakti in the following words by giving an example:

"Abide in Me, and I in you. As the branch cannot bear fruit of itself, except it abide in the vine; no more can ye, except ye abide in Me."

"I am the vine, ye are the branches; he that abideth in Me and I in him, the same bringeth forth much fruit; for without me, you can do nothing."

"As the Father hath loved Me, so have I loved you; continue ye in my love."　　　B

Like the Lord, a Master has a finite and an infinite aspect, and it is by devotion alone that we are able to see him in both of these aspects. We can see the form of the Master with the eyes of our devotion. Then we shall see that the light of His eyes is spread over the entire universe. A Master may be compared

to an ocean, and a disciple to a rivulet that flows into
and merges itself in the ocean. Thus the disciple
completely loses his identity in the ocean-like spirituality
of his Master.

> "As a lover and a beloved meet and are happy in the intoxi-
> cation of their union and feel that they are one and are at
> that time absolutely unaware of happenings in the world
> beyond their physical bodies, in the same manner, when a
> devotee communes with God, he feels much greater happi-
> ness and goes far above pain and desires, because this
> happiness is the consummation of all desires."

The currents of love emanating from the heart of
a devotee strike against the heart of the Master, draw
power from it, and return to the heart of the disciple
with a double force. In this manner the spiritual
powers of the Master enter the heart of the disciple
and it appears to him that the Master has become one
with him, and he himself feels one with the Master.
Once the disciple is in communion with the Guru, all
the gates of bliss and happiness are open to him.

The contemplation of a devotee is always fixed
on the form of the Guru, and he thinks about his
Master day and night. His attention is centered on
him uninterruptedly. When he dies the soul will go
where the Guru is. It cannot go anywhere else.

> "And he who at the last hour remembers me only and then
> departs—leaving the body—enters into Me. Of that there
> is no doubt."

> "Whatever form a man continually contemplates, the same
> he remembers at the hour of death, and to that very form he
> goes."

> "On me fix thy mind, to me bring thy devotion, to me offer
> thy sacrifice, to me make thy obeisance, then to me indeed

shalt thou come. Solemn is my promise to thee, for thou art dear to me." C

By devotion to the Lord, the entire attention of a devotee is dyed in the remembrance of the Lord—all actions are surrendered to Him. As a result the devotee is freed from the shackles of the world. Devotion frees one from fear, pleasure and pain, and brings instead bliss, peace of mind, satisfaction of the heart and contentment.

One who has been asleep for so many births is awakened, his cycle of birth and death is finished, he crosses the ocean of this world, and achieves Salvation. In other words, he is able to reach the highest region of Spirituality. The soul is merged in the Truth, goes into the Court of the Lord and is honored there.

CHAPTER 10

AWE, AFFECTION AND WORSHIP

Everyone, whether a human being or not, has some fear. No one is entirely free from it. It is only the Lord who is not afraid of any one, as He is the creator of all. He has no co-sharer or companion.

If one wishes to become fearless he should worship the Lord. As one thinks, so he becomes. The worship of the fearless One makes you fearless also. The Lord is immanent or dwelling within you.

"And I became Fearless, all fears vanished,
And the Protector, protected me, yea.
Such is thy munificence, O Lord,
That all my objects are achieved."   A

If there is fear of anything in this world, it means that one has not realized the Lord.

"When there is realization, there is no fear;
Where fear lives the Lord is not.
O Saints, remember this, for Kabir has said it after great deliberation."   4

There is no need to be afraid of anybody other than the Lord.

"Except the Lord there is none other to be afraid of."   A

Of whom can one stand in awe? Only of one about the existence of whom he is certain. There can be no fear of one whose existence is doubted. Therefore, whenever there is fear of the Lord, there is an ever present belief in His existence.

When man is afraid of the Lord, he constantly remembers Him and he cannot commit any sin. Awe and affection are thus born. It is for remembering the Lord that all worship is performed. If, while performing actions, there is no remembrance or awe of the Lord, then these actions and duties lead nowhere.

Gurus place great emphasis on awe for spiritual development. When there is awe, there is a strong desire to find means to remove it. It serves as a reminder every moment that one should strive to achieve one's object. For this reason, one makes quick progress.

Man's days are numbered. It is not known when they will end. Every day, every hour, every minute brings us nearer to that great change called death. On its arrival, the soul leaves the gross, astral and the ethereal bodies and goes to higher regions. This body is the field of actions. One can do actions in this body alone. In this body man can know himself and become indistinguishable from the Lord. The fear that the goal may not be realized before the end of this life, and that this human birth would therefore be in vain, compels a man to become spiritual. Not to know one's own self, and to spend day and night in sin is to commit suicide. He who is afraid of not knowing his own self and of passing his days in sin and thus committing suicide and not knowing the Lord, is in awe of Him and takes steps to free himself from this fear and to know the Lord through himself. In this way he escapes the fear of death. Those who are not in awe of the Lord always live in fear of death and rebirth.

"Those who are in awe of the Lord have no fear;
Those without it have much to fear.
O Nanak, this mystry is only solved when one enters
His presence."
A

We do not see the Lord, then why should we be
in awe of Him? He is manifest in the Master. On
meeting a Master, awe for the Lord comes to us of
itself. The Master knows everything in our heart.
When we see the Master, we know Him. He knows
us inside out and we become afraid of our own actions.
We try to rid ourselves of them and easily become
pure. On one side is our awe of Him; on the other
is His remembrance and upward pull. Awe forms in
the mind and is mingled with affection, and this gives
us an opportunity for self-improvement.

Maya, the deceptive illusion of the world, is very
powerful. The universe in reality changes every
moment, and nothing in it is eternal or remains in the
same state, although it appears to us to be eternal and
everlasting. The intellect may for a moment believe
it to be illusory, but the heart does not admit it to be
so. When a Master is found and one takes on His
color, then the curtain of Maya becomes a little
loosened and he begins to see the illusory nature of
the world. He begins to understand the causes of the
fall of the soul, of the troubles in this world, and
begins to take steps to remove them from his own life.
He begins to believe that the Lord is all powerful.
He begins to love Him. He then sees His will working.

"It is by Guru's grace that one is filled with Lord's Fear,
And by good fortune God abides in one's mind.
Through God's Fear one controls the mind
And through the Word, one's sense of ego is destroyed." A

Awe is inspired only by meeting a true Master. This awe, created by the Master's extraordinary beauty and magnetism, gives rise to pangs of love.   One feels a peculiar sensation of love and abandon.   When the devotee is in front of the Master both his heart and soul are attracted to him.   In that state, under the influence of awe, the eyes get filled with tears, but the devotee cannot go beyond the limit of propriety.   He cannot remain quiet and yet he cannot speak.   He becomes tongue-tied.   This state defies description. A lover may be in the room of the Beloved, but cannot utter a syllable.

Awe and love are mentioned together as well as separately by the Gurus.   One always thinks of and remembers the one he loves.   When one loves a beautiful and divine Being, the remembrance of this Being always attracts him and remains present in his inner mind.   Such love, which is tinged with awe, becomes true affection.   When there is such love, affection grows.

What a beautiful picture has been drawn of awe and affection by Guru Nanak Sahib using the illustration of a goldsmith's shop.   He says that in the shop of purity of body and mind the devotee should patiently beat the anvil of wisdom with the hammer of knowledge.   He should kindle the fire of the practice of austerities with the bellows of awe.   He should then make nectar in the crucible of affection, distilling it by constant remembrance of the reality of the Lord.   That is the real factory in which the Shabd is generated.

"There the goldsmith patiently hammers the anvil of wisdom with the hammer of knowledge,

Kindles the fire of austerities with awe, and moulds the reality in the vessel of love."

Worship

Worship means to serve or praise some higher and sublimer being than one's self in order to gain spiritual benefit. Nowadays wherever one looks one finds only outer worship prevalent. Hindus, Muslims, Christians and Sikhs and those belonging to other religions are all engaged in outer worship. Churches, mosques and temples are all religious places, and people regard bowing their heads and offering flowers before them as worship. Persons whose inner vision has not awakened, worship lifeless idols and tombs by placing flowers on them. But all their efforts are of no real spiritual worth.

It is strange that he who lives in the natural mosque (the body), which was constructed by the Lord with His own hands, should undergo hardships in man-made mosques.

The real and beneficial worship is the inner worship, which is not performed by the hands and feet or by the mouth, but by the mind and heart.

"O Mother, what should I offer to the Lord?
I do not find any beautiful flower or any other thing that is worthy of Him;
Neither incense, lights, sweets nor scents;
How is Thy servant to worship Thee?"

"By offering the body and mind we attain the Lord, through the grace of the Master.
There is no other way of worship.
O Ravidas, what will be your fate?"

9

When the worshiper progresses, he sees the Lord in His full glory. He sees that flowers and other beautiful things are already there, and there is no need to offer them. Even the body, the mind and our wealth are no longer ours. Then how can we offer anything?

The Lord is the basic substance or essence of all forms and of the formless. How can we worship Him? The Lord as the Shabd or Name pervades the whole of the universe. Name and Shabd are the Lord, and worship of them is worship of Him. The Saints teach that real worship consists in remembrance and repetition of the Name of the Lord. This is acceptable to the Lord. Most of the people do not do this and are following a wrong path.

"That repetition, those austerities, that fast and that worship is fruitful, which promotes love for the Lord. Except the love of the Lord, all other attachment is false and is forgotten in a moment."   A

Until a man rises to higher and finer regions where he can himself worship the Lord, it befits him to worship His incarnation, the Master. The disciple should, therefore, while contemplating on the human form of the Master with his outer eyes, progress inwardly and see the illuminated form of the Master within. When the heart of the devotee meets the heart of the Master, then the melody of the Shabd will be heard. Devotion to the Master is a step leading to spiritual relationship. Worship of the Master is worship of the Lord. Gurus place great emphasis upon this. One should worship both the Lord and the Master to gain salvation.

The devotees who perform outer worship say prayers, but the lovers of the Lord leave the body and then say prayers by going inside.   The devotees say prayers five times a day at fixed hours, but the lovers listen to the inner voice every moment.

CHAPTER 11

INTENSE LONGING

Bireh (intense longing) is the name of the active state of love. A lover who possesses bireh does not wish to lose sight of the Beloved even for a moment. Whenever he is not able to see Him or happens to be separated from Him, a feeling of pain stabs his heart and he feels an inner anguish. But the taste of this pain of separation is in no way less sweet than that of being with the Beloved. This is called Bireh.

Bireh has various stages. The first is the recollection of one's Beloved, accompanied by longing and contemplation. This condition of recollection and contemplation becomes so strong that a devotee's attention is completely diverted to the form of his Beloved, which always remains fixed in his mind's eye. The Beloved becomes the sustainer of his life, and he will not leave Him.

The two are merged into one, and a state of complete calmness and tranquility is achieved. In this state the devotee loses his own self and sees his Beloved everywhere. A heart that has true love for the Beloved is naturally happy and feels a current of ecstasy when he sees or meets Him.

Why is intense longing created? Simply because our soul has not been able to succeed in getting what it actually longs for. Just as a mother becomes restless at the time of separation from her son, or a wife from her husband; just as a fish is in anguish without water;

in a similar manner our soul is intensely restless because of its separation from the Lord.

This intense longing always surges up like a wave or current in the heart and refreshes the mind with remembrance of Him. As a result, the heart's agony is assuaged by continuous remembrance and contemplation of the Lord. This creates a feeling of happiness. It is a stepping-stone, over which a seeker has to tread to attain communion with the Lord.

In order to meet the Beloved, intense longing comes first, in the same manner as flowers bud and bloom on a fruit tree before it can bear fruit. Where there are no flowers, there can be no fruit. Similarly, where there is no bireh, there can be no meeting with the Beloved. In other words, this longing is a prerequisite for meeting the Lord.

In the state of intense longing, every cell of the body becomes restless with the memory of the Beloved, and without meeting Him or seeing Him the heart is not appeased. We seek out those whom we call Saints because they have achieved communion with the Lord, and we beseech them to help us in meeting the Lord. Inside of us there is an urge to meet Him and we cannot live without Him.

"O my Master, help me to meet my God. My mind and body are hungry to meet Him. I cannot live without seeing my Lord, and there is an intense and restless longing in me."   A

The history of the lives of all the Saints reveals the intensity of their desire and loging for the Lord. The people of the world eat, drink and are happy with the worldly pleasures, and sleep soundly at night. But a lover weeps and sighs, and is wide awake the whole night long in his longing to meet the Beloved. Such

a soul pines to meet the Lord and cries out: "O, will
it ever be possible for these eyes to see Him!"

"Without the Lord every cell of my mind and body is in a state
of anguish, and there is no sleep in my eyes. I am suffering
in mind and body from the pain of separation. The poor
doctors cannot diagnose my malady. Like one addicted to
intoxicants and drugs, I cannot live without my Beloved
even for a single moment. Those who have an intense desire
to meet Thee are not interested in anything else."   A

"The Lord is not with me and it is a dark night, with lightning
bringing fear to my mind. My bed is lonely. I am without
my Lord. The pain is so intense that death is preferable to
it."   A

Intense longing has a very deep influence because
of its powerful current of energy. Once it is established, no other impressions can enter the mind. Such
a devotee completely forgets his body and his clothes,
because he is being pulled by the magnet of the remembrance of the Lord, and his mind is completely
absorbed in contemplation of the Lord. If we are
being pulled towards something or somebody all the
time, we will ultimately merge into that form.

There are innumerable people in the world who
are longing for worldly objects, but in this longing
they are interested only in material things. It is
most difficult for people of this kind to follow the
path of Spirituality. There is no worldly method by
which one can find release from this world. All
longings are worthless with the exception of an intense
longing for the Lord. All others lead to distraction.
Shamas Tabriz told Maulana Rum:

"O my son, there are nine signs which distinguish the lovers
of God:

1. They heave cold sighs.

2. The face is pale. The devotee wishes to have communion with the Lord but it is not in his power. Every time he thinks of the Lord he cries out and the tear drops from his eyes are hardly able to extinguish the burning fire in his heart.

3. The eyes are always wet.

4. He eats sparingly.

5. He sleeps little.

6. Deep sleep does not come to him.

7. He sighs continually.

8. He is restless (impatient to behold the Lord).

9. He moans continually."

"When the fire of separation kindles in the heart and the smoke from it is not visible, only he who has experienced it, or who has kindled it, knows it is there. Only one who has been wounded knows the pain. No one else does. This fire burns within, not outside, and it produces water in the form of tears which try to extinguish the fire."   **4**

"No one has been united to his Beloved through mirth. Whoever has attained communion with Him has done so after shedding many tears. If it were possible to meet the Beloved while laughing and in a state of comfort, why should one suffer the anguish of separation? The people of the world are happy. They eat and sleep. Kabir alone is unhappy. He is awake and is crying."

"O Kabir, keep away from the life of pleasure and attach yourself to crying, for without it how can you find your Beloved!"

Kabir continues:

"My eyes, like those of a mad man, are searching for you every minute. You do not meet me. I am not happy, and am ever in a state of pain and tension. My body is emaciated. Now I am only a skeleton of bones. It is my misfortune that even now my Lord has not come to me. This separation has eaten up all my bones and my body, and has made me dead while still living. Like a powerful army, this separation has surrounded me. It does not permit me to die nor does it allow me to live, and my life is slowly ebbing away in anguish. I am suffering bireh in the absence of my Lord, and separation is troubling me every minute. Day and night I have no rest, and my breath is gradually growing less and less."

In this intensity of love the soul forgets the entire world. It cannot learn to stop thinking of the Lord even for a single second.

"The whole day is spent in looking towards the path from which my Beloved is to come, and the night is spent in the same manner. Unable to meet the Beloved, I am restless and my heart is troubled. That day will be an auspicious one when my Master will take me by the arm and make me His own. And I shall sit in the shade of His Lotus Feet." 4

Mira Bai says:

"I have been counting the stars and passing the whole night in wakefulness. When will the time of happiness come, O God! My Lord, meet me and be never again separated from me. O Lord, since you have been separated from me, I have been restless. If I listen to hymns in your praise, my mind becomes restless, for I find solace only in songs of intense longing for You. With my eyes open wide I am looking at the path (whence You will be coming) and the night has become as long as half a year. To whom should I tell my story of separation? O my friend, to whom should I relate the story of my separation and intense longing? It is cutting through my heart like a saw. When will Mira's Lord meet her and give her joy by removing her anguish!"

Buddha sought refuge in the jungles in search of the Truth, and his body became extremely emaciated. Likewise, we may study the life of any other Saint and we will find the same account of intense longing due to separation. Whoever has traveled the path of God-Realization had to cross the river of sighs before he could meet Him. It is indeed true that one has to tread that path through tears. Maulana Rum says:

"O man, if you wish to reach the Home of God, you should go by way of the ocean of tears, for it is only in that way that you will be able to reach Him. Dry prayers, dry counting of beads, dry reading of scriptures, and dry eyes as well as dry heart—all these are like going along a barren path towards God. But if you had gone through water (tears), you would have reached Him without any difficulty."

Shamas Tabriz says:

"Those whose eyes are weeping for the Darshan of the Beloved will one day surely behold Him. In love, weeping acts as a ladder. When you make a ladder of your eyes, then you will automatically be speeding towards the sky. The ocean of the Beloved's grace reaches from one end to the other, and no place is without it. But this fire of intense longing due to separation is for the purpose of ripening the faith of the followers on this path."

Maulana Rum further says:

"Weeping is like the clouds, and longing is like the heat of the sun. Just as the sun's heat is the cause of bringing rains from the clouds, by which this world remains in existence; similarly, separation, longing for Him and restlessness—all these are like fires which make the currents of grace and mercy of God burst out, as the rain does from the clouds, and pacify the hearts of devotees. Tears in the eyes and pain in the heart are the two pillars between which we pass to go within."

Through longing caused by separation a devotee washes away his bad thoughts with his hot tears, and remembrance of the Lord takes their place. But this longing can be awakened only by true love and not by crocodile tears.

Such a noble and rewarding longing is awakened only in the hearts of those who have pure and unadul-

terated love for the physical manifestation of God—
namely, the living Master. A disciple must have
true spiritual love for the physical form of his Master.
And when he sees the resplendent form of the Master
inside by means of the spiritual practice performed
with love, he is then attached to that unique form also
and to the Shabd emanating from it. He would
never wish to be separated from this. By separation
from the physical form of the Master, longing is
produced to meet Him inside. And when a devotee
does not see the form inside, the absence of the form
produces a great restlessness and anguish in the mind.

> "Last night, throughout the night, I could not sleep with my
> Beloved, and every part of my body is aching. If this is my
> condition after His absence for one night, what is the state of
> those who never meet Him, and how do they pass their
> nights?"
> A

The longing due to separation from the Lord has
a unique sweetness. Those who are blindly following
the dictates of the mind and are fully entrenched in
the worldly luxuries of "eat, drink and be merry"
cannot experience that sweet taste. Intense longing
and crying for the Lord always turn into happiness.
They are really blessed who are so fortunate as to be
gifted with this condition.

> "In the state of longing and its pain, the things of the world
> appear bitter. Only the Name of the Lord is sweet."
> "When this longing is produced in a person, he becomes
> eligible to merge in the Truth."
> 4

Longing produces love and veneration for the
Beloved. God is Love. Therefore, the devotee comes
nearer to the Lord in proportion to the degree of his
longing. He also realizes in greater degree the value

of his Beloved, so much so that the pure and noble form of the Beloved is always fixed in his mind.

The remedy for one who is in this state of suffering lies in the hands of the Beloved. He alone can remove it by granting His Darshan.

CHAPTER 12

THE RESULTS OF LOVE

When St. John became so old that he was not able to walk and was able to speak only with great difficulty, another follower of Christ took him to a gathering of children to deliver a sermon. He raised his head and said: "Little children, love one another." Once again he said this and then repeated it a third time, after which he was silent.

At that the people closest to him said, "Good man, haven't you anything more important to say to these children?" To this he replied: "I give this advice over and over again, because of all the qualities, that of love is the greatest need of mankind. If you would love each other and the current of love would fill your minds, you would possess all other good qualities. Love, and all things shall be added unto you."

If we could experience true love, we would be our own physicians and could bring peace and happiness to ourselves. Then all our pain and sadness because of our separation from the Lord, which are caused by our not understanding the principles of love, would vanish; and the radiant currents of joy would fill and invigorate our minds.

It is love alone that can give peace and happiness. Without it life is dry and worthless, and even the joys of heaven are of no value. A palace will appear as dreadful as a graveyard to a person who is bereft of love. But even the ill-furnished and dilapidated huts are beautiful if they are brightened with the spark of love. Through love, even jungles become filled with happy life; and without love, populated cities may appear bleak.

It is by the magic of love alone that a lover removes the covering of his pleasure and pain, happiness and sorrow, knowledge and ignorance. In love, gain or loss are equal.

Love brings to the lover the quality of concealing the bad qualities of others. Love hides all evils and bad things. In a lover's eyes the beloved appears to be pure and free from all evils. He sees the spark of his beloved in everybody. Therefore he talks sweetly to the liking of all. His attention never turns towards the faults or defects of anyone in this world. Why should he then criticize or talk of anyone? Criticism is the outcome of the absence of love.

In love, all the bad qualities of the mind and intellect such as anger, sloth, talking ill of others, hatred, and so forth, are removed, and we are able to control our mind by means of love. Love reigns over everything. It is so beautiful that wherever it abides, anger, hatred, and other similar emotions cannot exist.

"Those in this world who have love for the Lord, possess real knowledge, and if by chance they utter any harsh words, they do not hurt anybody because they do not forget the spirit of love and therefore love everybody. They are the chosen ones of God." 8

Love only gives, and takes nothing. Love is such a unique quality that whosoever gets it has no other desire left in him. Love makes a man selfless and free from all care. In love, there is never any question of taking, because it knows only how to give.

Love inspires generosity and obliterates selfishness, because it has no ulterior motive. If everyone in the world would live in the spirit of love, no worldly laws would be necessary. We need these laws because all have not learned to live in love, and as a result the world is entangled in a network of animal-like tendencies.

If we could learn to love ourselves, our neighbors, our country and the whole of mankind, and God Himself, we should no longer be in need of worldly laws, because love begets love. Then there would be no lack of harmony or trust among the nations, and the only ruling power would be that of love. Christ says:

"Thy kingdom come. Thy will be done on earth, as it is in heaven."

A lover achieves strength to bear all kinds of troubles and tortures. People of the world are unable to bear slander but a lover becomes indifferent to it. His soul receives such strength that he does not succumb to any ailment. Love is a perfect remedy for all inner ailments.

All things become easy in the presence of love. A person under the influence of love performs the most difficult tasks with comparative ease. Through love, even impossible things become possible, "Love knows no burdens; love has no burden." You may have to work very hard. There may be a great burden of responsibilities on your shoulders. But if you clearly understand the law of love, all these difficulties will be performed by love without trouble. "He does much who loves much."

If a person loves a certain type of work, he works at it incessantly because love feels no burden. A lover does not mind burdens and he therefore gladly accomplishes work beyond his capacity. He never complains of his inability to do any work because he considers himself capable of doing every type of work in the atmosphere of his love. Love gives him such energy that he does not consider anything impossible.

"If the path of love is beset with oceans, mountins, forests and endless deserts—all these appear to be equal to only one step forward on account of love."

Just as rain is a blessing for the earth and enables it to produce multicolored flowers and beautiful shrubs and trees, in the same manner, when tears from the eyes fall on the earth of the heart, the buds of the secrets of the knowledge of God burst into blossoms.

A place where there is love becomes sanctified by it. In that environment there is a powerful current of exaltation, but it can be felt only by a heart that is filled with love. If we perform our domestic and other worldly duties with love, we shall enjoy our life in comfort and without any worries, because in the presence of love, the mind and intellect are powerless to disturb one's inner calmness. Love does not influence only human beings. Even animals and birds are subject to its elevating influence.

Love itself is the beginning and the end. It is a pure emanation of God's current, which enters the heart of a pure person and spreads its influence all round, thus purifying the entire area. The heart of a lover is pure, and at the same time those who have the opportunity of meeting him cannot escape his purifying influence. If one comes across such pure souls, his heart is so greatly influenced that he feels as if purity had entered into him from head to foot.

The state of a person's mind is always reflected on his face. Happiness or pain, love or hatred are reflected in his expression, and if he speaks, then everything in his mind comes out clearly into the open.

When a spark of love for the Lord is lit in a person's mind, it cannot be concealed. His very eyes disclose it. Even if the mouth is locked, love will burst out in the form of teardrops from the eyes.

> "Love cannot be concealed once it has entered a person's heart. He does not speak it out but his eyes reveal it. Once love enters a man's heart it keeps him happy at all times, for he then becomes free from worries, and the currents of love flow out from him automatically."   4

The religion of a lover is nothing but love, under the influence of which a unique type of concentration and a feeling of loneliness enter his mind. His thoughts pass beyond the limits of union and duality. If one imbibes even a small particle of love, he will consider the whole world worth no more than a straw. The heart of one who has tasted even a few drops from the cup of love, finds no taste at all in the worldly pleasures. He desires neither heaven nor salvation.

After some time the disciple's condition becomes one of love and there is an intense desire of the heart for the Lord. By remembering the Master, who is the manifestation of the Lord, the disciple begins to long for his Darshan; tears automatically roll down his eyes, and the soul becomes restless. The restlessness of the soul makes him forget himself. The repetition of the Names becomes so intense that the disciple becomes completely absorbed in it and forgets his own self. Guru Ram Das says:

"My Master who is God incarnate has captured my heart and I am restless to have his Darshan."

This state cannot be described in words, because such a person is full of the ecstasy created by the elixir of Love and is awakened into a state of super-consciousness (bliss). Those who are devoid of love for the Master cannot understand this condition. In the fire of love, everything else in the mind of the lover is annihilated.

To forget one's self is the fundamental principle of love. All the desires of a lover narrow down to the will of the Beloved. His whole self is dissolved into the Beloved. When there is no self, then where are the desires?

"When I was, He was not. When He is, I am not. The lane of Love is so narrow that it can hold one but not both."   4

The unique quality of love is this: If a seed of love is sown into its field, it is followed by pain, burning, separation. These are the crops that grow. The lover sometimes complains, "O, why did I ever love?" Sometimes he berates his eyes and reprimands them for ever having cast a glance on the Beloved. He will not speak about this subject to anyone, who is not able to understand the condition of his heart, for to talk of the pain of one's heart to a person who has never felt such pain is to invite more pain. He, however, keeps the Beloved within his eyes, wherever his eyes go.

"That eye is fortunate which sheds pearls of tears in the remembrance of its Beloved. That heart is fortunate which is burning in separation from its Lord, because every spell of remorse is accompanied by a unique happiness. A person whose only aim is towards this end is the most fortunate one."

Only one whose mind and body are engulfed in the ocean of love can know the condition of love. No other person can do so. A lover is beside himself because of his intense longing, and people call him mad. But having tasted this unique love, he is so happy in it that he cares nothing for the world and passes his time in a state of constant love for the Lord. Guru Arjun says:

"O God! Your humble servant has become absorbed in the elixir of your Love and now that he has tasted it, he will never leave it."

True union and one-pointed attention come only with love. The spiritual progress achieved by means of meditation over a number of years can be had in a moment through love, because the union of inner sight takes the lover immediately to the goal. This is real love and this is true yoga. In fact, this is the be-all and end-all. This should be our aim. This should be our goal, and this should be our fast, our prayers, our meditation and everything else.

Truth is love and it resides in our heart. Love is Nam. It is deeply engraved in our mind and in our body. Whoever tries to search for it, gets it. Love for the Lord is awakened in the disciples of a Master. Thus all their desires are satisfied and they worship only the Lord. They tread the path of Love and are fully engrossed in its bliss.

God is Shabd. God is Love. Therefore, Shabd is also Love. Saints are Shabd incarnate. They bestow the gift of Shabd on others. Those who practise Shabd and listen to the Divine Music become oceans of Love. They love everybody and by the currents of this Divine Love radiate a virtuous influence in this world.

God is Love. He is omnipresent. The soul is a drop of that ocean and it swims like a fish back into that ocean. Once the magnetic power of love establishes itself in a mind, it will never be destroyed.

The currents of God's love then enter into your heart and make you a lover of God. The love for God increases in proportion to the increase of love for the Master, and the devotee begins to see light inside.

Sometimes the light is in the form of lightning, sometimes stars are seen, and sometimes the stars burst and the sun and moon are visible. Sometimes the luminous and brilliant form of the Master is visible within, and this enables the soul to see higher spiritual regions within and to cross Brahm and Par Brahm.

The Master forbids the devotee to reveal these secrets to others, because it is against the law of God and of Nature to do so. By the grace of the Master these internal sights increase in number and intensity day by day; and by contemplation on the form of the Master the devotee's love for God is also gradually intensified, thus increasing his state of happiness into one of unalloyed bliss.

The madness of a lover's ecstasy brings before his eyes a new world which is beyond this physical region and beyond the region of mind, and he takes every word of the Beloved as a sweet command. To live in Him is the highest and sweetest elixir. It is even dearer than life. The current of love takes one beyond good and evil, belief and unbelief, to a state so sublime that it cannot be described. One who is intoxicated in this unique state of bliss—in which any thought of separation or communion is lost—becomes an embodiment of Love.

The mind of a lover is strong and deep like that of an ocean. It does not contain tempests of other thoughts. His aim is one-pointed and there is only one thought in his mind—that of the Beloved. When we love, then love becomes the sustainer of our soul, and our complete attention is concentrated in the Beloved. Then all superficial ties are cut, and the soul is freed from the shackles of this world and flies to the regions above. That highest region is its true abode.

In its true abode the soul enjoys at all times the bliss of union. Love transforms it from the material and physical attachments to the finer, spiritual regions, and the drop of the soul is merged in the ocean of the Lord.

Because of the love within himself, God is always his guide. He meets God, and God resides in his heart. The mind becomes satisfied. He goes to his Real Home, and is freed from the cycle of births and deaths.

INDEX OF SOURCES

MASTERS

1. ARJAN DEV—The fifth in the line of ten Sikh Gurus (1563-1606).
2. BHAI GUR DAS—A contemporary of the fourth, fifth and sixth Sikh Gurus, and who was acquainted with them.
3. HAFIZ—One of the greatest of Persian Poets and also a true Saint (1320-1389). He was born at Shiraz and spent his life there as a court poet.
4. KABIR—A well known Saint (1440-1518) who lived in Benares and preached and practised Surat Shabd Yoga.
5. MAULVI RUM—A well known Moslem Saint of Persia, (1207-1277), who was a devoted disciple of Shams-i-Tabriz.
6. MUINUDDIN CHISHTI—A renowned Saint of medieval times (1143-1233). He taught the practice of the Word at Ajmer in Rajputana.
7. NANAK—The famous Saint of the Punjab, the first of the ten Sikh Gurus (1469-1539).
8. RAM DAS—The fourth in the line of ten Sikh Gurus (1534-1581).
9. RAVI DAS—A Saint of northern India who was a cobbler by profession.
10. SAHJO BAI—An eighteenth century woman Saint of Rajputana. Born in high caste, she became a disciple of Charan Das.
11. SARMAD—A Moslem Saint who was executed as a heretic by the orders of Aurangzeb, the Mogul King of Delhi.
12. SHAMS-I-TABRIZ—A Moslem Saint (1147-1247) who settled at Multan and was flayed alive because he rebelled against the outward forms of worship.
13. SHEIKH FARID—A Muslim Saint (1181-1265), born near Multan in northwestern India. He spent most of his life in the southern Punjab.
14. SWAMI JI—The Great Saint and Founder of what is now known as the Radha Swami Faith, Science and Philosophy. His real name was Seth Shiv Dayal Singh. (1818-1878).
15. TULSI SAHIB—A great Poet-Saint of Hathras (1788-1848), an exponent of Sant Mat and the author of the Ghat Ramayana.

SCRIPTURES

A. ADI GRANTH—The sacred scriptures of the Sikhs, compiled by the fifth Guru Arjan Dev. It contains, teachings of the various Sikh Gurus as well as of other Saints.

B. BIBLE—The Scriptures of the Christian faith.

C. GITA—Or Bhagvadgita, literally,"The Song of the Lord". It embodies the teachings of Lord Krishna, and is the most popular book on Hindu Philosophy.

D. MAHABHARAT—The great epic poem of the Hindus.

E. SAR BACHAN—Literally, Essential, True or Important Words. The name of a book by Swami Ji.

F. UPANISHAD—The philosophical and mystical part of the Vedas, the holy books of the Hindus.

GLOSSARY OF ORIENTAL TERMS

ANAMI—The Nameless; the Absolute; the Highest Deity, Radha Soami, the Ruler of the eighth and the Highest Spiritual Region.

ASTRAL—The first spiritual region.

BHAJAN—A form of spiritual practice. Applying the spirit to listening to the Internal Word or Shabd.

BIREH—The pain of separation; intense longing; pain of one who has been separated from the Beloved.

BRAHMAND—Literally, the ego of Brahm; the entire universe over which Brahm has jurisdiction.

CAUSAL—The second spiritual region.

DARSHAN—Vision or sight, particularly of some Saint or holy person.

DERA—Camp or Colony. In this book the name refers to the Radha Soami Colony, situated on the banks of the River Beas in the Punjab.

DHYAN—Contemplation; a form of spiritual practice; esoterically, beholding the form of the Master within.

GURMUKH—Literally, one whose face is turned towards the Guru; one who has completely surrendered himself to the Guru; a highly advanced soul which has cast off the three coverings and has reached Par Brahm.

GURU—Literally, one who gives light; Spiritual Teacher; Master.

GURU BHAKTI—Devotion to, and worship of a Guru.

KAL—Literally, Time or Death; the Negative Power; the name given to the Power that controls all the three worlds which are perishable. Kal rules and regulates the whole universe—gross subtle and causal—and will not let anyone cross his threshold to enter the realm of Sat Purush until that soul has been thoroughly cleansed of all desires and attachments.

KARMA—Action and re-action; the law of action and reaction; the fruit of or result of past thoughts, words and deeds. There are three types of Karma:

    1. Pralabdh, that portion of our karma which is allotted to this life and is responsible for our present existence. It is also called Fate or Destiny.

2. Kriyaman, the result or fruit of new actions performed during the present life.

3. Sinchit, those karmas which still remain to be taken out of our own stored-up lot and are to be worked off or to bear fruit in future incarnations.

MAYA—Illusion; phenomenal universe; all that which is not eternal, is not real or true, is called 'maya'. The veil of illusion which conceals the vision of God from our sight.

NAM—See Shabd.

PINDA—The physical and material universe; region of lower mind and matter.

RADHA SOAMI—Appellation of the Supreme Lord God. Soami literally means Lord, and Radha means soul—hence, it means "Lord of the Soul".

SANT MAT—The Teachings of the Saints; the Science of God-Realization, practised while living in this world. It is the Science of merging in the Supreme Creator, just as the drop merges in the ocean. This can be accomplished only under the guidance of a True Master in the physical form. We are in the physical form and need someone in the physical form to instruct and guide us to that Power within, which leads to the Supreme Being. Moreover, the presence of the Master is essential to guide and to protect us during the course of our Spiritual Journey. It is a natural Science and is complete in every human being regardless of race, color or creed. But the Key is with the Master, and He gives it to all whom He accepts.

SAT DESH—SACH KHAND—Literally, the True or Imperishable Region; esoterically, the fifth Spiritual Region, presided over by Sat Purush.

SAT GURU—A Master or Spiritual Teacher who has access to the fifth Spiritual Region.

SAT PURUSH—God; True Lord, who presides over Sat Lok and all the universes below it.

SATSANG—Literally, True Association; Association with a Saint or Perfect Master is external Satsang, and association of the soul with Shabd within is the Internal Satsang. The highest form of Satsang is to merge with Shabd and to engage in the prescribed meditation. When a congregation is addressed by a Master, that is also Satsang. Even to think about Him and His teachings is Satsang.

SEVA—Service—by wealth, body, mind or soul.

SHABD—Word; Sound; Audible Life Stream; Sound Current, Nam. As the soul manifests in the body as consciousness, the Word of God manifests Itself as Inner Spiritual Sound. There are five forms of the Shabd within every human being, the secret of which can be imparted only by a True Master.

SIKH—Literally, disciple; the followers of Guru Nanak and his nine successors are known as Sikhs. The name also applies to one who has reached the first Spiritual Region within.

SIKH GURUS—Guru Nanak, the first of the Sikh Gurus, was followed by nine others, each appointed by his predecessor, as is the age-old custom when there is an unbroken succession of Saints. The ten Sikh Gurus were:

1.	Guru Nanak	(1469–1539)
2.	Guru Angad	(1504–1552)
3.	Guru Amar Das	(1479–1574)
4.	Guru Ram Das	(1534–1581)
5.	Guru Arjan Dev	(1563–1606)
6.	Guru Har Govind	(1595–1644)
7.	Guru Har Rai	(1630–1661)
8.	Guru Har Kishan	(1656–1664)
9.	Guru Teg Bahadur	(1621–1675)
10.	Guru Gobind Singh	(1666–1708)

The Sikh Gurus were obliged to turn their followers into a military as well as a spiritual army shortly after 1600, due to fierce attacks launched against them by the Mogul Emperors of Delhi. Under Guru Gobind Singh, the Sikhs took new names having the suffix 'Singh' (Lion) attached to them. This custom has been followed by the Sikhs since that time.

SIMRAN—Repetition; remembrance; a form of spiritual practice.

SURAT—Soul; consciousness; inner attention. As consciousness in the body is due to the presence of the soul, hence the soul is called 'surat' or consciousness.

SURAT SHABD YOGA—The practice of the Sound Current; the union of the soul with Shabd; the spiritual exercise by which the current of consciousness is applied to the hearing of the Sound within; joining the mind and the attention to the Sound Current.

YOGA—Literally, means union; esoterically, spiritual exercises; practice; meditation in the spiritual sense; any system which leads to or aims at the union of the soul with God.

INDEX

(Prepared by satsangis in the U.S.A.)

INFORMATION AND BOOKS
ARE AVAILABLE FROM:

The Secretary
Radha Soami Satsang Beas
P.O. Dera Baba Jaimal Singh 143204
District Amritsar, Punjab, India

Radha Soami Book Dept.
P.O. Box 242
Gardena, CA 90247 USA
Phone 213-329-5635

CANADA

Dr. J. Khanna, 5550 McMaster Road, Vancouver V6T 1J8, B.C.

Mr. Reginald S. Davis, R.R. 1 Crapaud, Prince Edward Island, COA 1JO

U.S.A.

Mr. Roland G. deVries, 10901 Mill Spring Drive, Nevada City, California 95959

Col. E.R. Berg, U.S. Air Force (Ret'd), 4001 Mavelle Drive, Minneapolis, Minn. 55435

Mr. Roy E. Ricks, 651 Davis Street, Melrose Park, Ill. 60160

Mr. Henry F. Weekley, 2121 No. Ocean Blvd., Apt. 1108E, Boca Raton, Fla. 33431

MEXICO

Mr. Jorge Angel Santana, Cameta 2821, Jardines Del Bosque, Guadalajara, Jalisco

SOUTH AMERICA

Dr. Gonzalo Vargas N., P.O. Box 2666, Quito, Ecuador

Mr. Leopoldo Luks, Ave. Maracay, Urb. Las Palmas, Qta Luksenburg, Caracas, Venezuela

Mrs. Rajni B. Manglani, c/o Bhagwan's Store, 18 Water St., Georgetown, Guyana

WEST INDIES

Mr. Thakurdas Chatlani, 2A Gittins Avenue, Maraval, Trinidad

Mr. Sean Finnegan, P.O. Box 2314, Port-au-Prince, Haiti

Mr. Bhagwandas Kessaram, c/o Kiddies Corner, Swant Street, Bridgetown, Barbados

ENGLAND

Mrs. F.E. Wood, Willow Cottage, Worple Road, Leatherhead, Surrey

SWEDEN
Mr. T. Gunther, Skakeltorp 6018, 441 00 Alingsas

DENMARK
Ms. Inge Gregersen, Askevenget–15, 2830 Virum

HOLLAND
Mr. Jacob Hofstra, Geulwijk 6, 3831 LM Leusden

WEST GERMANY
Mr. Rudolf Walberg, Falkenstr. 18, D–6232 Bad Soden/Taunus

AUSTRIA
Mr. Hansjorg Hammerer, Sezenweingasse 10, A–5020, Salzburg

SWITZERLAND
Mr. Olivier de Coulon, Route de Lully, 1111 Tolochenaz

FRANCE
Count Pierre de Proyart, 7 Quai Voltaire, 75007 Paris

SPAIN
Mr. H.W. Balani, Balani's International, P.O. Box 486, Malaga

PORTUGAL
Mr. Alberto C. Ferreira, R. Machado dos Santos 20, 2775 Parede

GIBRALTAR
Mr. Arjan M. Thadani, Radha Soami Satsang Beas, P.O. Box 283

ITALY
Mr. Ted Goodman, Via Garigliano 27, Rome 00198

GREECE
Dr. Constantine Siopoulos, 11 Kanari Street, Athens–134

CYPRUS
Mr. Hercules Achilleos, Kyriakou Matsi 18,
Pallouriotissa—T.K. 9077, Nicosia

WEST AFRICA
Mr. Krishin Vaswani, Vaan-Ahn Enterprise Ltd., P.O. Box 507,
Monrovia, Liberia

Mr. Nanik N. Balani, Kewalram (Nig.) Ltd., P.O. Box No. 320, Lagos, Nigeria

EAST AFRICA
Mr. Peter Kivumbi, P.O. Box 664, Masaka, Uganda
Mr. Sohan Singh Bharj, P.O. Box 47036, Nairobi, Kenya
Mr. D.N. Pandit, United Timber Traders Ltd., P.O. Box No. 1963, Dar-es-Salaam, Tanzania
Mr. David Bowskill, P.O. Box 11012, Chingola, Zambia
Mr. Vernon Lowrie, P.O. Box 690, Harare City, Zimbabwe

SOUTH AFRICA
Mr. Sam Busa, P.O. Box 41355, Craighall, Transvaal 2024
Mr. R. Attweli. P.O. Box 5702, Durban 4000

MASCARENE ISLANDS
Mr. P.C. Nuckchady, P.O. Box No. 49, Rose-Hill, Mauritius

ISRAEL
Mrs. H. Mandelbaum, P.O. Box 2815, Tel Aviv–61000

U.A.E.
Mr. Jiwatram Lakhiani, P.O. Box 1449, Dubai

KUWAIT
Mr. & Mrs. Ghassan Alghanem, P.O. Box No. 25549, Safat, Kuwait

AFGHANISTAN
Mr. Manak Singh, c/o Manaco, P.O. Box 3163, Kabul

SRI LANKA
Mr. D.H. Jiwat, Geekay Ltd., 33 Bankshall Street, Colombo–11

NEW ZEALAND
Mr. Tony Waddicor, P.O. Box 5331, Welesley St. P.O., Auckland 1

AUSTRALIA
Dr. John Potter, Long Wood Road, Heathfield, South Australia 5153

INDONESIA
Mr. G.L. Nanwani, Yayasan, Radhasoami Satsang Beas, JL. Kelinci Raya No. 32A, Jakarta Pusat
Mr. Odharmal Chotrani, 51 Djl. Bubutan, P.O. Box 144, Surabaya

SINGAPORE
Mr. Bhagwan Asnani, 1806 King's Mansion, Singapore–1543

MALAYSIA
Mr. N. Pal, c/o Muhibbah Travels Agency, Sdn. Bhd.,
  46 Jalan Tanku Abdul Rahman, Kuala Lumpur 01–07

THAILAND
Mr. Harmohinder Singh Sethi, Sawan Textiles, 154 Serm Sin Kha,
  Sampheng Street, Bangkok–2

HONG KONG
Mrs. Cami Moss, Hongkong Hilton, G.P.O. Box No. 42
Mr. Gobind Sabnani, G.P.O. Box 3906

PHILIPPINES
Mr. Kay Sham, P.O. Box 2346 MCC, Makati, Metro Manila

JAPAN
Mr. L.H. Parwani, Radha Soami Satsang Beas, 2–18 Nakajimadori
  1–Chome, Aotani, Fukiai-ku, Kobe–651

*   *   *   *   *   *   *   *

FOR OTHER FOREIGN ORDERS
WRITE TO:
Mr. Krishin Babani, Buona Casa Bldg., 2nd Floor, Sir P.M. Road,
  Fort Bombay–400 001, India

Addresses changed since the book was printed:

BOOKS ON THIS SCIENCE

Swami Ji Maharaj
1. *Sar Bachan*

Baba Jaimal Singh
2. *Spiritual Letters* (to Huzur Maharaj Sawan Singh: 1896–1903)

Huzur Maharaj Sawan Singh
3. *Discourses on Sant Mat*
4. *Philosophy of the Masters* (*Gurmat Sidhant*), 5 vols. (an encyclopedia on the teachings of the Saints)
5. *My Submission* (introduction to *Philosophy of the Masters*)
6. *Philosophy of the Masters* (abridged)
7. *Tales of the Mystic East* (as narrated in satsangs)
8. *Spiritual Gems* (letters: 1919–1948)

Sardar Bahadur Jagat Singh Maharaj
9. *The Science of the Soul* (discourses and letters: 1948–1951)

Maharaj Charan Singh
10. *Die to Live* (answers to questions on meditation)
11. *Divine Light* (discourses and letters: 1959–1964)
12. *The Path* (first part of *Divine Light*)
13. *Light on Saint Matthew*
14. *Light on Sant Mat* (discourses and letters: 1952–1958)
15. *Quest for Light* (letters: 1965–1971)
16. *Saint John, the Great Mystic*
17. *Spiritual Discourses*
18. *Spiritual Heritage* (from tape-recorded talks)
19. *The Master Answers* (to audiences in America: 1964)
20. *Thus Saith the Master* (to audiences in America: 1970)
21. *Truth Eternal* (a discourse)

Books about these Masters

1. *Call of the Great Master*—Diwan Daryai Lal Kapur
2. *The Living Master*—Katherine Wason
3. *With a Great Master in India*—Dr. Julian P. Johnson
4. *With the Three Masters*, 3 vols.—from the diary of Rai Sahib Munshi Ram

Books on Sant Mat in General

1. *A Soul's Safari*—Netta Pfeifer
2. *In Search of the Way*—Flora E. Wood
3. *Kabir, the Great Mystic*—Isaac A. Ezekiel
4. *Liberation of the Soul*—J. Stanley White, Ph.D.
5. *Message Divine*—Shanti Sethi
6. *Mystic Bible*—Dr. Randolph Stone
7. *Mysticism, the Spiritual Path*, 2 vols.—Prof. Lekh Raj Puri
8. *Radha Soami Teachings*—Prof. Lekh Raj Puri
9. *Ringing Radiance*—Sir Colin Garbett
10. *Sant Mat and the Bible*—Narain Das
11. *Sarmad, Jewish Saint of India*—Isaac A. Ezekiel
12. *Teachings of the Gurus*—Prof. Lekh Raj Puri
13. *The Inner Voice*—Colonel C.W. Sanders
14. *The Mystic Philosophy of Sant Mat*—Peter Fripp
15. *The Path of the Masters*—Dr. Julian P. Johnson
16. *Yoga and the Bible*—Joseph Leeming

Mystics of the East Series

1. *Saint Paltu*—Isaac A. Ezekiel
2. *Saint Namdev, His Life and Teachings*—J.R. Puri and V.K. Sethi
3. *Tulsi Sahib, Saint of Hathras*—J.R. Puri and V.K. Sethi
4. *Tukaram, Saint of Maharashtra*—C. Rajwade
5. *Dadu, the Compassionate Mystic*—K.N. Upadhyaya, Ph.D.
6. *Mira, the Divine Lover*—V.K. Sethi
7. *Guru Ravidas, Life and Teachings*—K.N. Upadhyaya, Ph.D.
8. *Guru Nanak, His Mystic Teachings*—J.R. Puri